Walter Scott and Contemporary Theory

ALSO AVAILABLE FROM BLOOMSBURY

Blake, Wordsworth, Religion, Jonathan Roberts
Eighteenth-Century Literature and Culture, Paul Goring
Everybody's Jane, Juliette Wells
Romanticism, Sharon Ruston
Romanticism Handbook, Edited by Joel Faflak and Sue Chaplin

Walter Scott and Contemporary Theory

EVAN GOTTLIEB

B L O O M S B U R Y

LONDON • NEW DELHI • NEW YORK • SYDNEY

Bloomsbury Academic

An imprint of Bloomsbury Publishing Plc

50 Bedford Square	175 Fifth Avenue
London	New York
WC1B 3DP	NY 10010
UK	USA

www.bloomsbury.com

First published 2013

British Library Cataloguing-in-Publication Data
A catalogue record for this book is available from the British Library.

ISBN: HB: 978-1-4411-8253-1
PB: 978-1-4411-2022-9
ePub: 978-1-4411-3354-0
PDF: 978-1-4411-2874-4

Library of Congress Cataloging-in-Publication Data
Gottlieb, Evan, 1975–
Walter Scott and contemporary theory/Evan Gottlieb.
p. cm.
Includes bibliographical references and index.
ISBN 978-1-4411-2022-9 (pbk.) – ISBN 978-1-4411-8253-1 (hardback) –
ISBN 978-1-4411-2874-4 (ebook) – ISBN 978-1-4411-3354-0 (ebook)
1. Scott, Walter, Sir, 1771–1832–Criticism and interpretation. I. Title.
PR5341.G67 2013
823'.7–dc23
2012039248

Typeset by Deanta Global Publishing Services, Chennai, India
Printed and bound in India

Contents

Acknowledgments

Putting Scott together with contemporary theory may not immediately sound like a natural fit, but everyone at Bloomsbury unfailingly shared my enthusiasm for this book. Many thanks to David Avital and Haaris Naqvi for encouraging me to undertake a more ambitious study of Scott's novels, when my initial idea was simply to write a "reader's guide" to *Waverley*. Thanks also to Laura Murray for help preparing the final manuscript. Closer to home, I am grateful to all of the students at Oregon State University who have gamely participated in my classes and seminars, especially on theory, over the past decade. In this regard, and for consistently challenging me to broaden my theoretical interests and refine my critical understandings, special thanks to Taylor Boulware, Rubèn Casas, Adam Drury, Michael J. Faris, Sarah Ghasedi, Lauren Karp, Brian Lindsley, Brian Martin, Emily Nashif, Rebecca Schneider, Jessica Travers, and Chris Villemarette. Thanks also to the members of the OSU Theory Reading Group, especially Anita Guerrini, Kirsi Peltomaki, and Jillian St. Jacques, for indulging my various theoretical passions; and to Anita Helle, Director of the School of Writing, Literature, and Film at Oregon State University, for her support with regard to scheduling and funding. I also want to thank the organizers and participants at the academic conferences where portions of this book were first presented: the 7th Quadrennial International Scott Conference in Laramie, Wyoming; the Northeast American Society for Eighteenth-Century Studies conference in Hamilton, Ontario; and the Colloquium on Corporeality and Spirituality in the Works of Walter Scott at the University of Paris-Sorbonne. Finally, my very sincere thanks go to Adam Beach, Adam Drury (again!), Ian Duncan, Penny Fielding, Caroline Jackson-Houlston, and Matthew Wickman for providing invaluable feedback and encouragement regarding the structure and purpose of this study.

This book is dedicated to my family, and especially to my younger son, Liam, for his good humor and good sense. I hope both he and his older brother James continue to become sharp critical thinkers and, perhaps one day, as fond of Scott's fictions as I am.

Introduction

Everything you always wanted to know about Scott but were afraid to ask Contemporary Theory (and vice versa)

At the age of fifty-four, Sir Walter Scott, one of the most prolific and popular writers of his era, decided to keep a journal.[1] It would, he wrote in the opening entry for 20 November 1825, serve both private and public functions: "I have all my life regretted that I did not keep a regular [journal]. I have myself lost recollection of much that was interesting and I have deprived my family and the public of some curious information by not carrying this resolution into effect."[2] At the time, Scott could have little idea of the hardships he would soon experience. Only two months later, he would declare bankruptcy after the simultaneous collapses of the printing and publishing business in which he was heavily invested; and the following May, his beloved wife Charlotte would die unexpectedly. Nevertheless, for the next six years until his own untimely death, Scott would keep his resolution to write in his journal as frequently as possible.

The posthumously published *Journal* is a trove of information and opinion concerning the life and times of an author often said in his own day to have no rival in British literature save Shakespeare. Regardless of whether Scott intended his journal for eventual publication—its high degree of playfulness and conscious self-fashioning suggests that he did—he clearly relished the opportunity not only to record the daily goings-on of his busy household and worldly affairs, but also to reflect on his abilities and shortcomings as an author. Some of the most fascinating passages in the *Journal* give us Scott's apparently uncensored opinions regarding both his and others' literary talents. One entry records his views of Jane Austen, at the time a far lesser-known author than Scott, whose novel *Emma* he had presciently reviewed almost a decade earlier:

> Also read again and for the third time at least Miss Austen's very finely written novel of *Pride and Prejudice*. That young lady has a talent for describing the involvements and feelings and characters of ordinary life which to me is the most wonderful I ever met with. The Big Bow wow strain I can do myself like any now going but the exquisite touch which renders ordinary common-place things and characters interesting from the truth of the description and the sentiments is denied to me. What a pity such a gifted creature died so early.[3]

This striking passage displays Scott's characteristic blend of insight, wit, self-deprecation, and gentle condescension toward his female counterparts. If Scott were alive today, he would likely be surprised but, on the basis of the above assessment, perhaps not astonished to find that Austen has now far outstripped him in popularity, both among lay readers and most critics and scholars.

Austen has long received her due as a serious writer; "the Author of Waverley," as Scott was known until he revealed himself in January 1827, has only recently been returned to that station. Despite penning novels set on multiple continents and in periods ranging from the Middle Ages to the present day, Scott's reputation dwindled during the second half of the nineteenth century to a writer of picturesque Scottish romances and boys' adventure stories. By the early twentieth century, Leslie Stephen's faint praise of Scott as providing excellent reading for convalescents had morphed into E. M. Forster's acerbic rhetorical question, "Who shall tell us a story? Sir Walter Scott, of course."[4] Even Northrop Frye, who along with David Daiches was one of the few Anglo-American critics of the mid-twentieth century to hold Scott in much esteem, suggested that he most enjoyed reading the Waverley Novels while traveling by plane, since their "formulaic techniques" rendered them reassuringly familiar and ideal for passing the time.[5]

Scott's return to critical respectability did not truly begin until the 1962 English translation of the Marxian critic Georg Lukács' seminal study *The Historical Novel*. By praising Scott's depictions of the clashes of social and economic forces that bring about historical change, Lukács may have been promoting his own version of dialectical materialism, but he was also reviving Scott's reputation as a literary craftsman whose fictions deserved careful attention. For Lukács, the Waverley Novels are noteworthy not only for showing the effects of historical change on the common people who lived through them, but also for the way their heroes usually embody a "neutral ground" in order to "bring the extremes whose struggle fills the novel . . . into contact with one another."[6] Of the subsequent major studies of Scott in the 1960s, Alexander Welsh's *The Hero of the Waverley Novels* continues to be the most influential. Like Lukács, Welsh treats Scott as a substantial writer whose fictions reflect Britain's and Europe's historical transitions from an aristocratic to a bourgeois order. Welsh also emphasizes the inherent conservatism of Scott's sociopolitical outlook, embodied especially in his creation of "passive" heroes whose inevitable survival typically ensures the appropriate transfer of landed property and patriarchal authority from one generation to the next.[7]

Though Scott studies languished again in the 1970s, the New Historicism of the 1980s spurred several more studies of Scott's evolution and accomplishments as a novelist and cultural commentator.[8] But it was largely thanks to a series of ground-breaking, historically oriented texts in the 1990s that Scott fully reassumed his central position in both the history of the novel and the Romantic era, that important hinge between the eighteenth and nineteenth centuries, which witnessed so many revolutions in the political (e.g. American, French, Haitian), economic (agricultural, industrial, financial), cultural (e.g. the 1807 abolition of the British slave trade), and aesthetic spheres.[9] In these contexts, Ina Ferris locates in Scott's career the masculinization of the professional author; Ian Duncan and Fiona Robertson each put Scott squarely at the center of the novel's generic development from Gothic romance to nineteenth-century realism; Robert Crawford and Katie Trumpener establish the Waverley Novels' influences on both Celtic and British modes of national imagining; and James Chandler demonstrates how Scott's handling of history is essential to the development of modern forms of historicism.[10] These remarkable studies—each of which placed Scott back into dynamic exchanges with other authors and ideas of his time—were followed by a series of more tightly focused monographs in the 2000s, especially Catherine Jones' *Literary Memory: Scott's Waverley Novels and the Psychology of Narrative*, Caroline McCracken-Flesher's *Possible Scotlands: Walter Scott and the Story of Tomorrow*, Julian Meldon D'Arcy's *Subversive Scott: The Waverley Novels and Scottish Nationalism*, and Andrew Lincoln's *Walter Scott and Modernity*.[11] (A number of other wider-scale monographs from this decade, led by Duncan's *Scott's Shadow: The Novel in Romantic Edinburgh*, continued to give Scott a prominent place in their critical narratives of British literary and cultural history.[12]) As further evidence of Scott's renewed critical vitality and respectability, special journal issues and book collections devoted to his works have multiplied.[13] The last few years have seen the publication of several more monographs primed to extend our appreciation and understanding of Scott's contributions to additional areas of literary and cultural history.[14]

Clearly, "the Great Unknown," as Scott was affectionately referred to for most of his career, is no longer unknown to literary scholars and critics, and *Walter Scott and Contemporary Theory* is deeply indebted to all of the above scholarship. This study differs from its predecessors, however, by its focus on putting Scott into dialogue with a wide variety of cutting-edge theorists, philosophers, and critics. My methodology, thus, purposefully echoes that of Slavoj Žižek's *Looking Awry: An Introduction to Jacques Lacan through Popular Culture*. Explaining his approach in that book, Žižek declares that

> [*Looking Awry*] mercilessly exploits popular culture, using it as convenient material to explain not only the vague outlines of the Lacanian theoretical edifice but sometimes also the finer details missed by the predominantly academic reception of Lacan . . . On the other hand, it is clear that Lacanian theory serves as an excuse for indulging in the idiotic enjoyment of popular culture.[15]

To adopt one of Žižek's favorite expository strategies, let me paraphrase this passage to better suit my own purposes:

> *Walter Scott and Contemporary Theory* thoroughly explores Scott's Waverley Novels, using them as convenient material to explain not only the vague outlines of the contemporary theoretical edifice but sometimes also the finer details missed by the predominantly philosophico-political reception of contemporary theory . . . On the other hand, it is clear that contemporary theory serves as an excuse for indulging in the wise enjoyment of Scott's oeuvre.

With a less polemical voice, and by balancing the relative importance of the two areas of inquiry—but with equal zest for my subjects—my working premise is that Žižek's unorthodox methodology represents an effective way to use (contemporary) theory and (literary) practice to shed mutual light on each other's inner workings. By juxtaposing pairings of Scott's early and later novels with major contemporary theoretical concepts, *Walter Scott and Contemporary Theory* uses theory to illuminate the complexities of Scott's fictions while simultaneously using Scott's fictions to explain and explore the state of contemporary theory.

Why Scott?

Why choose Walter Scott's fictions as the "convenient material" for this type of study? Arguably, there exists a handful of other British writers whose literary legacies are broad and deep enough to support the kind of critical and interpretive work I do in this book (including Shakespeare, Dickens,

George Eliot, Joyce, Woolf, and Rushdie). In this regard, my own lack of familiarity with the intricacies of these authors' oeuvres merely mitigates against *my* suitability for the task at hand, not theirs. But there are other, more objective reasons why Scott's fictions make particularly fertile ground for the seeds of contemporary theory to take root and grow. Some of these have already been alluded to in my brief synopsis of the modern history of Scott criticism, but they bear repeating in greater detail.

Despite being long associated with poetry, the Romantic era can just as properly be understood as the age of the novel's rise to hegemony.[16] Moreover, like its historical period, the Romantic novel represents an integral hinge between its eighteenth- and nineteenth-century generic neighbors. As Robert Miles explains,

> [The Romantic novel] was a continuation of an eighteenth-century form. Many of its chief practitioners subscribed to the late Enlightenment belief in a rational, political, public sphere. Its principle modality is symbolism, the propensity to rise above the literal in an attempt to form what we would now call ideological perspectives.[17]

An Enlightened view of society and human nature, combined with a renewed interest in the symbolic and the immaterial: this unusual synthesis—which helped make this period's novelists frequently appear immature, eccentric, or simply mediocre to the Victorians and Moderns who succeeded them— is what now makes Romantic-era novelists so fascinating to contemporary critics and scholars.[18] Within this dynamic period, moreover, Scott was the undisputed king of fiction. From the appearance of his first novel, *Waverley*, in 1814, through at least 1850, no novelist in Britain was more popular than Scott. The sheer abundance and availability of his writings meant that he positively saturated the print market for the first half of the nineteenth century in verse (including his early, two-volume collection *Minstrelsy of the Scottish Border* [1802–03] and nine original "metrical romances"), nonfiction prose (including the nine-volume *Life of Napoleon Buonaparte* [1827–28] and the four-volume *Tales of a Grandfather* [1828–31]), and of course fiction: 23 full-length novels, plus several novellas and short stories.

Scott was well aware of the improbability of his own productivity. Playfully stoking the public's wonderment that one author could write so much, in the Introduction to *The Betrothed* (1825) he imagines a boardroom meeting wherein various characters from his previous fictions debate whether to form a joint-stock company and incorporate in order to produce future Waverley Novels even more efficiently (possibly with the help of a steam engine). They cannot agree, however, and eventually the Author of Waverley himself interrupts their meeting to proclaim that he is turning his attention away from fiction toward history. Scott thereby inserts a canny advertisement for his forthcoming *Life of Napoleon* into his latest novel while simultaneously underscoring the anarchic fecundity of his imagination. *The Betrothed*'s introduction, thus, highlights another aspect of Scott's literary output that makes it particularly suitable for illuminating and exploring some of contemporary theory's central concerns: his combination of authorial interests and strategies appears simultaneously modern and (as I explain below) even postmodern. The era in which Scott lived and wrote was particularly dynamic and tumultuous for Britain. In geopolitical terms, it began with the United Kingdom losing its most important colonial possession, America; it ended with Britain, having successfully led the Allied powers against Revolutionary and then Napoleonic France, well on its way to becoming the world's first superpower and reconstituting its imperial ambitions through eastern expansion. In economic and technological terms, Britain began the Romantic era ahead of its competitors, thanks to its ongoing "agricultural revolution" of the eighteenth century; this advantage in turn allowed it to become by the 1830s the most productive and industrialized nation on the planet.[19] Such momentous changes brought equally substantial alterations to Britain's sociopolitical fabric: women's rights, the status of minorities (including Catholics and black slaves), workers' rights, and voting laws all underwent substantial revision.

If Scott's historical moment made him well positioned to represent fiction- ally the sociopolitical passage to modernity, taking full advantage of what Jacques Rancière calls modern literature's mission as a "symptomatology of society,"[20] then his primary choice of genre was equally fortuitous. Scott did not single-handedly create the historical novel, but he certainly brought it to popular and literary fruition.[21] In his own day, he was celebrated for his ability to bring historical subjects and characters vividly to life; the current critical renaissance of Scott studies, following Duncan's lead in *Modern Romance and Transformation of the Novel* (where he in turn builds on Fredric Jameson's influential typologies in *The Political Unconscious*), has added a renewed appreciation of the Waverley Novels' synthesis of the older tradition of prose romance, associated with the aristocracy, and the new priorities of an emergent realism, associated with the growing bourgeoisie. If the writing of history is the means by which the present comes to terms with the past and sets its course for the future, then the historical novel becomes in Scott's hands the premiere literary genre for accomplishing these goals in a format simultaneously entertaining and instructive.

There is another element of Scott's oeuvre that makes it especially suitable for theoretical intervention and analysis: its habitual self-referentiality. Repeatedly, the Waverley Novels draw attention to their dual status as commercial objects and literary fictions. The introduction to *The Betrothed* not only envisions a fantastical meeting of characters from previous Waverley

Novels, but also allows them to draw attention to the business side of Scott's novelistic labors, as the opening call to order by the "Preses" (a Scots term for moderator) demonstrates:

> Gentlemen, I need scarcely remind you, that we have a joint interest in the valuable property which has accumulated under our common labours. . . . It is, indeed, to me a mystery how the sharp-sighted [public] could suppose so huge a mass of sense and nonsense, jest and earnest, humorous and pathetic, good, bad, and indifferent, amounting to scores of volumes, could be the work of one hand, when we know the doctrine so well laid down by the immortal Adam Smith, concerning the division of labour.[22]

The double register of these observations would be remarkable even were they limited to acknowledging that the Waverley Novels may be regarded simultaneously as "valuable property" and "a mass of sense and nonsense." (In a brilliant public relations move, Scott had already published a mildly critical review of several of his earlier fictions.) The tacit admission that his productivity was, or at least could be, in inverse ratio to the quality of his creative output, dispels any lingering doubts regarding Scott's self-consciousness as a modern author in a competitive literary market.[23] To diversify his product, as well as to maintain his ruse of anonymity, Scott invented multiple authorial and editorial personae. All of this has led Jerome J. McGann to describe Scott's style as a kind of Romantic postmodernism: "Scott is not simply a kind of fantastical historian . . . he makes a parade of his imaginary moves."[24] For McGann, the anachronism of calling Scott postmodern is warranted insofar as it helps us appreciate the effects of his deployment of a variety of self-reflective metafictional devices. Scott's unparalleled combination of the Romantic/ modern (of historical moment, subject matter, and favored genre) and the postmodern (of style and approach to his profession and subject matter) contribute to making him an ideal author for reading through, and occasionally against, contemporary theory.

Why *contemporary* theory?

This brings me to the second half of my title. There are really two relevant questions here: Why theory? And why *contemporary* theory?

The term "theory" is purposefully, even productively, ambiguous. Situated somewhere between the abstractions of much traditional philosophy and the applied nature of most literary criticism, theory tends to be simultaneously more open-ended than the former and more global in its scope and ambitions than the latter. The etymology of the word, deriving from the Greek *theoria*, embraces both observation and reflection. In this light, Jonathan Culler provides a solid starting point for defining its contemporary iterations: "Works of theory characteristically function not as demonstration but as speculation – ideas whose range of applicability is not known in advance. Theory is analytical, speculative, reflexive, interdisciplinary, and a counter to common-sense views."[25] Culler uses "analytical" not to denote the tradition of mostly Anglo-American philosophy that eschews ontological questions in favor of strictly logical ones, but rather to signal any investigative intellectual procedure. Following Culler, "theory" as I understand it has more in common with what is broadly called Continental philosophy: those lines of theoretical inquiry, radiating outward from Europe, that ask after first principles both ontological (regarding being) and epistemological (regarding knowing). Since roughly the mid-twentieth century, moreover, such inquiries have been increasingly oriented toward the generation of critical problems and perspectives, especially regarding the status quo (be it political, social, aesthetic, or commonsensical, in Culler's idiom), rather than toward the consolidation of timeless answers or rigid dogmas. In particular, most although not all theory tends to be critical of the normative claims of Western modernity, which Peter Wagner summarizes as "the idea of the autonomy of the human being as the knowing and acting subject, on the one hand, and, on the other, the idea of the rationality of the world, that is, its principled intelligibility."[26]

Academic literary criticism since at least the 1970s has been heavily influenced by theoretical innovations, but theory and criticism are congruent, rather than identical, critical and interpretive projects. In general, the former tends to be more holistic and ambitious than the latter. Even the most avant-garde literary criticism still tends to be textually oriented, whereas theory takes as its objects of inquiry the overlapping realms of the human and the social in their widest purviews. As such, theory is well suited for generating provocative interpretations of the historical novel, a literary genre that purposefully and self-consciously embraces both the "real" of historical fact and the "fiction" of authorial craftsmanship.[27] Furthermore, inasmuch as Scott's historical novels in particular tend to juxtapose the past and the present, they are already engaged in asking some of the same questions about modernity that theory excels at pursuing.

My wager in this book, moreover, is that *contemporary* theory is particularly suited to this task. This might initially seem odd at first glance, considering that not so long ago "the death of theory" was being loudly proclaimed in some circles. But to paraphrase Mark Twain, these rumors were greatly exaggerated. In retrospect, what seems to have run its course is what is often called "high theory": the humanistic and social scientific work, mostly emanating from France in the decades following the tumultuous events of

1968, largely inspired by the "linguistic turn" in earlier twentieth-century philosophy (i.e. by modern philosophy's turn toward language as the ultimate medium of human expression and social action).[28] The development and legacy of this linguistic turn—generally traced back to the structural linguistics of Ferdinand de Saussure and forward to the deconstruction of Jacques Derrida, the historicism of Michel Foucault, and the structural psychoanalysis of Jacques Lacan—have been tracked many times.[29] Suffice it to say that even as the Derridean and Foucaultian models of theory were dominating Anglo-American Humanities departments in the 1980s and 1990s, the work of many other Continental theorists was gradually becoming available in English.[30] Just as the supposed "death of theory" in the early 2000s was being pronounced, a number of these theorists—many of whom I discuss in the following chapters—were in fact primed to breathe new life into the theoretical enterprise.

Walter Scott and Contemporary Theory does not, however, argue that we should no longer be reading Derrida, Foucault, or the other illustrious theorists of their generation; on the contrary, both of these theorists feature prominently in this text, albeit with emphasis on their late-career work, some of which has only recently been translated into English. They are included here, that is, not as representatives of "high theory," but as participants in the project of contemporary theory alongside those younger writers and thinkers—including European authors like Giorgio Agamben and Slavoj Žižek, and North Americans like Judith Butler and Manuel DeLanda—whose body of work mostly succeeds that of the 1968 generation. None of these theorists' ideas can be summed up succinctly or even exhaustively. Moreover, a book that moves repeatedly between theory and literature can only hope to discuss some of the most salient aspects of contemporary critical thought; I hope readers will follow their own interests and explore more fully those theorists whose ideas and approaches they find most compelling. For my part, I have tried to avoid favoring one theoretical "school" or methodology over another, and instead have looked for commonalities and continuities among those whose ideas seemed most compelling and relevant to my purposes.

The theorists discussed in the following chapters neither follow one critical program nor acknowledge one intellectual origin; indeed, several pairs of them (Derrida and Habermas; Foucault and Jean Baudrillard; Butler and Žižek) have publicly, strongly disagreed with one another. Taken together, however, their common identification with progressive, in many cases radical political positions becomes apparent. This orientation by itself is not unique to contemporary theory; many twentieth-century philosophers and writers, from Adorno to Sartre, also identified with Communist or antifascist parties and movements. But, the explicit political commitment of many contemporary theorists is especially notable in our supposedly postideological age, in which a pernicious notion of "fair and balanced" continues to obfuscate the real stakes of much public debate and policy. Theory gives us the intellectual tools to cut through that fog, dispensing with most of what passes for common sense in order to offer a variety of more challenging, troubling, and ultimately more substantial methods and frameworks for the critical study of many facets of culture, politics, the human, and (as we will see in my conclusion) perhaps even beyond.

It remains for me to say something regarding the specific Waverley Novels and critical concepts that I have chosen to engage with in *Walter Scott and Contemporary Theory*. Clearly, other selections were possible—with such large bodies of work from which to choose, some Scott novels necessarily had to be left out (although almost every well-known Waverley Novel is represented), and at least several important contemporary theoretical concepts are also absent.[31] Nevertheless, the novels and theoretical topics I have settled on are, I think, equal parts representative and complementary. Each main chapter focuses on a pair of Scott novels, one from early and another from later in his career, in order to demonstrate both continuities and transformations in his writing and thinking.[32] The novels in question are read primarily with reference to one or more contemporary critical concepts. Again, different combinations of novels and ideas were possible, but I feel strongly—and hope the reader will agree—that my chosen pairings shed constructive light on all elements involved. Those already familiar with Scott's novels will, I hope, discover new avenues of inquiry, thanks to the theoretical vistas offered here; those already well versed in contemporary theory should find that Scott's oeuvre offers intriguing opportunities for exemplifying, illuminating, and occasionally problematizing theory's various methods, assertions, and conclusions. As each chapter builds on the materials discussed in those previous to it, a relatively comprehensive yet dynamic picture of Scott's fictional oeuvre and the state of contemporary critical theory should emerge. If readers come away from this book with a greater understanding of the complexities and pleasures of *both* the Waverley Novels *and* contemporary theory, I will have amply achieved my goals.

1

Subjectivity, or *Waverley* and *Ivanhoe* with Žižek

In his foundational study, *The Hero of the Waverley Novels*, Alexander Welsh delineates the developmental arc of the archetypal Scott protagonist. Frequently caught up in a historical crisis much larger than he is capable of fully comprehending, the "Waverley Hero" must learn to give up his childish, idealistic attachments to premodern, "romantic" causes—especially Jacobitism, that anachronistic allegiance to the former Stuart monarchs of Scotland and England—in order to claim his place as a respectable member of modern society. In a more recent preface, Welsh reiterates this reading of the Waverley Novels' politicojuridical vision of individual and social maturation, asserting that "Scott's novels embrace a contractual ideal for society, frequently contrasted with feudal and patriarchal custom."[1] As Welsh himself recognizes, the Rousseauvian social contract was in fact unpopular with the Tories of Scott's day, who much preferred Hobbesian ideas of sovereignty-from-above to republican-sounding notions of "the general will" as the basis for social cohesion.[2] Nevertheless, Welsh effectively underscores the image of Scott as an uncritical (if occasionally ambivalent) promoter of an essentially conservative vision of modern subjectivity, one founded on men's willing renunciations of their anarchic desires in favor of "proper" familial and national commitments. (I say "men" advisedly, because this is a thoroughly *masculine* picture of civilized modernity, one that relegates women mostly to traditional supporting or seducing roles, which Welsh ingeniously identifies in Scott's novels with the "blonde heroine/dark seductress" dichotomy.)

In its general outline, there is much to admire in Welsh's persuasive interpretive scheme. Nonetheless, as I intend to demonstrate, we can greatly enhance, as well as complicate, Welsh's insights by thinking more closely about the specific ways in which Scott's fictions promote particular versions of modern subjectivity. By "subjectivity," moreover, contemporary theorists almost always mean something more specific than simple "individuality." To clarify the stakes of this distinction, and to probe more deeply into Scott's constructions of subject formation in *Waverley* and *Ivanhoe*—still arguably Scott's best-known and most influential novels—this chapter draws on the ideas of Slavoj Žižek, one of the most prolific, provocative theorists of contemporary subjectivity.

Waverley and the subject of modernity

Seen in the traditional critical light described above, the main plot of Scott's first novel, *Waverley, or 'Tis Sixty Years Since*, reads like an early nineteenth-century instruction manual on how to win friends and influence people. As the novel's oft-forgotten subtitle implies, *Waverley* is self-consciously set 60 years in the past, on the eve of the second major Jacobite Rebellion.[3] With the 1707 Act of Union between England and Scotland little more than a generation old, and the Hanoverian line of British monarchs only slightly more established, Great Britain is very much still a work in progress as the novel begins.[4]

Into this moment is thrust Edward Waverley. Even as a child, Waverley instinctively mediates between the various factions struggling to establish their hegemony. Foremost among these are his father, Richard, and uncle, Sir Everard, who have been estranged since the former, excluded from the family's landed inheritance due to the laws of primogeniture, abandoned his hereditary Jacobitism to seek political fortune with the Hanoverians. Father and uncle are partially reconciled, however, by 5-year-old Waverley's charming antics upon first spying his uncle's emblazoned carriage. By way of explanation, the urbane narrator jokes that "I know not whether the boy's nurse had been a Welch-woman or a Scotch-woman, or in what manner he associated a shield emblazoned with three ermines with the idea of personal property, but he no sooner beheld this family emblem than he stoutly determined on vindicating his right to the splendid vehicle on which it was displayed."[5] Despite its apparent unimportance, a passage like this already contains many of the hallmarks of Scott's career-long ingenuity: it simultaneously plays on readers' assumed familiarity with the stereotype of excessive Celtic genealogical pride, associates the young Waverley, despite his thorough Englishness, with the more peripheral (some would say internally colonized) nations of the British state, and establishes a seemingly natural bond between a male heir and his familial property.

The stage is, thus, set for Waverley, equal parts cipher and conduit, to play his small role in a much larger clash of sociopolitical forces, the outcome of which will decide his fate as well as the course of history. Thanks to Lukàcs, this format is now widely understood as evidence of Scott's deployment of a proto-Marxian materialist dialectic. Although Lukàcs declines to connect Scott directly to Hegel, such a move is unnecessary, for the Author of Waverley and Marx in fact share a different but equally important intellectual influence: the Scottish Enlightenment. As a student at the University of Edinburgh in the 1780s, Scott would have learned the conjoined historicist methodologies pioneered by earlier luminaries like David Hume and Adam Smith. First, there was stadial theory, in which all societies are seen to progress, programmatically if not inevitably, through three or four discrete stages, from hunting-gathering through pasturage to modern commercialism. (It was this insight that a society's mode of production determines its social relations that most impressed Marx.[6]) Second, he would have encountered conjectural history, in which gaps in the historical record are filled by speculation based on presumed knowledge of a given society's stage, combined with an understanding of the supposedly timeless, universal qualities of human nature. As many scholars have noted, the Scottish Enlighteners likely built these theories from materials gathered quite close to home; from their mostly academic perches in the rapidly developing cities of the Scottish Lowlands, figures like Smith, Adam Ferguson, and William Robertson needed only to look northward to see a Highland social fabric that, up until the aftermath of the 1745 Rebellion, was still largely woven from traditional feudal strands.

As an officer in the British army, Edward Waverley eventually makes his way into those Scottish Highlands, where he witnesses firsthand both the glories and the deprivations of pre-1745 Highland clan culture. We are prepared for Scott's superficially haphazard but entirely careful construction of this situation by the way he skillfully manipulates readers' expectations in *Waverley*'s introductory chapter. Demonstrating his familiarity with the range of generic options available to a Romantic-era novelist looking to create a new, eponymous protagonist, Scott slyly protests that

> I had only to seize upon the most sounding and euphonic surname that English history or topography affords, and elect it at once as the title of my work, and the name of my hero. But, alas! What could my readers have expected from the chivalrous epithets of Howard, Mordaunt, Mortimer, or Stanley, or from the softer and more sentimental sounds of Belmour, Belville, Belfield and Belgrave, but pages of inanity, similar to those which have been so christened for half a century past?[7]

His choice of "Waverley," Scott explains, is designed to avoid all preconceptions: "I have therefore, like a maiden knight with his white shield, assumed for my hero . . . an uncontaminated name, bearing with its sound little of good or evil, excepting what the reader shall hereafter be pleased to affix to it."[8] Yet even as he invokes the language of heraldry—the very thing that will soon fatefully attract young Waverley to his uncle's carriage—to claim that he is founding a fresh fictional genealogy, Scott remains disingenuous about the motives behind his choice. For one thing, as some critics have pointed out, "Waverley" was not an entirely uncorrupted name; on the contrary, many of Scott's readers (if not Scott himself) would have been familiar with an earlier Romantic-era novel, Charlotte Smith's *Desmond* (1792), which prominently features a "Waverly." Moreover, as few readers fail to notice, Scott's choice of surname for his protagonist carries the relatively obvious homonymic connotation of "wavering," which sharply describes his protagonist's inconstancy with regard to the various forces—familial, political, national, and sexual—that push and pull him throughout the novel.

Especially given its hero's notable malleability, it makes sense (despite Franco Moretti's claims to the contrary[9]) to read *Waverley* as a kind of early British *bildungsroman*, that is, as a Romantic-era case study in what theorists today call "subject formation" or "subjectivation." The idea that individuals are made rather than merely born is not new; indeed, opposition to the Platonic idea that we are each born in possession of full knowledge of ourselves and our world, and simply need to be reminded, presumably by a wise teacher like Plato's Socrates, of what we once knew, is almost as old as the Platonic tradition itself. From a contemporary theoretical perspective, one of the most convincing and provocative accounts of subject formation derives from Jacques Lacan, who reinterpreted Sigmund Freud's psychoanalytic theories in light of twentieth-century insights concerning the structural dimensions of language. Where Freud generally regards people as guided by biologically derived drives of which they are largely unconscious, Lacan sees individuals as motivated by unconscious desires that are not only intangible but also formed primarily by their interactions with others. For Lacan, in other words, the social world of language and culture—which he calls the symbolic order—necessarily precedes the individual, who only finds her place in it insofar as she "agrees" (in a manner that is necessarily incomplete and therefore ongoing) to its naming of her. The individual is subjectivized, first and foremost, by submitting to the "Name of the Father." On a literal level, this acceptance—which of course has already happened by the time the subject is old enough to realize it—is embodied in the patriarchal Western tradition of assuming the father's last name; figuratively, it entails accepting the "Law of the Father" as well, that is, the primacy of the masculine signifier ("the phallus," for Lacan, which takes the place of the biological penis in Freud's theories) in the symbolic order.

There is much more, of course, to Lacan's theories. At this point, however, let us stop with the further recognition that the Lacanian phallus is essentially an "empty" signifier, meaning that its role is to suture or hold together the Symbolic in order to maintain the appearance of the latter's consistency against intrusions of "the Real": those unsymbolizable, "impossible" points of reality (although this is not the only way to understand the Real, as we will see) that regularly challenge the symbolic order's coherence. With this insight, we reach one entry point into the thought of the Slovenian philosopher, writer, and cultural critic Slavoj Žižek, who deploys a unique synthesis of psychoanalysis, Marxian theory, and Continental philosophy in his voluminous output. His early work is very interested in "the symptom" as both a psychoanalytic and a Marxist concept, for in each, the symptom (whether on the body or the body politic) makes manifest the latent or hidden contradictions of the entity in question (whether the individual patient or the social order).[10] In his later work, Žižek frequently attends to the previously undertheorized Lacanian concept of the Real, often suggesting that it is in fact an *effect* of the contradictions of the symbolic order rather than their preexisting *cause*.[11] Together, Žižek's readings of the symptom and the Real are important components of one of his most fundamental contentions (itself a synthesis of philosophical, psychoanalytic, and political perspectives): that what we experience as "reality" is largely a phantasmatic structure. In other words, for Žižek, our ideological-symbolic understanding of the world is not superimposed upon an already existing reality, as in Marx's original definition of ideology as operating like a camera obscura, projecting an upside-down image of the world. Instead, ideology-as-fantasy structures our very experiences, not just of the world at large, but also of ourselves and our place in it.[12]

We can see many of the abovementioned processes at work with surprising clarity in Scott's first novel. If Waverley is from the start a particularly pliable fellow, then this may be because he enters a symbolic order that is unusually or exaggeratedly inconsistent. Lacking a strong, authoritative father figure, Waverley is brought up by a host of patriarchal substitutes: his absent-minded uncle, Sir Everard; his staunchly Jacobite aunt, Rachael, who regales him with tales of his ancestors' royalist sacrifices in the English Civil War; and an indulgent, equally Jacobitical tutor (whose seditious writings later threaten to incriminate Waverley even though he has never read them). The rest of Waverley's education, Scott informs us, is mostly filled with "a surfeit of idle reading" in his uncle's copious library, where Waverley freely helps himself to French memoirs "scarcely more faithful than romances," "chivalrous and romantic" Spanish adventure stories, and Norse epics.[13] Allowed to read "rather to awaken the imagination than to benefit the understanding," Waverley is almost comically unprepared for the military profession that awaits him, having at best a tenuous grasp on (or place in) the normal sociosymbolic coordinates of early eighteenth-century Britain.[14]

Accordingly, it does not prove particularly difficult for him to be drawn into the conspiracy forming around the secret return of the dethroned Jacobite heir Prince Charles Stuart. From the moment Waverley takes leave of his new regiment, stationed on the southeast coast Scotland, to visit Sir Everard's old friend, the Baron of Bradwardine, close to the Highland line, Waverley is primed to believe he is now beginning to live the "romance" he has hitherto only read about.[15] In a pattern that will be repeated (albeit with significant variations) in subsequent Waverley Novels, Waverley's geographical movement northward—from England to the Scottish Lowlands, then the Borders, then the Highlands—is not just a movement back in time, as per Scottish Enlightenment stadial theory, but also an apparent movement from English/Hanoverian reality to Scottish/Jacobite romance and fantasy. (That there were English Jacobites—although few if any chose to join their Scottish counterparts in the 1745 Rebellion, dooming its chances of success—and also many Hanoverian Lowlanders, are facts mostly ignored by Scott to simplify the lines of historical conflict.)

To convey his sense that he is crossing a threshold, not just into another place and time, but into another genre, Waverley's entrance into the Lowland village of Tully-Veolan is focalized almost entirely from his perspective.[16] One of the first things he notices, we are told, is that "The houses seemed miserable in the extreme, especially to an eye accustomed to the smiling neatness of English cottages."[17] Yet even as the "realistic," Enlightened cast of Waverley's mind initially has him noting everything about Tully-Veolan that does not meet his modern (English) standards, he quickly begins assimilating what he sees to the "romantic" (Jacobite) perspective implanted in him since childhood: "Three or four village girls, returning from the well or brook with pitchers and pails upon their heads, formed more pleasing objects, and with their thin short-gowns and single petticoats, bare arms, legs, and feet, uncovered heads and braided hair, somewhat resembled Italian forms of landscape."[18] This aestheticizing gaze, especially when focused on the village's eligible females, is resumed later in the same paragraph, when we learn from Waverley's thoughts that "among the young women, an artist might have chosen more than one model whose features and form resembled those of Minerva."[19]

By the time Waverley is drawn yet farther north, thanks to some strategic cattle stealing by the Highland bandit Donald Bean Lean, he is deeply involved in imagining both himself and those around him as characters in a chivalrous romance. Thus, even when Bean Lean turns out to look nothing like what Waverley expects—"Waverley prepared himself to meet a stern, gigantic, ferocious figure . . . Donald Bean Lean was the very reverse of all these"[20]— the fantasy that supports Waverley's increasing abandonment of his previous existence is now too strong to be disrupted by mere facts. Žižek offers an explanation of this phenomenon through one of his favorite ideological examples: the phantasmatic logic of anti-Semitism. What might have happened, he asks in *The Sublime Object of Ideology*, when a typical citizen of 1930s Germany, "bombarded by anti-Semitic propaganda," confronted his perfectly friendly and respectable Jewish neighbor?

> Does not this everyday experience offer an irreducible resistance to the ideological construction? The answer is, of course no. If everyday experience offers such a resistance, then the anti-Semitic ideology has not yet really grasped us. An ideology is really 'holding us' only when we do not feel any opposition between it and reality – that is, when the ideology succeeds in determining the mode of our everyday experience of reality itself.[21]

As we will see, perhaps the Highland/Jacobite "hold" on Waverley is never as strong as it initially appears. Nevertheless, as Waverley journeys into the waiting hands of the ambitious Highland chieftain Fergus MacIvor (whose cosmopolitan manners, learned at the French court of the exiled Stuarts, Waverley notes but again fails to assimilate critically), he appears to accept fully his increasingly immersive Jacobite experiences. The well-known scene in which Fergus' devoted sister, Flora, seduces Waverley to their cause by singing a translated Gaelic air while accompanying herself on a small harp, is so overtly theatrical as to be almost parodic: Scott repeats his "romantic" description of this set-piece, staged against the backdrop of a waterfall at twilight, no less than three times, and emphasizes that Waverley imagines himself "like a knight of romance . . . conducted by [a] fair Highland damsel."[22] Yet even when Flora's "spell" is broken by the sudden appearance of Fergus and his hunting dogs, Waverley does not allow such quotidian details to disturb his fantasy-supported view of "reality" (just as Žižek's exemplary anti-Semite takes the Jewish neighbor's appearance of normalcy as simply another sign of his dangerous treachery).

Waverley's "conversion" to the Jacobite cause is complete—at least temporarily—when, with the Rebellion in full swing, he meets Bonnie Prince Charlie himself in occupied Edinburgh. Having already been accused of desertion by the British army, Waverley is carefully conducted by Fergus through the halls of Holyrood Palace (the monarch's official Scottish residence) into "a presence-room fitted up with some attempt at royal state."[23] Despite this scarcity of props, Waverley is immediately fascinated by the Prince:

> Unaccustomed to the address and manners of a polished court, in which Charles was eminently skillful, his words and his kindness penetrated the heart of our hero, and easily outweighed all prudential motives. To be thus personally solicited for assistance by a prince, whose form and manners, as well as the spirit which he displayed in this singular enterprize, answered his ideas of a hero of romance . . . gave Edward, in his own eyes, the dignity

and importance which he had ceased to consider as his attributes. . . . the time, besides, admitted of no deliberation, – and Waverley, kneeling to Charles Edward, devoted his heart and sword to the vindication of his rights![24]

Feeling cast out of one sociosymbolic order—what Žižek, following Lacan, calls the big Other—Waverley now eagerly accepts the place offered him in another. Clearly, he is gratified by the Prince's personal invitation to join the Jacobite cause. But, Waverley is also pleased here in a more precise psychoanalytic sense: by having his "romantic" fantasy appear to come true, his "ideal Ego" is restored to him in the form of (what he fantasizes is) the Other's positive view of him. As Žižek frequently points out, however, this ideal Ego must be differentiated from the harrowing "Ego-Ideal," in which the subject identifies with (what he fears is) how his life truly appears to the Other: "as a vain and repulsive spectacle."[25] In fact, Waverley has already experienced a version of this abjection in his earlier interview with a British army officer who charged him with "spreading mutiny and rebellion" as well as "desertion," and ordered him taken to jail in Stirling (during which journey Waverley was freed in an ambush and eventually guided to Edinburgh).[26]

Which is the real Edward Waverley: Jacobite hero, or Hanoverian deserter? As the novel demonstrates, answers to this kind of identity-determining question—like the terms of the question itself—are formed at least as much by the operations of forces beyond the subject's control, as by the subject himself. Following the timeline of historical events, Scott has Waverley participate as a Jacobite in only one battle, at Prestonpans. Here, he manages to avoid killing any fellow Englishmen, but again experiences the disorienting effects of being forced to identify with his lowly Ego-Ideal when, hearing the English voice of his former commanding officer give final battle commands to the other side, Waverley has the first of several apparent epiphanies:

> It was at that instant, that looking around him, he saw the wild dress and appearance of his Highland associates, heard their whispers in an uncouth and unknown language, looked upon his own dress, so unlike the which he had worn from his infancy, and wished to awake from what seemed at the moment a dream, strange, horrible, and unnatural. "Good God," he thought, am I then a traitor to my country, a renegade to my standard, and a foe . . . to my native England![27]

The concluding phrase, "my native England," gives certain indication of where Waverley's loyalties ultimately lie. At this battle, the Jacobites prove victorious, however, and so he remains on their side; in a moment of seemingly spontaneous compassion, he also saves an English colonel from certain death. Although Scott gives no hints (save in the above passage) that Waverley harbors ulterior motives in the heat of battle, this act of mercy proves crucial to his eventual reconciliation with the Hanoverians. Furthermore, even as Charles Stuart's forces enjoy further successes pushing through the Borders and into northern England, the consistency of Waverley's Jacobitical fantasy begins to dissolve as he realizes that Flora does not love him and that Fergus has been using their friendship to garner credit with the Prince.

By early December, having pushed as far south as Derby, the Jacobite army fatefully decides to turn back toward Scotland. Although Scott again refrains from confirming whether Waverley plans any of his actions, when he is caught in a chaotic nighttime skirmish and becomes separated from the retreating Jacobites, Waverley effectively uses his situation to begin disentangling himself from their rebellion. It is at this pivotal moment where most critics locate Waverley's true maturation, which Welsh and others have identified as his transition into adulthood, modernity, and Britishness. Along these lines, Waverley's entire Jacobitical episode now begins to appear structurally akin to the psychoanalytic process that Žižek, again following Lacan, calls "traversing the fantasy." Rather than learning to free oneself from a given fantasy, as traditional Freudian therapy would prescribe, "traversing the fantasy" involves totally identifying with it in order to "pass through it". To appreciate what this entails, we need first to familiarize ourselves with the famous Lacanian insight that one's desire is always the desire of the Other. Žižek has shown that although this insight is central to Lacan's understanding of subjectivity throughout his career, its meaning changes significantly. In the 1940s, the phrase "Desire is the desire of the Other" initially designates desire's paranoiac, envious quality: "I desire an object only insofar as it is desired by the Other," in Žižek's paraphrase.[28] By the middle of Lacan's career, however, this formulation changes its meaning: desire now becomes structured in advance by one's position in the symbolic order, such that one's desire is always effectively the desire of the big Other (designated with a capital "A"). In Lacan's late work, finally, what previously appeared to be the desire of the big Other becomes instead (as the symbolic order itself is revealed to be illusory, artificial[29]) the "impenetrable, enigmatic" desire of the small other ("a"), the ultimate phantasmatic object itself.

"Traversing the fantasy," then, requires identifying with one's fantasy (insofar as fantasy is always the articulation of a desire) so strongly and thoroughly that one ultimately realizes its emptiness: an emptiness that in turn must be recognized as belonging, not only to oneself, but also to the Other.[30] But does Waverley ever reach this point? That is, does he renounce Jacobitism and emerge on the far side of the "fantasy" of the 1745 Rebellion, recognizing that Bonnie Prince Charlie, far from being the representative of the (phantasmatic) big Other, is in fact just another inscrutable "objet petit a," an objectification of Waverley's own self-(mis)recognition? Or does Waverley merely give up identifying with one fantasy—the "romance" of Jacobitism—in order to (re)identify with another?

For answers, let us turn to the well-known passage where Scott most explicitly conjoins Waverley's rejection of Jacobitism with his supposed assumption of a mature, British identity. Waiting out the Rebellion—which, as Scott's readers well knew, would end in utter defeat for the Jacobites at Culloden on 16 April 1746—at a farmhouse in Cumberland, Waverley is finally at leisure to review his recent past and take stock of his current situation. As the narrator explains,

> it was in many a winter walk by the shores of Ulswater, that [Waverley] acquired a more complete mastery of a spirit tamed by adversity, than his former experience had given him; and that he felt himself entitled to say firmly, though perhaps with a sigh, that the romance of his life was ended, and that its real history had now commenced.[31]

"He was soon called upon," the narrator adds, "to justify his pretensions to reason and philosophy." In a recent reading of this passage, Celeste Langan observes that Waverley's "sigh" both supplements and displaces the need for him to actually "*say* his adieus," so that "We are told only that Waverley 'felt entitled' to announce an end to an era, the commencement of another – in short, to mark a period."[32] Langan links Waverley's exhalation to Scott's evocation of that ultra-Romantic idea, the "spirit of the age" (*zeitgeist*). His sense of entitlement, however, remains problematic. On its surface, the above passage suggests that Waverley's choice to forego the "romance" of his earlier life and embrace "real history" is entirely voluntary; this is, after all, apparently the moment when he finally overcomes his wavering, makes a decision, and firmly sticks to it. Yet, Scott specifies that Waverley achieves "mastery" of a spirit (his own) that is *already* "tamed by adversity." What can this redoubling mean? I think we are presented here with what Žižek frequently identifies as one of the key ideological features of modern society: the paradox of the "forced choice, of [the] freedom to do what is necessary . . . I have to do freely what I am expected to do."[33] (One of Žižek's favorite examples is the freely chosen yet entirely requisite endorsement of the democratic process by any public figure in the West.) Having already, albeit not entirely consciously, recognized the hopelessness of the Jacobite cause, Waverley now takes it upon himself to commit fully to the only real choice he has left: the Hanoverian monarchy.

This requirement to choose what amounts to the only available choice produces a particular yet generalizable kind of person: the barred or split subject. Although this Lacanian paradigm is frequently presented as a transhistorical phenomenon, in *Tarrying with the Negative: Kant, Hegel, and the Critique of Ideology*, Žižek offers an intriguing account of its potential historical origins. The barred subject as the paradigmatic subject of modernity comes into being, he hypothesizes, on the far side of the most significant rebellion in Romantic-era history: the French Revolution. Characteristically reading Hegel through Lacan, Žižek explains how the dialectic of *bildung* begins as a rational exchange between the subject and the State (perhaps the biggest "big Other" of the modern era): "in exchange for his increasing alienation, for sacrificing a further substantial part of himself the subject receives honor, wealth," and the other benefits of modern societal legitimacy.[34] Eventually, the subject ends up exchanging "everything" for "nothing," as everything that might constitute her "radical particularity" is sacrificed for the ontological nullity that is her place in the symbolic order. The historical moment of this irrational (unbalanced) exchange—the ultimate "forced choice"—is the Terror of the French Revolution, during which every French citizen lived under threat of immediate execution.[35] The only way to forestall the anxiety raised by the constant threat of the guillotine, Žižek speculates, was to effect the ultimate dialectical reversal (the Hegelian "negation of negation") and identify oneself as completely as possible with the death-dealing power of the State, thereby "internaliz[ing] this force of negativity and recogniz[ing] in it [one's] own essence."[36] As a result of this passage to modern subjectivity, however, the traces of one's own "radical particularity" remain only as a series of "pathological" obstacles that must be repressed in order to maintain one's successful identification with the (void of the) big Other.

As a historical account of the French Revolution, this Hegelian/Žižekian paradigm is certainly open to debate. But as an allegory of the modern subject's emergence, "through a violent abstraction from all its particular roots and determinations" into a socially functional yet radically self-alienated entity "which is as such foreign to, incompatible with, enjoyment," it is a troublingly productive critical narrative.[37] At any rate—especially if we keep in mind that Scott's representation of the Jacobite uprising in *Waverley* can itself be read as a metacommentary on the French Revolution[38]—does this formulation not help explain why Waverley so readily, yet so dispassionately, embraces his own post-Rebellion life with the bloodless Rose Bradwardine, daughter of the Baron whose Lowland estate Waverley thereby stands to inherit? With Bonnie Prince Charlie fled back to France, Fergus and his followers either killed in battle or executed after summary trials, and an already ghost-like Flora retiring to a Continental nunnery, both Waverley's choice to return to the Hanoverian fold (facilitated by his father's sudden death and the mediation of the Englishman, Colonel Talbot, whose life Waverley saved) and his decision to marry Rose (whom he discovers saved his life when she alerted Prince

Charles to Waverley's earlier capture) are so overdetermined as to be almost parodic.

In short, the Jacobite failure is the condition of Waverley's triumph. Seen in this light, *Waverley*'s final chapters ought to make us rather uneasy. We learn, for example, that Waverley's future kindnesses to Fergus' displaced and suppressed clansmen earn him the nickname "Friend of the Sons of Ivor," and watch as Talbot, who secretly purchased the Baron's ruined estate after the Rebellion at "a very great bargain," returns it—nostalgically restored to its former Lowland glory—to Bradwardine.[39] Most discomfiting is Scott's description of a new painting of Waverley and Fergus in full Highland regalia, with the MacIvor clan descending a rocky pass in the background, proudly displayed in the Baron's refurbished dining hall; the painting's scene never took place, it turns out, but was concocted in an Edinburgh artist's studio after the fact.[40] It is tempting to scour these details for evidence that Waverley recognizes their inauthenticity. Such knowledge would be akin to the psychoanalytic logic of fetishistic disavowal: "I know very well . . . (e.g. that women don't have penises) . . . but nevertheless (I will act as though I don't know this, by focusing on their feet/hair/ etc.)." For Žižek, such logic not only is analogous to the sociopolitical bad faith identified by Peter Sloterdijk as "cynical reason," but also explains how ideology manages to operate despite the general public's hazy awareness that the fantasy of the symbolic order frequently only imperfectly captures their subjective experiences: "one knows the falsehood very well, one is aware of a particular interest hidden behind an ideological universality, but still one does not renounce it."[41] This is why, as Žižek often points out, ideology resides finally in one's behavior: it is in what one does, not merely in how one thinks.

Waverley's "bad faith" is so deeply hidden, even to himself, that almost no trace of it can be heard in his own pronouncements. If we listen closely, however, overtones of Sloterdijk's "cynical reason" may be heard in the studied urbanity of Scott's narrative voice in *Waverley*, especially as it moves the novel toward its retroactively inevitable-seeming conclusion. Consider, for example, the barely suppressed irony with which Scott describes the moment when Waverley commits his affections to the Baron's daughter: "To Rose Bradwardine, then, he owed the life which he now thought he could have laid down to serve her. A little reflection convinced him, however, that to live for her sake was more convenient and agreeable."[42] Yet when, with regard to the reception of the fraudulent portrait, Scott's narrator announces that "The whole piece was generally admired,"[43] readers must recognize that, notwithstanding the novel's famous final chapter (which I discuss at the start of the next chapter), its remaining characters—those who are still living, that is, and have not perished like the noble Evan Dhu along with the Jacobites' ambitions—seem to have adopted *en masse* the aestheticizing, phantasmatic gaze that Waverley turned on the village of Tully Veolan at his initial arrival. As for Waverley himself, his exchange of any remaining "radical particularity" for his position in the reconstituted symbolic order is so complete that few traces of self-consciousness, much less self-criticism, can be found in him as the novel that bears his name draws to a close. The culminating feast in the Baron's restored manor-house, presumably only the first of many over which Waverley will now placidly preside, entirely validates Žižek's contention that "Repetition announces the emergence of the law, of the Name-of-the-Father . . . the event that repeats itself retroactively receives, through its repetition, its law."[44]

The figure of the Jew and the failure to act in *Ivanhoe*

Waverley ends with the successful reintegration of the surviving characters—led, of course, by the protagonist himself—into the reigning sociosymbolic order. As we have seen, this movement maps quite neatly onto Waverley's actual movements through eighteenth-century Britain, from England to Scotland and back again.[45] Using *Waverley* in its turn as a map or blueprint from which to generalize about the rest of Scott's novels, however, can be a mistake. While many of Scott's subsequent novels take up similar themes, almost everything that Scott wrote after *Waverley* tends to complicate its patterns and conclusions, even when they seem compatible.

Such complications can be seen clearly if we move from *Waverley* to *Ivanhoe* (1819), still Scott's best-known, most widely recognized novel. This was the first Waverley Novel to feature an exclusively English historical setting, one that far predates either Scott's own memories or the oral traditions that he frequently drew from for his previous fictions. Worried that he was exhausting the public's interest in Scottish themes and topics, Scott muses explicitly in *Ivanhoe*'s "Dedicatory Epistle"—written in the voice of one of his many fictional mouthpieces—on the dangers of his new approach. Maintaining his public anonymity, Scott has the introductory letter's addressee suggest that "the charm [of the previous Waverley Novels] lay entirely in the art with which the unknown author had availed himself . . . of the antiquarian stores which lay around him, supplying his own indolence or poverty of invention, by the incidents which had actually taken place in his country at no distant period."[46] Along with *Waverley*'s "Postscript, which should have been a Preface," I will return to *Ivanhoe*'s introduction in greater detail in Chapter 2. For now, I want merely to address the potential difficulty that *Ivanhoe*'s late-twelfth-century setting presents for a critical approach to subjectivity. While the eighteenth-century setting of many other Waverley Novels makes them roughly synonymous with the emergence of recognizably modern thought and society in the West, *Ivanhoe*'s setting in the "period towards the end of the reign of Richard I" is clearly premodern.[47] Can contemporary theory— most (although not all) of which is designed to address phenomena specific to Western modernity—speak about representations of such a moment?

There are at least two reasons to answer "yes." The first is specific to Scott's case: no matter their historical period, every Waverley Novel features characters with recognizably modern psychologies. This is a consequence, I think, of Scott's enlightened belief in the supposed timelessness of human nature, combined with his understanding that, to attract and hold the interest of readers, "the subject assumed should be, as it were, translated into the manners, as well as the language, of the age in which we live."[48] In the later nineteenth and early twentieth centuries, this was frequently seen as a weakness of Scott's non-Scottish and pre-eighteenth-century writings; now it is more generally appreciated as a strategy for producing the novels' ongoing relevance.[49] The second, which potentially applies not only to modern representations of premodern times (like *Ivanhoe*) but also to the cultural productions of those premodern periods themselves, involves invoking an insight best formulated by Joan Copjec. The historicist requirement that "the past must be understood in its own terms," Copjec argues, overlooks the fact that no era, like no person, is entirely accessible to itself; accordingly, "*no historical moment can be comprehended in its own terms*."[50] Granted, the notion of an ever-present absence or lack at the heart of the subject is itself at least partially a psychoanalytic formulation. Nevertheless, Copjec's critique of historicism serves as a useful reminder that, when carried out thoughtfully, theoretical interventions into even the distant past can cast critical illumination forward as well as backward.

Such is certainly the case for *Ivanhoe*. The novel nominally focuses on the adventures of a disinherited Saxon knight, Wilfred of Ivanhoe, who has returned to England after accompanying Richard I on his ill-fated Crusade to the Holy Land. Thematically, however, *Ivanhoe*'s main interest is in delineating the conflict of civilizations following the Norman conquest. Unlike the radically unsettled nature of *Waverley*'s mid-eighteenth-century backdrop, Scott imagines late-twelfth-century England as a place of clearly demarcated oppositions. The greatest distinction he draws, not surprisingly, is between the Norman victors and the vanquished Anglo-Saxons who are now their inferiors. Early in the novel, for example, the jester Wamba explains the distinction between the terms for a live pig and a slaughtered one in an explicitly hierarchical register: "so when the brute lives, and is in the charge of a Saxon slave, she goes by her Saxon name [swine]; but becomes a Norman, and is called pork, when she is carried to the Castle-hall to feast among the nobles."[51] Scott frequently exaggerates the differences between the two primary peoples of England, in fact, the better to facilitate the multiple reconciliations he eventually arranges between them. Yet while he pays a great deal of attention to dress and costume in *Ivanhoe*, he is admittedly not always consistent about such details. While the Saxon thane Cedric and his beautiful ward Rowena are carefully coutured in traditional Saxon gear, for instance, Cedric's Saxon thrall, Gurth, is described as wearing the traditional clothing of the Norman peasantry. Likewise, on the linguistic plane, although Scott correctly notes that Normans and Saxons mostly continued to speak two separate languages, he first violates the historical record by anachronistically suggesting that they have already developed a shared "lingua Franca" in which to communicate, and later erroneously suggests that this imaginary synthetic dialect eventually became English.[52]

Regardless of whether these inconsistencies are intentional or accidental, the pattern they present stands out: two races, differing in language, custom, and costume, with a shared history of violent antipathy, whose eventual synthesis is nevertheless already anticipated. As the complete mingling of Norman and Saxon would not take place for several centuries, however, Scott forgoes the kind of happy ending with which *Waverley* concludes—in which the marriage of the English Waverley and the Scottish Rose Bradwardine literally unites former enemies—in favor of something a little more measured. The eventual union of Ivanhoe and Rowena, a descendant of Alfred the Great, maintains Saxon purity (although Cedric had hoped to marry his ward to Aethelstane, a descendent of Edward the Confessor), but it is effectively presided over by Richard I—the Norman king whose legitimacy is ultimately acknowledged by the proud Cedric. The Saxon thane's acceptance of the Norman monarch, in turn, becomes the springboard from which Scott can launch his optimistic assessment of England's unified future, as he describes how "the countenance which [Richard] afforded on this and other occasions to the distressed and hitherto degraded Saxons, gave them a safer and more certain prospect of attaining their just rights, than they could reasonably hope from the precarious chance of a civil war."[53] The fact that Ivanhoe can marry whomsoever he wants *and* receive his father's blessing (unlike Waverley, whose marriage to Rose is facilitated by his father's untimely death) suggests that Scott's tale of early England actually achieves more closure than his first novel, at least on the level of psychosocial stability represented by the Law of the Father.

Fittingly, the costs of this achievement are even more boldly highlighted in *Ivanhoe* than in *Waverley*. This is due primarily to the presence of two characters who remain excluded from either the Norman or the Saxon camp: Isaac, "the Jew of York," and his daughter Rebecca. Critics have generally praised Scott's tolerant portrayals of these figures, especially given the anti-Semitic stereotypes prevalent in early nineteenth-century Britain. Additionally, readers have frequently noted that the "romantic chemistry" between Ivanhoe and Rebecca seems far stronger than that between Ivanhoe and Rowena. Although the novel is nominally about its eponymous knight's quest to win back Rowena's hand, the plot itself is driven by Ivanhoe's ever-deepening relationship with Rebecca. The seeds of their romance are planted early, when Ivanhoe spontaneously alerts Isaac to a planned waylaying by the minions of the Templar knight, Brian de Bois-Guilbert. Later, after being wounded at the tournament of Ashby-de-la-Zouch, Ivanhoe is cared for by Rebecca, who refuses to abandon him even when they are both in danger; later still, the Saxon knight engages in single combat with the corrupt Templar to save Rebecca from being burned as a witch. Although he does not actually have to kill Bois-Guilbert, who dies of an apparent heart attack just as the duel commences, it is clear that Ivanhoe is as willing to stake his life for Rebecca as she is for him.

Their impassioned relationship develops, moreover, against a backdrop of near-unremitting anti-Semitism. Nearly every non-Jewish character in the novel says or does something bigoted at some point in *Ivanhoe*. Even the "heroic" characters are not free from this habit: Robin Hood (Locksley), who makes several pivotal appearances, thinks nothing of directing casual insults at Isaac, and Ivanhoe's immediate "compassion" for the older man is mixed with "contempt."[54] Nevertheless, such moments pale in comparison to the abuse that Isaac routinely absorbs from the novel's less tolerant characters. At Ashby-de-la-Zouch, caught between Prince John's sneering regard (as Richard's usurping brother, he needs access to the capital of the York Jews) and the tournament crowd's utter contempt, Isaac is first humiliated by Wamba, then relieved of his gold by John, and finally left to "the derision of those around him."[55] Beautiful Rebecca, meanwhile, consistently finds herself the object of unwanted male attention. The "lovely Jewess," as she is repeatedly called (once by Prince John, twice by the narrator), seems to attract admirers as much for her subaltern status as for her beauty, such that when Bois-Guilbert exclaims "would to Heaven that we had never met, or that thou hadst been noble in birth and Christian in faith," the reader strongly suspects that it is precisely her forbidden Jewishness that makes her so irresistible to the Templar.[56]

David Simpson observes that "Scott consistently has a hard time offering a critique of anti-Semitism without claiming (albeit in a smaller voice) that there are aspects of the Jewish character and culture that seem to invite it."[57] Rather than see this ambivalence as Scott's failure, or even as a regrettable feature of the age in which he wrote, however, we are now in a position to recognize it as symptomatic of a larger pattern that Žižek's blend of psychoanalysis and ideology critique can identify. Earlier, with regard to the way a fully successful ideology entirely structures the subject's relationship to her or his lived experience, we saw Žižek invoke the logic of anti-Semitism whereby the Jewish neighbor's appearance of normalcy actually confirms the anti-Semitic stereotype of the deceitful, conspiratorial Jew. But why do such stereotypes exist at all? On several occasions in *Ivanhoe*, Scott explains the hatred of Jews in twelfth-century England as stemming from their professional access to the country's supply of specie, which was continually depleted and therefore always difficult to obtain.[58] Later, he gives Rebecca a series of powerful, quasi-Shakespearean speeches during her captivity at Templestowe, in which she refutes Bois-Guilbert's characterization of Jews as a "degraded nation . . . head[s] bent down before each petty noble, and . . . look[s] only terrible to the shivering and bankrupt debtor" by reminding him that "Thou has spoken the Jew . . . as the persecution of such as thou has made him. . . . industry has opened to him the only road to power and to influence, which oppression has left unbarred."[59] And yet Scott's own undeniably ambivalent portrayals of Jews—especially his repeated descriptions of Isaac as cowardly to the point of effeminacy—attest that anti-Semitism is far more deep-seated and irrational than any logical, historically specifically account can fully explain.

Žižek's explanation is founded on the idea that anti-Semitism is "perhaps the purest incarnation of ideology as such."[60] (For this reason, I think, some critics have mistaken Žižek's consistent return to the subject as evidence of his own anti-Semitism.) The anti-Semitic figure of "the Jew" goes far beyond the scapegoat function normally attributed to it. Instead, Žižek sees "the Jew" as the exemplary *point de capiton*, or "quilting point," that allows an otherwise contradictory and self-conflicting symbolic order to appear coherent to itself. The essence of a quilting point, ironically, is that it has no essence—like the Lacanian *objet a*, the *point de capiton* "has no positive consistency" outside of the system itself: "the *point de capiton* is rather the word which, *as a word*, on the level of the signifier itself, unifies a given field, constitutes its identity."[61] It does not add anything new to the cluster of conflicts and contradictions that already characterizes a given sociosymbolic order. It simply gives a name to the excess of signification already generated by these contradictions. This act of naming allows a given ideological field to preserve its appearance of consistency—figuratively, to stitch itself together—through the *point de caption*. Thus, the "quilting point" is not a symbol in the traditional sense of representing the abstract qualities of what it symbolizes in a concretized form; rather, it is a symptom of the fundamental antagonisms, contradictions, or deadlocks it both crystallizes and masks.

For the anti-Semite, it should now be obvious, the figure of "the Jew" is the ultimate *point de capiton*. Blaming Jews for society's ills not only explicitly attributes those problems to the interference of a foreign entity (an explanation, perhaps, for Scott's decision to clothe Rebecca consistently in "Eastern" dress), but also implicitly prevents the internal causes of social antagonism from being actively interrogated: "Society is not prevented from achieving its full identity because of Jews: it is prevented by its own antagonistic nature, by its own immanent blockage, and it 'projects' this internal negativity into the figure of the 'Jew'."[62] In *Ivanhoe*, these internal antagonisms include not just the strife between Normans and Anglo-Saxons, but also the differing interests of monarch and nobles, and the gap between the chivalric code's idealistic veneration of women and their real treatment as mere objects of exchange between men. By this logic, if "the Jew" ever were to be removed fully from the body politic—as, for example, Nazi Germany horrifically attempted—another *point de caption* would need to be found to take its place (the homosexual, the Communist, or the terrorist, for example).

In fact, *Ivanhoe* achieves its measure of closure through a similar movement. In the form of Isaac and Rebecca's departure for Grenada, Scott anticipates the Jews' actual expulsion from England in 1290, but with the added irony that the Jews of Spain would in turn face exile two centuries later if they did not convert to Catholicism. Thus, whereas in *Waverley* Scott uses the Jacobite defeat at Culloden to signal the removal of the last threat of radical difference from Britain's unified modernity, the self-imposed exile of Isaac and Rebecca at *Ivanhoe*'s conclusion does not dispel England's pervasive anti-Semitism as much as confirm it. By this point in the novel, after all, it is clear that no union between Rebecca and a Gentile will take place: Ivanhoe has married Rowena, and Bois-Guilbert is dead. Even when alive, moreover, Bois-Guilbert is certain that marriage with Rebecca is out of the question, both because of his Templar oath and her supposed racial inferiority. When he makes her a last-ditch proposal, it is to become his mistress, not his wife. Still, by proposing that he and Rebecca flee England together, Bois-Guilbert shows a measure of real courage:

> "Listen to me, Rebecca," he said, softening his tone; "England – Europe – is not the world. There are spheres in which we may act, ample enough even for my ambition. We will go to Palestine, where Conrade, Marquis de Montserrat, is my friend – a friend free as myself from the doting scruples which fetter our free-born reason – rather with Saladin we will league ourselves, than endure the scorn of the bigots whom we contemn."[63]

Bois-Guilbert's ability to imagine a symbolic order other than England's current status quo is encouraging, and his reference to Saladin as a figure of freedom anticipates that character's subversive appearance in Scott's *The Talisman* (1825) 6 years later. Yet, Rebecca correctly recognizes that the Templar's plans are self-serving fantasies, and we are meant to cheer when she tells the prideful Bois-Guilbert that she prefers death to becoming his lover.

By contrast, as mentioned above, readers have long bemoaned that Scott does not write an authentically happy ending that would allow Ivanhoe and Rebecca to stay together. Especially if they were to remain in England, such a union might approach what Žižek calls a true "Act." The ethicopolitical Act, in Žižekian parlance, is related to the psychic movement of "traversing the fantasy" insofar as the latter often facilitates the former (although some of Žižek's examples suggest that the two moments can happen concurrently). But in fact the Act—related, but not identical to Alain Badiou's notion of an "Event," as we will see—goes farther than the traversal, since it is designed not merely to make explicit the ideological coordinates of the symbolic order in which the subject is located, but also to alter those coordinates: "An Act always involves a radical risk . . . it is a step into the open, with no guarantee about the final outcome – why? Because an Act retroactively changes the very coordinates into which it intervenes."[64] The key word here is "retroactively," which confirms that an Act assumes its properly ethical dimension only *after the fact*, that is, after it has succeeded in altering the situation in which it will be interpreted. In other words, as Žižek says, one undertakes an Act by "engaging oneself into a kind of Pascalean wager that the Act itself will create the conditions of its retroactive 'democratic' legitimization."[65]

Two additional qualifications are elaborated elsewhere in Žižek's capacious oeuvre. First, the Act may involve cutting oneself loose from the current symbolic order by a violent deed that, even more troublingly, is frequently directed at oneself or the objects of one's greatest libidinal attachments; citing several such moments in popular movies of the 1990s, Žižek explains that "by cutting himself loose from the precious object through whose possession the enemy kept him in check, the subject gains the space of free action."[66] Second, a legitimate Act, to be differentiated from mere "libertarian pathetic outbursts," must be followed by a true willingness to work to create a new, revolutionary order; indeed, it is on this ground that Žižek criticizes other contemporary theorists for holding views of political revolution that ultimately depend upon and perpetuate their own marginalization.[67]

One can only speculate how any of this would play out in *Ivanhoe*, however, as no such Act occurs. Again, Bois-Guilbert perhaps comes closest when, desperate to avoid fulfilling the Grand Master's order that he duel any challenger to ensure Rebecca's execution, he momentarily imagines "renounc[ing] present fame and future ambition" by fleeing into exile with her.[68] Such renunciation, for a character like the Templar, would be akin to the self-wounding that Žižek says may unbind the subject from the symbolic order that constitutes him; the very exile that Bois-Guilbert proposes, however, undercuts the revolutionary potential of such an unbinding by converting resistance into mere flight. For his part, Ivanhoe hardly dreams of any such subversive action. Having asked for and been granted his father's favor, he seems perfectly content with his marriage to Rowena, apparently neglecting even to inquire about Rebecca's whereabouts. The revelation that the Black Knight, Ivanhoe's frequent collaborator throughout the novel, is really Richard the Lionhearted amply confirms the reconstitution of a Law of the Father that was never truly challenged to begin with.

By contrast, Rebecca—having survived not only Bois-Guilbert's kidnapping but also the Templars' sentence of execution—is if anything stronger and more attractive at *Ivanhoe*'s conclusion than when she was first introduced. Her final interview with Rowena, as Duncan observes, shows both her character and beauty to greater advantage than those of the Saxon princess.[69] But does Ivanhoe's union with Rowena even qualify as the generic, happily-ever-after ending of Romance? Or might Scott be offering the fictive equivalent of what Žižek calls a "parallax gap," after the phenomenon whereby a single object appears to change location when viewed from two different perspectives?[70] At *Waverley*'s conclusion, let us recall, we are confronted with the paradox whereby what we have been told is the culmination of Waverley's passage into "real life"—his marriage to Rose—instead becomes visible as yet another kind of fantasy. In *Ivanhoe*'s penultimate paragraph, by contrast, this perspectival slippage is reversed:

> [Ivanhoe] lived long and happily with Rowena, for they were attached to each other by the bond of early affection, and they loved each other the more, from the recollection of the obstacles which had impeded their union. Yet it would be inquiring too curiously to ask, whether the recollection of Rebecca's beauty and magnanimity did not recur to his mind more frequently than the fair descendant of Alfred might altogether have approved.[71]

If the first sentence provides the expected Romance ending, the second quietly but firmly implies that this fantasy will only hold up as long as Ivanhoe's psyche is not "too curiously" or closely examined. To do so, Scott's narrator implies, would be to discover that, appearances to the contrary, neither Ivanhoe nor Rowena is fully satisfied by their socially sanctioned "happy ending" together. This is a far more realistic ending than many have wanted to recognize. (Hence the popularity of the stage and fictional adaptations of *Ivanhoe* that focused on Rebecca and Ivanhoe's relationship, even occasionally letting them remain together if not married.[72])

In both *Waverley* and *Ivanhoe*—the watershed novels of his career—Scott presents elaborate fictions that conclude with their protagonists firmly enmeshed in their respective symbolic orders. Both Waverley and Ivanhoe appear to accept, even to embrace, their subjectivities as constituted by their successful reidentifications with the big Other (the symbolic orders that they themselves, of course, are helping to construct and maintain). Yet, the seeds of doubt that Scott plants in each novel's concluding moments maintain a gap between the appearance of these protagonists' happiness and the hollowness at the center of their (admittedly fictional) being. Is it too much to think that Scott here reflects the modern self-doubt of the Cartesian cogito, which Žižek observes "is not a substantial entity but a pure structural function, an empty place (Lacan's $ [barred subject])—as such, it can emerge only in the interstices of substantial communal systems"?[73] Certainly, we may see in Ivanhoe's disavowed regret traces of what another important theorist of modern subjectivity, Judith Butler, identifies as the melancholy constitutive of the contemporary subject. Butler's ideas will be taken up in more detail in Chapter 3, where we will see whether her (and Homi Bhabha's) notions of performativity and hybridity offer alternatives to the highly polarized versions of subjectivity (radically self-divided or violently liberated from the existing order) put forward by Žižek. First, however, I want to turn to a second major theme in contemporary theory which Scott's Waverley Novels take up with extraordinary vigor: historicity.

2

Historicity, or *The Antiquary* and *Redgauntlet* with Koselleck and DeLanda

*W*averley was an astonishing success. Selling for one guinea apiece, the original print run of 1,000 sold out within the month of its publication (July 1814), and three more printings were produced before the end of the year. Despite lacking an author's name on the title page, it seems that many people took *Waverley*'s authorship for granted; in his *Life of Sir Walter Scott* (1837–38), J. G. Lockhart, Scott's son-in-law, writes that:

> "In truth, no one of Scott's intimate friends ever had, or ever could have had, the slightest doubt as to the parentage of Waverley. . . . Nor do I believe that the mystification ever answered much purpose among literary men of eminence beyond the circle of his personal acquaintance."[1]

Men, of course, were not the only ones to see through Scott's playful deception right from the start; as Austen wrote to her sister after reading *Waverley* for the first time,

> "Walter Scott has no business to write novels, especially good ones. – It is not fair. . . . I do not like him, and do not mean to like Waverley if I can help it – but fear I must."[2]

With characteristic irony, Austen leaves unclear whether she fears she must like the novel (or the character?) because of its innate appeal, or because the public had embraced it so readily.

In fact, not all of the novel's initial reviews were wholly positive. Ina Ferris notes that "John Wilson Croker of the *Quarterly* [*Review*] wished that the author had written a history; the crusty *Critical Review* . . . disliked it enormously; and John Scott, soon to be editor of the important liberal *London Magazine*, did not think it ranked with 'our best novels.'"[3] But one thing all the reviewers seemed to agree on was that no one before Scott had made historical subjects and figures come to such life on the novelistic page. In Croker's view, "the interest and merit of the work is derived, not from any of the ordinary qualities of a novel, but from the truth of its facts."[4] In this vein, William Hazlitt, looking back on just the first decade of Scott's novelistic career, could already assert that "Sir Walter has found out (oh, rare discovery!) that facts are better than fiction; that there is no romance like the romance of real life . . . With reverence be it spoken, he is like the man who having to imitate the squeaking of a pig upon the stage brought the animal under his coat with him."[5] Hazlitt's idea of reverence is characteristically irreverent. Nevertheless, his porcine imagery encapsulates the early consensus that, as one reviewer more tactfully put it, Scott possessed a "nature [that] vibrated to the touch of the past."[6] In the twentieth century, critics began to find a great deal more sophistication in the Waverley Novels' treatment of the historical record. As discussed previously, it is Lukàcs who makes the most compelling early case for Scott as an active shaper of historical narratives, rather than merely as their passive vessel or transmitter; although he does not grant Scott anything approaching Hegel's historical self-consciousness, he does credit him with "the intensification and dramatic compression of events" necessary to bring out what Lukàcs believed was the proper "deep unity" between historical movements and their lead actors.[7] More recently, incisive contributions by a number of scholars have continued to clarify and further explore the sophistication of Scott's understandings and representations, not just of history but also of historicity.[8]

Before going further, I want to address in more detail what critics and theorists meant by these two related but crucially distinct terms. The major critical insight generated by theorists of history in the closing decades of the twentieth century was precisely the differentiation of these concepts. For previous generations, this was not a difference that mattered; traditional historians and historians of ideas alike generally assumed that, with the proper training and resources, "facts" about the past could be recovered from historical accounts, which could in turn be read as more-or-less accurate descriptions of "what really happened" (excluding evidence of bias or fabrication). There were of course *theories* of history—including the Scottish Enlightenment's stadial theory, which became for Hegel the idea of history as "an unfolding 'dialectic of spirit',"[9] as well as less sophisticated versions of historical explanation like Thomas Carlyle's "great man" theory—but there were few theories of *history* as a textual practice or mode of representation.

Spurred by the linguistic turn, however, the early 1970s saw the publication of a succession of major studies that together establish two significant critical insights: first, that any given historical text or record is essentially discursive in nature; and second, that a fundamental break or shift in Western historical consciousness took place somewhere around the late eighteenth and early nineteenth centuries. With regard to the former, we can look to Hayden White's formalist argument that modern historical writings "contain a deep structural content which is generally poetic, and specifically linguistic, in nature"; with regard to the latter, we can cite Michel de Certeau's assertion that "Modern Western history essentially begins with the differentiation between the *present* and the *past*," in conjunction (and, perhaps, partial competition) with Foucault's observation that the Modern Age is distinguished from its Classical predecessor by the way in which "man enters in his turn, and for the first time, the field of Western knowledge."[10] Notwithstanding their disagreements, these theorists helped establish that what we have access to in a given historical account is not history as such but "historicity": what Ruth Mack, in a recent study of Scott's eighteenth-century predecessors, calls the "historical quality" of such writings.[11]

The historicity of a given text is indexed by both the degree and kind of self-awareness it manifests regarding the relation between its own moment of composition and that of the past it claims to represent. James Chandler argues that such self-consciousness reaches its modern apex in the Romantic era: "What makes Romantic historicism distinctive is the quality and extent of its interest in what might be called 'comparative contemporaneities.'"[12] Chandler draws on a crucial insight of the first theorist whose ideas I explore in this chapter: Reinhart Koselleck. Although Koselleck's *Futures Past: On the Semantics of Historical Time* was originally published in 1979, it was not made available in English until 1985, by which time the ascendancy of "high theory" may have overshadowed its reception in North America. I will be deploying Koselleck's ideas about historicity in relation to *The Antiquary* (1816), Scott's third and self-professed favorite novel. This chapter's second half then turns to Scott's most self-consciously metafictional novel, *Redgauntlet* (1824). Here, I introduce some of the recent ideas of Manuel DeLanda, whose very different paradigms for understanding historical change take their primary inspiration from the materialist philosophy of Gilles Deleuze.

Beginnings, endings, and Scott's sense of history

Let us turn first to what is probably the most frequently discussed single chapter in Scott's oeuvre: *Waverley*'s conclusion. Its title, "A Postscript, which should have been a Preface," immediately tells us something important about Scott's approach to history, at least at the start of his novelistic career. With regard to this unusual assertion of circular temporality, I have written elsewhere that "When beginning and ending are inextricably interwoven, the past is reconceived as the necessary complement of the present, available to Scott's readers only insofar as it confirms what they already know."[13] The knowledge I had in mind, of course, is the destruction of the Jacobite-Highland bloc which, in Scott's representation, threatened the modern British nation-state. In this sense, the final chapter of *Waverley* appears to confirm the inevitability of historical progress. This interpretation is supported by the well-known passage where Scott delineates the magnitude of Scotland's transformation since the conclusion of the 1745 Jacobite Rebellion (when the novel ends):

> The gradual influx of wealth, and extension of commerce, have since united to render the present people of Scotland a class of beings as different from their grandfathers, as the existing English are from those of Queen Elizabeth's time. . . . But the change, though steadily and rapidly progressive, has, nevertheless, been gradual; and, like those who drift down the stream of a deep and smooth river, we are not aware of the progress we have made until we fix our eye on the now-distant point from which we set out.[14]

At first glance, Scott's simile appears to anticipate Arthur Eddington's famous "arrow of time" analogy, especially insofar as a river's natural flow is in one direction only. But in the Scottish Enlightenment's stadial theory, although social progress moves through a series of universal stages, it is nowhere given that every society necessarily moves through *all* of them. Scott goes this one better: not only is progress not a given—the Jacobites, in the above image, are stranded on the banks of the river of time, rather than moving forward in its flow—but it is also highly relative, insofar as "progress" can be appreciated primarily by measuring one's perceived distance from some previous historical moment. Scott's imagery thereby invokes what Johannes Fabian calls the "allochronic" discourse of anthropology, in which the object of observation is typically "placed in a time other (usually earlier) than that in which the writing anthropologist places himself or herself."[15]

Yet when we place Scott's "river of time" within *Waverley's* larger looped structure, in which its final chapter not only could have been but *should have been* prefatory, then the novel's historicity becomes more complex again. Indeed, I want to argue that it anticipates the basic axiom of Koselleck's historical theory: "chronology and lived time coincide but diverge . . . the former is a datum against which temporality can be registered, but . . . this conception is itself the outcome of the structure with which we endow lived events."[16] The relationship between our lived experience and our larger sense of time passing, in other words, is neither hierarchical nor nested but mutually informing: we make sense of the former against the backdrop of the latter, but that backdrop in turn is constructed from the conceptual materials available to us in the present moment. This insight can change our sense of the historical perspective Scott establishes in *Waverley*, because although temporal progress may appear inevitable (like a river flowing in one direction, or a postscript that is already virtually present at a novel's opening), that appearance is a function of the position from which it is enunciated. In *Waverley*, this recognition is muted and its implications played down; in *The Antiquary*, as we will see, it arguably determines the novel's overarching historical perspective.

The other major statement by Scott regarding historicity, to which we can now return, is *Ivanhoe*'s "Dedicatory Epistle." Like *Waverley*'s frame chapters, this piece is a prime example of what Gerard Genette calls "paratexts": those "undefined zone[s]" of a text, "between inside and outside," that function simultaneously as its limits and its contact points with the wider world to which it refers and in which it circulates.[17] Since *Ivanhoe* was the first Waverley Novel to deal exclusively with English history, Scott uses the occasion to address some of the new challenges it presents. Presenting *Ivanhoe* as a found manuscript discovered in the home of one of *The Antiquary*'s characters, its introductory letter is credited to an English antiquary, Laurence Templeton, who defends it from presumed criticisms.

Anticipating complaints that *Ivanhoe* lacks the authenticity of previous Waverley Novels (which all generally featured times—within living memory— and places—within Scotland—to which Scott had relatively direct access), Templeton claims that such reproaches "do not appear to me to be altogether insurmountable," since having to rely on textual sources is the lot of every historian who works in periods that lie outside living memory.[18] The other predicted complaint that Templeton addresses is rather more difficult to answer; this is the question of whether *Ivanhoe*'s Anglo-centric history will attract a sufficient number of readers. The appeal of the previous, Scottish-themed Waverley Novels is summarized neatly: "If you describe to [an English reader] a set of wild manners, and a state of primitive society existing in the Highlands of Scotland, he is much disposed to acquiesce in the truth of what is asserted"—primarily, Scott hints, out of ignorance.[19] Writing historical fiction about an Englishman's own ancestors, by contrast, raises greater obstacles because "the same worthy person, when placed in his own snug parlour, and surrounded by all the comforts of an Englishman's fireside, is not half so much disposed to believe that his own ancestors led a very different life from himself." The problem of everyday experience, thus, reasserts itself, since the conveniences and securities of contemporary life make it difficult for the typical reader to believe

> that the shattered tower, which now forms a vista from his window, once held a baron who would have hung him up at his own door without any form of trial; that the hinds, by whom his little pet farm is managed, a few centuries ago would have been his slaves; and that the complete influence of feudal tyranny once extended over the neighbouring village, where the attorney is now a man of more importance than the lord of the manor.[20]

The common thread connecting all of these examples, of course, is the development of what Ellen Wood identifies as one of the major pillars of Western modernity: "legal-rational political authority."[21] At the same time, Templeton's use of the now-obsolete term "hinds" for farm workers serves as an unintentional reminder that every document inevitably becomes antiquated, which is to say historical.

This predicament—that it is the fate of every document or account to become displaced from the moment of its composition—raises a further question: how is the historical novelist to ensure that her or his production, taking place as it does in a previous era, remains relevant and compelling for contemporary readers? *Waverley*'s introductory chapter provides one answer by claiming (with the Scottish Enlighteners) a transhistorical basis for human nature, such that the historical novelist's business is with "those passions common to men in all stages of society, and which alike have agitated the human heart" throughout time.[22] *Ivanhoe*'s "Dedicatory Epistle" likewise takes up this theme, describing the "large proportion of manners and sentiments which are common to us and our ancestors."[23] But it also stakes a more provocative claim. Refuting the expected criticism that "by thus intermingling fiction with truth, I am polluting the well of history with modern invention," Templeton asserts the necessity of making historical materials accessible to contemporary readers:

> It is true, that I neither can, nor do pretend, to the observation of complete accuracy, even in matters of outward costume, much less in the important points of language and manners. But the same motive which prevents my writing the dialogue of the piece in Anglo-Saxon or Norman-French, and which prohibits my sending forth to the public this essay printed with the types of Caxton or Wynken de Worde, prevents my attempting to confine myself within the limits of the period in which my story is laid. It is necessary, for exciting interest of any kind, that the subject assumed should be, as it were, translated into the manners, as well as the language, of the age in which we live.[24]

Scott understands the historical novelist as a kind of mediator or translator between the past and the present, for whom not just languages, but also manners and even actions must be converted into terms and modes that will make sense to contemporary readers. The trope of translation indicates Scott's recognition that historicity leads an essentially discursive existence. Accordingly, the best way to communicate the impact of a given historical moment may require something other than absolute fidelity to the terms in which it was initially experienced. In the previous chapter, this insight was expressed via Copjec's psychoanalytically inflected claim that no historical age understands itself completely. Now, we can add that Scott anticipates Koselleck's idea that the very notion of history (as chronology) we use to explain and situate our contemporary moment is itself a product of that moment.

Finally, potential complaints regarding the inauthenticities or anachronisms of Scott's rendering of historical details in *Ivanhoe*—or, for that matter, in later English-themed Waverley novels such as *Kenilworth* (1821) and *Woodstock* (1826)—are rendered at least partly moot in advance by Templeton's ready admission, near the end of *Ivanhoe*'s "Dedicatory Epistle," that he has "attempt[ed] . . . to frame for myself a minstrel cornet, partly out of the pearls of pure antiquity, and partly from the Bristol stones and paste, with which I have endeavoured to imitate them."[25] Now, Scott exchanges the trope of the historical novelist as translator for that of the historical novelist as counterfeiter. While a translation by its very nature signals its difference from the original, a counterfeit—here imagined as fake gems ("Bristol stones and paste")—attempts to pass itself off as authentic. Considered as a master trope for characterizing the historicity of the Waverley Novels in general, it confirms Scott's awareness of the obscure, permeable boundaries between fact and fiction, record and rhetoric, history and discourse, past and present.

Competing histories and historicisms in *The Antiquary*

Questions regarding the possible relationships between past, present, and future are central to both Koselleck's theories and to Scott's third novel. Anthropologists and linguists have long recognized that different languages encode different senses of historicity; whereas most Indo-European languages use an absolute tense system to signal when an action has taken or will take place, for example, Mandarin Chinese has no grammatical tense and therefore relies on context or the use of adverbs to imply temporality. Restricting himself to the development of a sense of history in Western culture, however, Koselleck asserts that prior to the Enlightenment, Europeans generally lacked a sense of futurity as we understand it today in terms of an unlimited horizon of potential. Instead, Koselleck proposes, they experienced the future primarily as it was prescribed by the Catholic Church's eschatological worldview: "Until well into the sixteenth century, the history of Christianity is a history of expectations, or more exactly, the constant anticipation of the End of the World on the one hand and the continual deferment of the End on the other."[26] The Christian doctrine that saturated Europe from the end of the Roman Empire through the beginning of the Renaissance mandated a historical perspective that, we might say, was not so much "apocalypse now" as "apocalypse sooner or later." Such a worldview, Koselleck points out, served the Church's interests by allowing it for several centuries to "utiliz[e] the imminent-but-future End of the World as a means of stabilization . . . enabling its self-constitution as world and as institution."[27] The catalyst for change, which Koselleck is careful to avoid suggesting occurred all at once, was the slow but inevitable rise of secularism.[28] This transformation is embodied and institutionalized in a document like the 1555 Peace of Augsburg, which concluded the conflict between Charles V and his Lutheran opponents by allowing German princes to choose between Catholicism and Lutheranism while remaining part of the Holy Roman Empire. In effect, Koselleck explains, the "compromise" of the Augsburg Settlement heralded the rise of a new principle of social and, by extension, temporal organization: "politics."[29] Eschatology was by no means dead—as Koselleck notes, Nostradamus issued his prophesies in 1555— but with the end of the world consistently delayed, and temporal concerns becoming ever more central for political leaders, the apocalypse became increasingly a matter of astrological or natural scientific speculation.

On this account, the sixteenth-century French thinker Jean Bodin gets specific credit from Koselleck, not just for his recognizably modern definition of state sovereignty (a topic to which I will return in Chapter 4), but also for splitting history into three distinct realms: the sacred, the human, and the natural. By doing so, Koselleck argues, Bodin established not only that human history could be conceived separately from its earthly and spiritual counterparts, but also that it "had no goal . . . but rather was a domain of probability and human prudence."[30] The stage was set for history to take on its recognizably modern conceptual structure of discrete but interconnected planes of temporality: past, present, and future. With regard to the latter, moreover, as political prediction came to replace religious/astronomical prophecy as the most relevant method of temporal anticipation, "The future became a domain of finite possibilities, arranged according to their greater or lesser probability."[31]

For Koselleck, the next major contribution to the understanding of human history is none other than the stadialism of the Scottish Enlighteners. With its "typical eighteenth-century mixture of rational prediction and salvational expectation," stadialism "inaugurated our modernity" by decisively detaching the future from the past.[32] This new, recognizably modern form of the future is characterized by two distinct features: the seemingly ever-growing rapidity of its approach and its essential unknowability. Together, these create both the characteristic anxiety of modern life and the sense of boundless possibility that the most optimistic (or naïve) commentators continue to promote. Yet, they also alter human experience in a less obvious, but perhaps even more significant way: as our desire to "hasten" the future becomes ever stronger, Koselleck notes, "This self-accelerating temporality robs the present of the possibility of being experienced as the present."[33] In other words, the unexpected (and frequently unperceived) cost of our modern construction of the future, as that which constantly must be anticipated yet cannot ever entirely be known in advance, is the virtual loss of the present, which becomes available for critical analysis only belatedly, as history. In this precise sense, Foucault's stated goal at the end of the introductory chapter of *Discipline and Punish*—"writing the history of the present"—is the only one available to the self-aware modern historian.[34]

Writing a history of the present is more or less what Scott explicitly sets out to do in *The Antiquary*. In the printed "Advertisement" placed before the first chapter, he explains that this will be his final novel: having written of "the age of our fathers" (i.e. the mid-eighteenth century) in *Waverley*, and "that of our youth" in his second novel, *Guy Mannering; or, The Astrologer* (1815), Scott claims that with *The Antiquary* he will bring his fiction up to "the last ten years of the eighteenth century" and thus complete the series.[35] This sense of anticipating the future extends into the narration's opening chapter, which finds a young man "grow[ing] something impatient" as he waits in Edinburgh for a coach to take him farther into Scotland. Thus begins yet another northward journey by a Waverley hero. This time, however, his adventure—at the end of which, like Waverley before and Ivanhoe after him, another wayward son will recover his patrimony—proves little more than a peg on which Scott hangs multiple meditations on the ways in which history can be lost, recovered, mediated, and deployed. This new emphasis is marked immediately by the fact that the eponymous character of Scott's third novel is not the Waverley Hero (here named Lovel), but rather the collector and historian Jonathan Oldbuck. As owner of the Scottish estate where Lovel ends up sojourning while he attempts to woo back the woman he loves, Oldbuck is frequently considered by critics to be Scott's greatest authorial self-portrait. Stern on the outside but kindhearted on the inside, Oldbuck's passions include collecting relics of Scotland's past, retelling stories of his Germanic family's Whiggish loyalties, and arguing with his Tory neighbor, the stuffy Sir Arthur Wardour (whose daughter is in fact the object of Lovel's affections).

When Oldbuck first shows Lovel his study, we are immediately immersed in the materiality of the antiquary's relationship with history:

> It was a lofty room of middling size, but obscurely lighted by high narrow latticed windows. One end was entirely occupied by book-shelves, greatly too limited in space for the number of volumes placed upon them, which were, therefore, drawn up in ranks of two and three files deep, while numberless others littered the floor and the tables, amid a chaos of maps, engravings, scraps of parchment, bundles of papers, pieces of old armour, swords, dirks, helmets, and Highland targets. . . . A large old-fashioned

oaken table was covered with a profusion of papers, parchments, books, and nondescript trinkets and gewgaws, which seemed to have little to recommend them, besides rust and the antiquity which it indicates.[36]

Although Lovel, like the reader, can initially see little more than "chaos" in this scene, Oldbuck seems, or at least claims, to know the exact identity and value of each text and artifact. His lengthy explanations of his treasures' provenances, as well as the skill with which he purchased or acquired them, form one of the book's recurring jokes. Yet, it is precisely the difficulty of ascertaining the "reality" of these values—if not also the authenticity of the pieces themselves—that *The Antiquary* consistently highlights. The materialization of the historical record in the form of manuscripts and artifacts would seem, at first glance, to be the most reliable kind of information regarding the past. Nevertheless, Scott repeatedly undercuts this assumption. Certainly, Oldbuck himself turns out to be a less than fully reliable interpreter of the past, whose explanations frequently bear the marks of his desire to vindicate Scotland's glorious past (as when, for example, he declares a ditch on his property evidence of an ancient Roman encampment) or to have triumphed in the marketplace (as when he admits to Lovel, "How often have I stood haggling upon a halfpenny, lest, by a too ready acquiescence in the dealer's first price, he should be led to suspect the value I set upon the article!"[37]). Yet as Yoon Sun Lee indicates, Oldbuck's patriotic traditionalism sits uneasily with his antiquarianism: the latter's reliance on present scarcity to determine the market value of artifacts leads to a radically decontextualized view of the very objects that patriotic traditionalism wishes to assign a more permanent value based on their historical significance.[38]

Moreover, *The Antiquary* resists fully endorsing either of these modes of historical valuation. Although traditionalism initially appears less self-interested, or at least less motivated by profit than antiquarianism, it is discredited insofar as it proves eminently open to abuse. In this vein, Sir Arthur's family pride—he boasts frequently of his ancient Scottish lineage, especially compared to Oldbuck's less distinguished, less native family history—is precisely what enables him to be repeatedly duped by the novel's semicomic villain, the swindling German adventurer Dousterswivel. (It is also what leads Wardour initially to oppose his daughter's marriage to Lovel.) As for Oldbuck, although we are told that he "was much more scrupulous [than Sir Arthur] in receiving legends as current and authentic coin"[39]—so much so that, as Matthew Rowlinson points out, when Sir Arthur tries to repay part of his debt to Oldbuck with old coins, the antiquary is more interested in their literal worth (as metal) than in their exchange value (as specie)—his historical interpretations often prove just as fallible. The most frequent agent of Oldbuck's embarrassments in this arena is Edie Ochiltree, a professional beggar or "gaberlunzie" and amateur local historian who takes special delight in deflating the titular antiquary's pretensions. As many critics have noted, Ochiltree's knowledge is primarily oral and experiential, whereas Oldbuck is consistently associated with print culture. In the novel's most amusing vignette of debunking, Oldbuck explains at length to Lovel his reasons for believing that the ditch on his newly purchased land is evidence of an ancient Roman encampment, paying special attention to an inscription found on the property, "A.D.L.L.," which Oldbuck claims "may stand, without much violence, for *Agricola Dicavit Libens Lubens* [Agricola willingly and happily dedicated (this)]."[40] His high-minded account of the ditch and inscription, however, is gleefully interrupted by Ochiltree, who claims eyewitness knowledge of the spot's identity as something more quotidian and much less ancient. According to the beggar, it is nothing more than a 20-year-old wedding site, whose ditch was part of a temporary rain shelter; "A.D.L.L." stands for "Aiken Drum's Lang Ladle," a joke at the groom's expense. The look on Oldbuck's face when he hears these revelations, Scott notes, is like that "of a damsel of sixteen, whose romance of true love has been blown up by some untimely discovery, or of a child of ten years, whose castle of cards has been blown down by a malicious companion."[41]

Like so much else in *The Antiquary*, however, even this history is open to debate. Several elements of Ochiltree's story appear just as "romantic" as Oldbuck's historical conjectures: "Aiken Drum" is the name of a character in a Scottish nursery rhyme—literally the man in the moon—who is said to play upon a "ladle" or spoon; the phrase "lang ladle" is also part of a Scots folk expression that translates roughly as "If you plan to sup with the Devil, make sure to bring a long spoon."[42] Regardless of whether Oldbuck is truly unaware of these folkloric provenances, or simply wishes to cut short his embarrassing debate with Ochiltree, this episode not only diminishes his status as the novel's premiere historical authority, but also exemplifies the potential for conflict between differently mediated modes of historical memory. Ironically for a novel that would seem to celebrate antiquarian lore, the authority of eyewitness knowledge is underscored later, albeit in a more serious key, when the revelations of the dying peasant woman, Elspeth Meiklebackit, lead to the discovery of Lovel's true identity as the heir of the local Catholic gentry, the Glenallans. Although Elspeth shuns any speculation on events she did not witness for herself—she refuses to guess at the contents of a long-ago conversation between the current Lord Glenallan's brother and his recently deceased mother, for example, on the grounds that "what they did or said I will not say, because I did not hear"[43]—her account is no less sensational for its veracity. It involves elements that would not be out of place in a Gothic romance: a secret, decades-old marriage between Eveline Neville and Glenallan; a false tale of incest, spread by Lady Glenallan to make her son renounce his union; an attempted suicide on the part of Eveline, after she is separated from her husband; and the clandestine birth of a male heir, who is whisked away from her dying mother and brought up in England as a Neville. Eyewitness accounts, it seems, are no less fantastic than other forms of historical memory.

Outside the realm of living memory—the realm which Scott's critics complained he was wrong to abandon in most of the Waverley novels from *Ivanhoe* onward—it becomes even harder to distinguish fact from fiction. As Koselleck observes in one of his many occasional essays, "What has happened, and has happened beyond my own experience, is something that I can experience merely by way of speech or writing."[44] The past's essentially textual nature underwrites one of the most amusing secondary plots of *The Antiquary*: Oldbuck's attempts to encourage Lovel to write an historical epic poem. "The Caledoniad; or, Invasion Repelled," will celebrate the victory of the ancient inhabitants of Scotland over the Romans. When Lovel points out that Agricola's forces were not in fact defeated, Oldbuck is undaunted: "No, but you are a poet – free of the corporation, and as little bound down to truth or probability as Virgil himself – You may defeat the Romans in spite of Tacitus."[45] Although Lovel never writes such a poem, the novel's final paragraph informs us that Oldbuck has completed all of the accompanying historical notes, which "will be at the service of any one who chuses to make them public, without risk or expence to THE ANTIQUARY."[46] We are left, in other words, with highly qualified assurance of the fictional existence of explanatory notes accompanying an imaginary poem on a historical event that never occurred. Besides being a characteristically elaborate joke, this conundrum is a wonderful illustration of Koselleck's observation of the effects of language's necessity for the transmission of history: "Viewed in retrospect, what has actually taken place is only real in the medium of linguistic fiction."[47]

"The Caledoniad" is not the only piece of what Koselleck calls "the fiction of the (f)actual" to lead a spectral existence in *The Antiquary*.[48] The novel also features an interpolated Germanic folk tale, "The Fortunes of Martin Waldeck," which Isabella Wardour reads aloud to the other main characters. This supernatural story, in which the eponymous hero accidentally finds goblin-gold, is said to have been transcribed from an account given by Dousterswivel, who has been cheating Sir Arthur with promises of discovering similarly buried treasure. In his notes to the Magnum Opus edition, Scott claims not to remember where he got the tale's idea; David Hewitt notes the existence of a sixteenth-century family of German copper miners named Waldeck and speculates that their story is "mythologized history."[49] From Koselleck's perspective, of course, "mythologized history" is a redundant expression in as much as every historical account necessarily departs from its irrecoverable origins. Nevertheless, Dousterswivel avers that his tale is a "vara true story" that has simply been mistranslated: "Miss Wardour, she is so sly and so witty, that she has made it just like one romance."[50] His motives for this claim are clear to readers, albeit not to Sir Arthur, who is thereby encouraged to continue funding Dousterswivel's fraudulent activities. Even as the German scoundrel obscures one truth, however, he inadvertently speaks another, since he not only confirms Koselleck's foundational observation that we necessarily construct and interpret narratives of the past in the light of present needs, but also anticipates how the fiction in which he himself is embedded—that is, *The Antiquary*—is constructed so as to conclude "just like one romance."

The agent of that conclusion, moreover, is none other than the lowly Ochiltree. Although Oldbuck is also skeptical of Dousterswivel's claims, it is ultimately the true-hearted beggar who proves the fraudster's undoing. His knowledge of local history, combined with his skepticism regarding written histories and market values alike, makes him the perfect foil to Dousterswivel's (as well as Oldbuck's) pretensions. Ochiltree is not without his own vanities—he likes to show off his picturesque appearance to best advantage—but unlike the German swindler or the Scottish antiquary, he lives in the present rather than the future or the past. Rebuffing the Wardours' offer to join their household after he helps rescue them from drowning, Ochiltree reminds Isabella that "I am the idlest auld carle that ever lived; I downa be bound down to hours o'eating and sleeping; and, to speak the honest truth, I wad be a vera bad example in ony weel-regulated family."[51] It is this "presentness," perhaps more than anything else, which makes Ochiltree essential to the novel's vision of a society that, for all its modernity, still clings to older ways of life as well. Although carriageways and the postal system are present in the (purposefully vague) north-east region of Scotland where *The Antiquary* takes place, these impersonal networks of transport and communication are still less important than the human networks Ochiltree mediates and manages. Such is the beggar's claim when further justifying his reluctance to reside permanently with Isabella and her family:

> And than what wad a' the country about do for want o' auld Edie Ochiltree, that brings news and country cracks frae ae farm-steading to anither, and gingerbread to the lassies, and helps the lads to mend their fiddles . . . and kens mair auld sangs and tales than a' the barony besides, and gars ilka body laugh wherever he comes? – troth, my leddy, I canna lay down my vocation, it would be a public loss."[52]

In his own eyes, at least, Ochiltree represents the last vestige of the "vanishing present" that for Koselleck characterizes our modern experience of temporality. Furthermore, especially insofar as he self-consciously plays this role, Ochiltree embodies the late eighteenth century's sense of itself as a transitional moment—a sense, Koselleck asserts, that was in fact unique to that era: "the experience of *transition* . . . marks the new epochal consciousness developed toward the end of the eighteenth century in which one's own time was not only experienced simultaneously as an end and a beginning but also as a period of transition."[53]

Scott conveys these experiences, moreover, while simultaneously ensuring that readers remain conscious throughout of the mediated nature of the "history" they are reading. In addition to the examples discussed above, the novel's fictionality is consistently highlighted in at least two ways. First, although most of the novel's geographic indicators suggest it takes place along Scotland's eastern coastline, certain details occasionally undercut this claim; most notoriously, just prior to the Wardours' near-drowning and dramatic rescue by Ochiltree and Lovel, Scott describes the sun setting, quite impossibly, "upon the edge of the level ocean."[54] In all likelihood, this is a genuine authorial error; nevertheless, it (and others like it, including several lapses in the narrative's internal chronology that are silently corrected in the new Edinburgh Edition[55]) effectively draws attention to the purely discursive nature of what we are reading. From a conventional historical perspective, such breaches of realism would appear to widen the gap between the Waverley Novels' status as fiction and the "truth" of the historical record. By contrast, from Koselleck's perspective, the incomplete closure of *The Antiquary* is its most "realistic" historical gesture. Its very inadequacy as a conventional historical document, that is, makes it exemplify what Koselleck calls the impossibility of any "*histoire totale*": "History takes place in the anticipation of incompleteness; any interpretation that is adequate to it therefore must dispense with totality."[56]

The Antiquary breaks with historiographical realism in a second way: by blatantly incorporating other genres into itself. As Hayden White and others have demonstrated, even (or especially) the most traditional historical narratives have their conventions and borrowings. But, *The Antiquary* makes its synthetic composition explicit. Most obviously, parts of it echo the Gothic romance, popularized in the last decades of the eighteenth century by Ann Radcliffe and her many imitators.[57] In particular, Scott's subplot involving the Glenallan family contains a laundry list of Gothic features: Catholicism, a vengeful parent, rumors of incest, suicide, family secrets, a lost (and found) heir. Not content to keep these conventions in the background, Scott builds an additional Gothic episode directly into the novel's early chapter via the night Lovel must spend in the supposedly haunted "Green Room" of Oldbuck's mansion. Afterward, readers expecting the nocturnal appearance of a ghostly Oldbuck ancestor to be rationally dispelled, as it would be in a Radcliffe novel, are half-disappointed: although Oldbuck chastises his guest for believing in the phantom, the family motto the specter shares with Lovel during its appearance—"Kunst Macht Gunst," or "Skill wins favour," as Oldbuck translates it—turns out to be authentic. It is also integral to the plot, since it motivates Lovel to continue pursuing Isabella's hand in marriage. Yet, "authentic" is not necessarily the right term here, for as David Punter observes, the German word "Kunst" can also mean "trick" or "artifice": an allusion, perhaps, to the slipperiness of language as well as to the multiple "plots" that keep both history in general and the history of *The Antiquary* in motion.[58] Either way, the manifest artificiality of *The Antiquary*'s Gothic interpolations is matched only by the artifice of the novel's conclusion, in which Edie's burning of Dousterswivel's fraudulent mining machinery is mistaken for a signal fire communicating an imminent French invasion. The false alarm is eventually revealed as such, but not before it leads to a morale-lifting gathering of the novel's community, as well as to the revelation of Lovel's true identity as the rightful Glenallan heir.[59] *The Antiquary*'s conclusion, thus, reconfirms Koselleck's insight that, in the time of modernity (*Neuzeit*) ushered in by the end of the eighteenth century, anticipating the ever-accelerating, ever-receding future becomes both more necessary and more impossible than ever before.

Redgauntlet's material histories

If any Waverley Novel is more self-conscious than *The Antiquary* about its own status as historical fiction, and in turn even more interested in querying the profiles of history and historicity alike, it is *Redgauntlet*. Subtitled "A Tale of the Eighteenth Century," and published just a few years before Scott's financial collapse, this late novel marks a return to the Jacobite themes that dominate Scott's early fictions. But unlike *Waverley* (which deals with the 1745 Rebellion) and *Rob Roy* (which is set against the backdrop of the earlier 1715 rebellion, as we will see in Chapter 3), *Redgauntlet* narrates a Jacobite Rebellion that never happened: a fictional second attempt, undertaken by an aging Charles Stuart, to infiltrate Britain, rally his supporters, and reclaim the British throne for his family. Scott's novels had, of course, always mixed historical events with fictional characters and imaginary situations, and just the year before, he had tried his hand at a contemporary novel of manners, *St. Ronan's Well* (1823).[60] Never before, however, had Scott put a patently imaginary event at the center of a full-length historical treatment. As the editors of the Edinburgh Edition demonstrate, Scott includes enough chronological details in *Redgauntlet* to allow a surprisingly accurate dating of its action, to July–August 1765.[61]

As well as being his only exercise in entirely "alternative history," the novel's structure is unique to Scott's oeuvre. The first volume is entirely comprised of letters sent between the two main characters, Darsie Latimer and Alan Fairford; here, Scott reproduces the epistolary format of popular eighteenth-century novels. The second volume interrupts this arrangement with two chapters of third-person narration, before adopting another popular eighteenth-century format, the journal entry, which is continued in Darsie Latimer's voice for seven chapters before returning to a third-person narration. Most of the second half's chapters are then focalized alternately by Latimer and Fairford, who spend much of the novel separated after the former is kidnapped by his estranged uncle and the latter sets out to rescue him. Only in the last two numbered chapters of Volume Three—in which Charles Stuart's abortive rebellion, for which he has been preparing with the help of Latimer's uncle, Hugh Redgauntlet, is quashed before it ever really begins—does a truly omniscient narrative voice reestablish itself. The final chapter nevertheless returns to epistolarity with a letter that resolves the characters' fates by citing a variety of further sources (newspaper articles, marriage records, eyewitness accounts). We are implicitly warned against complacently accepting the preceding narrative's authenticity, moreover, by the identity of this final letter writer: it is Dr. Dryasdust, the addressee of *Ivanhoe*'s "Dedicatory Epistle." After deploying a profusion of narrative styles and formats, in other words, Scott closes by reasserting the principle of fictionality at work in even the most "realistic" discursive account. (Along these lines, critics frequently cite *Redgauntlet*'s tragicomic subplot, the ridiculously labyrinthine legal case of Peebles v. Plainstanes.)

One feels tempted to say that *Redgauntlet* is effectively *The Antiquary* on steroids: it takes the earlier novel's themes of history's essentially discursive nature, and the modernity of our conceptions of temporality, and amplifies them tenfold. In what remains of this chapter, however, I would like to pursue a reading of *Redgauntlet*'s historicity that moves away from the discursive and conceptual frameworks posited by Koselleck, toward an altogether different kind of thinking about history. For if our historical experience is inevitably conditioned by our own historical moment—specifically, the conjoined qualities of *acceleration* and *openness* that characterize our modern relationship with the future and make our sense of history essentially "apprehended in terms of progress"[62]—then Koselleck's theories, in turn, are themselves products of our contemporary moment. This is not an argument against their validity or usefulness, but rather an index of the degree to which the application of Koselleck's ideas (like those of Foucault, de Certeau, White, and the other "discourse theorists" of history) is circumscribed by the same critical insights that drive them.

Let me briefly unpack this idea. As early as the 1960s, Foucault (among others) was arguing that our very concept of "man" or "humanity"—that supposedly transhistorical entity—is itself an historical construct.[63] Most poststructuralists responded to this insight by variously displacing, decentering, or fragmenting the position of the human in their work. Even as Foucault, Derrida, Julia Kristeva, Paul de Man, Jean-François Lyotard, and others shift their attention away from individuals and toward language or discourse as the primary agent of history, culture, and subjectivation, they arguably nevertheless retain an implicitly human-centered worldview. Who else but "man," after all, could be the final subject and object of language, the ultimate speaker and addressee of discourse? For those of us who came of age intellectually in the period of poststructuralism, the idea of thinking "beyond" or "around" linguistic mediation seems naïve at best. Yet, this is precisely what some of today's theorists are once again proposing. In this, they at least have the "high theory" example of Lacan, who, in addition to his language-centered approach to psychoanalysis, was also deeply interested in the potential of models and formulas for graphing the human psyche. More recently, Alain Badiou (whom I discuss in the Conclusion) has dug deeply into the ontological resources of mathematics to ground his philosophical theories in an objective bedrock.

Another strategy of the contemporary postlinguistic turn is prefigured in the alternately organic and mechanistic models and vocabularies deployed in the later decades of the twentieth century by Gilles Deleuze (often in collaboration with Félix Guattari). As with Badiou, I write at greater length about Deleuze and Guattari's pathbreaking work in my concluding chapter; their influence on contemporary theory, especially the varieties of posthumanism, can hardly be overstated. For now, however, I want to explore what happens if we focus, not on the discursive features of *Redgauntlet*'s representations of history and historicity, but rather on its materialist (or realist) investments. I propose to do this via the work of one of Deleuze's most illuminating contemporary interpreters: Manuel DeLanda.

Not surprisingly, books, manuscripts, letters, newspapers, and other texts appear regularly in Scott's fictions. But almost as often, chunks of solid matter occupy even more significant narrative positions. Sometimes, as in the Covenanters' tombstones that feature prominently in the introduction to *The Tale of Old Mortality* (1816), they help set the narrative in motion; elsewhere, like the titular amulet of *The Talisman* (1825), they become central to the plots in which they are embedded. Frequently, such objects came directly from Scott's life, as with the the prison door of the old Edinburgh jail that features in in *The Heart of Mid-Lothian* (1819). As Scott explains in a note to the Magnum Opus edition, when the jail was being torn down he had its substantial front door salvaged and rehung in his home; two years later it became an essential piece of the novel that gave the old Tolbooth a permanent place in literary history. Similarly, several pieces of Scott's justly famous personal collection—the Marquis of Montrose's sword and a rifle said to belong to Rob Roy MacGregor—seem to have provided the impetus for two other early Waverley Novels, *A Legend of Montrose* (1819) and *Rob Roy* (1817).[64]

At first glance, *Redgauntlet* appears to share little of this material motivation. Accordingly, critics have generally focused on its negotiation of the Jacobitical themes of his Scott's earlier fictions. While Bonnie Prince Charlie is young, dashing, and charismatic in *Waverley*, the Charles Stuart of *Redgauntlet* spends most of the novel wearily disguised as a Jesuit priest. Worse, support for the Jacobite cause is now so weak—except for Hugh Redgauntlet's stubborn attachment—that the Hanoverian regime cannot even be bothered to imprison the Stuart heir and his followers after exposing their meager plot:

> "You, sir – all – any of the gentlemen present," said the General, –"all whom the vessel can contain, are at liberty to embark uninterrupted by me; but I advise none to go off who have not powerful reasons, unconnected with the present meeting, for this will be remembered against no one." "Then, gentlemen," said Redgauntlet, clasping his hands together as the words burst from him, "the cause is lost for ever!"[65]

Redgauntlet recognizes that the government's offer of unconditional amnesty, combined with its willingness to allow Charles Stuart and his retinue to flee, effectively robs the Jacobite movement of its last vestiges of heroism and mystique. Denied the opportunity for martyrdom, much less success, the Cause is indeed "lost for ever."

This kind of analysis of Scott's discourse—one that focuses on his deployment and representation of "plot," understood as both the Jacobites' stratagems and the novel's narrative—provides a satisfying, "high theory" picture of its self-reflexive historicity. When we shift our gaze from the human to the material histories at stake in *Redgauntlet*, however, a somewhat different picture emerges. To do so, in effect, is to heed the force of DeLanda's observation in what is still probably his best-known book, *A Thousand Years of Nonlinear History* that as humans, we have a tendency to ignore or "underestimate the vitality of the processes of self-organization in other spheres of reality."[66] In many ways, this insight contains the key to what DeLanda calls Deleuze's "realist ontology": a perspective on the world that "grant[s] reality full autonomy from the human mind," while also striving to understand that reality from a nonanthropocentric perspective.[67] Although ontological realism does not deny the insights of poststructuralism and psychoanalysis with regard to the overdetermined, inevitably mediated nature of humanity's relation to reality, it does not accept the Kantian corollary that, as a result, nothing objective can be said or known about "the great outdoors" (to use Quentin Meillassoux's redolent phrase).[68] Nor does it retain the traditional Western metaphysical belief that reality has an unchanging core that might eventually become accessible to us.[69] Since at least Plato, the idea of "essence" has been invoked to explain the identity of things, "those fundamental traits without which an object would not be what it is," as DeLanda puts it.[70] What Deleuzian ontology sets out to do, however, is to disrupt and destabilize such Platonism by demonstrating how reality, understood as that which is both around us and includes us, is composed of processes rather than essences.

This "inherently dynamic" view of the world does not deny that "things" exist.[71] Instead, it entails two positive requirements: first, that reality be explained in immanent rather than transcendent terms; and second, that the appearance of static, stable "things" belies their fundamental evanescence. At the most basic level of reality, "things"—whether living or inert—can be described most accurately as temporary collections of matter, energy, and physical information.[72] Reality is always on the move, even if it appears otherwise to us. This, in effect, is DeLanda's clear-sighted explanation of the importance of the related terms "multiplicity" and "flow" in Deleuze's work. Together, multiplicity (the composition and arrangement of things) and flow (the speed at which they move and change) explain how even "the most stable and durable traits of our reality . . . merely represent a local *slowing down* of this flowing reality."[73] The rocks and mountains that appear to be among the most stable elements of our world, for example, are in fact transitory forms (one might even call them symptoms) created by underground lava flows, continental plate shifts, and the constant erosion that constitute the reality of our planet's geology. What applies to the so-called natural world, moreover, applies to us as well: "Similarly, our individual bodies and minds are mere coagulations or decelerations in the flows of biomass, genes, memes, and norms."[74]

This is an unusual and admittedly unsettling way to describe human beings. Nevertheless, a closer look at DeLanda's list of "ingredients" that go into making a human reveals some familiar items. The final two elements, memes (a term coined by Richard Dawkins to describe a replicable unit of cultural information) and norms, or socially sanctioned values, exist primarily at the human level, and account for the materials traditionally taken up by literary critics and theorists. The first two, by contrast, are biologically based, empirically verifiable, and seemingly outside the realm of theory. Nevertheless, when seen from the perspective of the flow of the world's multiplicities, they turn out to function similarly. In a discussion on how humans have historically altered the circulation of biomass, for example, DeLanda points out that since pigs eat the same foodstuffs as people but are very efficient converters of carbohydrates into protein, the domestication of hogs was essentially a method for transforming them into "living storage devices for unpredicted [grain] surpluses."[75] We are still dealing with the same "thing" here—the pig— whose linguistic denominations Wamba parses in *Ivanhoe*, but seeing it as a modular element in the changing history of material flows, rather than as a linguistic sign, provides a novel perspective that reintegrates humans into the world instead of confirming our separation from it.

In DeLanda's Deleuzian historiography, then, it is not a question of nature versus culture, but rather of how natural and cultural factors both operate according to process-based patterns. Although these patterns are recognizable and even partially predictable thanks to factors like the distribution and coordination of their various qualities, they are far from entirely knowable in advance. This is due neither to randomness nor to the interference or guidance of higher powers; as DeLanda observes, in a strictly materialist ontology, even overarching concepts such as "the Market" or "the State" become visible as "reified generalities" with limited explanatory power.[76] Such abstractions should be supplemented or even replaced, DeLanda argues, by the process that makes self-directed assemblages out of multiplicities and destabilizes their predictability: "emergence," or the spontaneous manifestation of "properties of a whole that are not present in its parts."[77] A simple example of this integral phenomenon is the interaction under certain conditions (or parameters) of two hydrogen molecules and one oxygen molecule to form an entirely new substance, water. A more complicated example of a whole spontaneously becoming more than the sum of its parts, which demonstrates the applicability of DeLanda's materialist approach to understanding human assemblages as well as natural ones, is the emergence, again under certain conditions (especially population density), of a community out of individual families.[78]

The idea of emergence has become increasingly important in DeLanda's recent work.[79] For our purposes, however, we need only deploy the more basic components of his methodology to uncover a different side—a more elemental substratum, so to speak—of *Redgauntlet*'s historicity. Hugh Redgauntlet has pinned his hopes of fomenting another Jacobite rebellion on his nephew, Darsie Latimer. His family has a long and troubled history of supporting the Stuarts, but at the novel's start, Latimer is neither a Jacobite nor even aware he is the Redgauntlet heir; precisely to prevent him from following in his predecessors' fateful footsteps, Latimer has been raised in Scotland, kept ignorant of his family history, and forbidden to enter England until he is 25 years old. Nevertheless, his uncle (under his alias, Herries) kidnaps him with the belief that, given time, he can "turn" Latimer to the Jacobite side. Redgauntlet seems to believe that his nephew is intrinsically, even genetically susceptible to supporting Charles Stuart. This faith in his nephew's latent Jacobitism is bolstered by the presence of a mark on Latimer's forehead that he appears to share with his Redgauntlet ancestors. The myth of the Redgauntlet mark is first introduced by an itinerant musician and balladeer, Wandering Willie, with whom Latimer travels early in the novel. In the course of telling a tale of the Redgauntlet family, Willie describes the moment when his own ancestor, Steenie Steenson, arrives to pay his overdue rents to Sir Robert Redgauntlet:

> The rental-book, wi' its black cover and brass clasps, was lying beside [Sir Robert]; and a book of sculduggery sangs was put betwixt the leaves, to keep it open at the place where it bore evidence against [Steenie] . . . as behind the hand with his mails and duties. Sir Robert gave my guidsire a look, as if he wad have withered his heart in his bosom. Ye maun ken he had a way of bending his brows that men saw the visible mark of a horse-shoe on his forehead, deep-dinted, as if it had been stamped there.[80]

Willie's narrative—popularly anthologized as "Wandering Willie's Tale"—proceeds to explain, with an effective mix of the comic and the supernatural, how Steenie's payment goes missing after Sir Robert's untimely death, and Steenie must travel to the underworld to retrieve the receipt.

The havoc caused by a "thing" that circulates without human agency—Steenie's payment turns out to have been stolen by Sir Robert's pet monkey—suggests that the course of history, even when viewed from the perspective of its human participants, is never entirely controlled by them. But it is the ominous Redgauntlet mark, which soon reappears in "Wandering Willie's Tale" on the face of Sir Robert's son when he becomes angry, that speaks most directly to *Redgauntlet*'s essentially realist ontology. To see this most clearly, let us return once more to DeLanda's nonanthropocentric perspective on reality. In *A Thousand Years of Nonlinear History*, he systematically traces materialist processes in three distinct but interrelated domains: the geological, the biological, and the linguistic. With regard to the second, he notes that natural and cultural factors mutually influence each other and sometimes even converge, not just on the level of the circulation of biomass (as in the previous example of pigs as protein storage units), but also on the genetic level. After all, without "the flow of genetic materials through generations . . . organized flesh would exist in forms as ephemeral as hurricanes . . . and, moreover, it could not evolve."[81] Still defying the Western tradition of viewing things as defined by essences, DeLanda stresses that "there is nothing necessary about these accumulations"; instead, they are "historical constructions, their defining traits a purely contingent collection assembled by means of selection pressures, which act as a genetic sorting process." It is these "selection pressures," usually some combination of natural and cultural factors, that are active; genes and their products, by contrast, are best understood "not [as] a blueprint for the generation of organic structure and function . . . [but rather] as constraints on a variety of processes that spontaneously generate order, in a way *teasing out* a form from active (and morphogenetically pregnant) flesh."[82]

DeLanda is talking specifically about the historical construction of species, but with a little critical license, his insights transfer well to Scott's representation of the Redgauntlet family line. Much of the novel takes the form of a drawn-out "tease" of Latimer's dawning comprehension of himself and his family lineage. Only when he spies the mark of the Redgauntlet genetic heritage on his uncle's face (some 100 pages after "Wandering Willie's Tale"), does the truth begin to dawn on him:

> he bent on me a frown so portentous, that no one who has witnessed the look can forget it during the whole of life. The furrows of the brow above the eyes became livid and almost black, and were bent into a semi-circular, or rather elliptical form, above the junction of the eye-brows. . . . this deep and gloomy contortion of the frontal muscles was not unaptly described, as forming the representation of a small horse-shoe.[83]

Soon after, Latimer and Redgauntlet engage in an impromptu staring contest, wrinkling their brows at each other, and when the former simultaneously catches sight of himself in a mirror, he reports that "I started again at the real or imaginary resemblance which my countenance, at that moment, bore to that of Herries."[84] "Real or imaginary": this phrase limns the two types of factors— natural ("real") and cultural ("imaginary")—that facilitate the selection of a given set of transferable traits. Hugh Redgauntlet, as we know, has staked his fate on the primacy of the natural: if the upside-down horseshoe which appears on the forehead when a Redgauntlet male becomes angry is really caused by a heritable genetic mutation, then Latimer will ultimately accept his familial identity and act accordingly (i.e. join the Rebellion). For Redgauntlet Sr., we might say, biology is, or at least ought to be, destiny.

At first, it seems that this will be the case. Although Latimer discovers that the mark on his forehead "could not be called forth by voluntary effort," the moment he becomes agitated it shows itself: "Angry and ashamed at being detected in my singular occupation [looking at his reflection], I turned round sharply, and, I suppose, chance produced the change on my features which I had been in vain labouring to call forth."[85] The involuntary nature of the mark's appearance momentarily seems to confirm its status as an index of what Redgauntlet calls the "mysterious law of nature" that he hopes will inexorably lead his nephew to commit to the Stuart cause.[86] Thanks to DeLanda, it is not difficult to identify Redgauntlet's crucial category error here: he is confusing a genetic legacy (the mark on the forehead) with a culturally conditioned one (the family's previous political loyalties). Yet as DeLanda's work consistently demonstrates, it is precisely the unstable, variable nature of the interactions between these two conditioning domains that makes the emergence and expression of a given trait or entity—be it a birthmark, a dynastic loyalty, a friendship, or a rebellion—so difficult to predict. This insight too is reflected in Scott's novel, inasmuch as an intermixing of natural and cultural "selection factors" is evident in the details of the mark's "origin story." As Redgauntlet eventually explains, the horseshoe mark is said to derive from a case of accidental infanticide: the heir of the very first Redgauntlet, Alberick, supposedly displayed the mark on his forehead after Alberick's horse fatally trampled his first-born but estranged son during battle. Just as he never stops to question the logic of his Jacobitical loyalties, Hugh Redgauntlet displays absolute faith in the veracity of this family legend. For readers, it is easy to see how this myth, like many origin stories, rationalizes a random occurrence (in this case, a genetic mutation) through a narrative of crime and punishment. Confusing the biological and the metaphysical, it anticipates Hugh Redgauntlet's later category error regarding Latimer's destiny.

Furthermore, as if to recognize this fact, almost as soon as the story of Alberick Redgauntlet is retold, the Redgauntlet "fatal frown" fades almost entirely from view,[87] never to play the commanding role that Redgauntlet had hoped and Latimer had feared. Indeed, when he finally learns his true family lineage, Latimer has surprisingly little trouble countering his uncle's arguments for supporting the Jacobites. At the conclusion of their climactic debate, Redgauntlet does "swear, by the mark that darkens my brow, that a new deed should be done – a new doom should be deserved" if Latimer actively obstructs his purposes[88]; but his threat is never carried out, and Redgauntlet ultimately accepts the Hanoverian offer of clemency accompanied by exile.

On the level of the human actors and political fortunes at stake in *Redgauntlet*, critics have correctly read the novel as a *bildungsroman* in which Latimer's rejection of a fatal, futile Jacobitism mirrors Britain's national maturity and Scott's own farewell to his youthful idealisms. But from the perspective of realist ontology that DeLanda makes available, Scott's novel also becomes legible as a tale of how material transmissions—whether of genes or memes—are always overdetermined by more than merely biological factors. The fates of the various main characters, cleverly reported in a concluding epistle by Dryasdust, make this plain. We learn that Redgauntlet eventually becomes the Prior of a strict Continental monastery, where he "never mentioned his own family" or British politics again, while Latimer apparently dies childless as well.[89] Fairford, by contrast, marries Latimer's sister, Lilias, thus facilitating the potential transmission of their genetic materials—but since female Redgauntlets apparently do not carry the "fatal frown," it seems this mutation will disappear from the genetic record.[90]

Are these simply two different ways to describe the same set of (fictional) events? Certainly. Nevertheless, the move from a discursive to a materialist frame of inquiry has the potential to alter significantly our understanding of what happens in our world—and why it matters. As DeLanda observes near the end of *A Thousand Years*, it prompts the recognition that we live in "a world that does not possess a ladder of progress, or a drive toward increased perfection, or a promised land, or even a socialist pot of gold at the end of the rainbow."[91] If we can learn to combine this existential humility with a truly "experimental attitude" to reality, says DeLanda, while at the same time avoid "confus[ing] the need for caution in our explanation of the non-linear possibilities of (economic, linguistic, biological) reality . . . with despair, resentment, or nihilism," then a more enmeshed, destratified, "positive, even joyful conception of reality" might in turn become available.[92] This would, I think, still count as progress—but it would be progress of a different, less hierarchical, linear, and anthropocentric sort than what the modern episteme has generally encouraged us to understand by that word.

Is "history without humans," so to speak, possible for us to consider seriously? To do so, will we first need to revise our very definitions of "the human"? In my conclusion, I revisit these questions by exploring the ideas of several contemporary "posthumanist" theorists. In the intervening chapters, however, I wish to hold in reserve the possibilities opened up by DeLanda's realist ontology, in order to explore the relations between Scott's oeuvre and the state of contemporary theory via several more conventionally human-centered, but no less productive and potentially illuminating, categories of critical inquiry.

3

Hybridity and performativity, or *Rob Roy* and *The Talisman* with Bhabha and Butler

The previous two chapters have begun with Scott and transitioned into theory. Now, I would like to reverse this pattern, and let theory take center stage first. In this chapter, I draw primarily on the ideas of two theorists already well known to many literary scholars: Homi Bhabha and Judith Butler. Despite their different backgrounds and intellectual engagements—Bhabha is closely associated with postcolonial studies, Butler with queer theory—they share a commitment to approaching the major topics and questions of contemporary theory through the lens of discourse. Their focus on the powerful agency of language, especially its ability to create effects of subjectivization in both its speakers and its addressees, means returning to theoretical ground that is perhaps not quite as cutting edge as the realist or materialist theory that is attracting increasing attention. Nevertheless, it would be a serious error for literary studies to abandon the path of discourse analysis. Even if Derrida's infamous exhortation that "Il n'y a pas de hors-texte" (best translated as "there is no outside-the-text") is no longer as commanding as it once seemed, his emphasis on the textuality of *all* human experience—its inevitable appearance as series of signs or traces in need of deciphering—is still deeply insightful and relevant to many critical undertakings.[1] Although the charge of anthropocentrism may stick, language is undeniably fundamental to the human experience. As Butler asserts in the introduction to *Excitable Speech: A Politics of the Performative*, "We do things with language, produce effects with language, and we do things to language, but language is also the thing that we do."[2] Language is at the very core of our humanity.

Discourse-centered theoretical approaches, moreover, need not focus on language or texts to the exclusion of other signifying entities, especially bodies. The ways in which various kinds of discourse contribute to produce the bodies they purport merely to describe is a key insight that connects Bhabha's and Butler's work back to Foucault's. In *Discipline and Punish: The Birth of the Prison,* a text closely associated with the rise of theoretical interest in the relations between discourse, power, and bodies, Foucault is clear that subjects are formed by and through the discourses and practices they alternately wield and are apprehended by: "the body is also directly involved in a political field; power relations have an immediate hold upon it; they invest it, mark it, train it, torture it, force it to carry out tasks, to perform ceremonies, to emit signs."[3] Power, in short, is productive: "[power] produces reality; it produces domains of objects and rituals of truth. The individual and the knowledge that may be gained of him belong to this production."[4] In his next major book, *The History of Sexuality* Vol. 1: *An Introduction*, Foucault subsequently introduces a third term, pleasure, which ensures that power (and the discourses through which it operates) cannot be mistaken for something easily escaped or undone; thus, his description of the "*perpetual spirals of power and pleasure*" around which discourses of sexuality coalesce.[5]

The most pressing critical questions in the wake Foucault's pioneering analyses appeared to be: how can the productive effects of discourse best be revealed?; and in what ways might we—the subjects who are produced by those effects—re-direct, co-opt, transform, or otherwise resist those same discourses in individually and communally empowering ways?[6] According to Foucault, we cannot ignore our own imbrications in the mutually reinforcing lines of power, knowledge, and pleasure. As a result, his analytical framework makes common resistance almost impossible, since every co-optation will inevitably be co-opted in its turn. Individual acts of resistance seem equally moot, especially since Foucault is notoriously hostile to psychoanalysis, the critical discourse that would otherwise seem most capable of engaging language's authority on its own symbolic terrain. (In a recently published translation of an interview given in 1978, Foucault explains that his deployment of the term "pleasure," rather than the more traditional psychoanalytic term "desire," reflects his skepticism regarding psychoanalysis' normalizing dynamics.[7]) For Foucault, the idea of resistance to power is best conceived in highly tactical, multiple, spontaneous, even evanescent terms.[8] As Jeffrey Nealon indicates, this does not mean that we should give it up, but rather that we must reconceive what it might look like: "The difficulty surrounding the question of resistance for Foucaultian social theory is not how to refine techniques for mining this scarce thing called resistance from underneath the encrusted surface of totalized power . . . but rather the question concerns ways to mobilize, focus, or intensify practices of resistance, insofar as they're already all over the place."[9] Nealon advocates an immanent, "glass half-full" reading of Foucault's understanding of the fully enmeshed nature of power and resistance.

Bhabha and Butler, I want to show, take something of the same approach. For both, if Foucault's power-knowledge-pleasure triad means there is no outside to the discourses that make and speak us as socialized subjects, then it also means that resistances to the normalizing effects of those discourses are already present and ongoing, even when the subjects in question are unaware of what they are doing. More, these contemporary theorists are much less hesitant than Foucault to reintroduce psychoanalytic concepts into their analyses of subjectivization.[10] The result, as I hope to demonstrate via two of Scott's most exciting Waverley Novels, is that questions of the nature and trajectory of human desire—as well as questions of ethnicity, nationality, class, and gender, to name other major sites of identity formation—can once more be asked. To help us follow the traces of these formations in *Rob Roy* and *The Talisman*, I will focus on two of the concepts most frequently associated with Bhabha's and Butler's work: hybridity and performativity.

Rob Roy and the limits of hybridity

At first, *Rob Roy* appears to follow the same trail blazed by Scott in *Waverley* and subsequently repeated (albeit with significant variations, as we have seen) in *The Antiquary*: a young Englishman travels north to Scotland, finds adventure and romance, and returns home a wiser and wealthier man. Rather than taking place during the 1745 Rebellion or at the end of the eighteenth century, *Rob Roy* is set further back in time, during the run-up to the 1715 Jacobite uprising. This change of era, in turn, entails a host of differences; indeed, *difference*—one of high theory's key terms[11]—turns out to be central to Scott's concerns in *Rob Roy*. In the lengthy "Introduction" he added to the Magnum edition, Scott explains his title character's appeal in language that also reflects his ideas regarding the novel as a whole: "It is this strong contrast betwixt the civilized and cultivated mode of life on the one side of the Highland line, and the wild and lawless adventures which were habitually undertaken and achieved by one who dwelt on the opposite side of that ideal boundary, which creates the interest attached to his name."[12] Yet even here, the delineation of stark differences between England (and the Lowlands) as a place of commercial modernity, predictable and boring, versus the Highlands as a space of primitive excitement is undercut by Scott's description of the line that separates them as "ideal" rather than real. As we will see, Rob Roy himself repeatedly crosses this line with almost alarming ease and speed. Such crossings confirm that the kind of strict demarcation Scott invokes above is in fact mostly absent from his novel. On the contrary, while differences of various kinds are important in *Rob Roy*, they are repeatedly shown to be partial rather than complete, constructed rather than natural, and inherently open to deconstruction. Scott's ready admission in the Magnum introduction that it was his publisher's idea to call the novel *Rob Roy*—the eponymous outlaw himself appears only sporadically—merely confirms the inadequacy of the paradigm of static difference Rob purportedly represents.

Frank Osbaldistone, the novel's narrator and true protagonist, encounters a variety of differences long before he crosses the border into Scotland. Although his overbearing father insists that he prepare to take over "the great [mercantile] house of Osbaldistone and Tresham," Frank is more interested in literature than commerce.[13] Readers of previous Waverley Novels will not be surprised that *Rob Roy* opens with yet another young man resisting paternal authority. The novel's first-person narration, however, is much more unusual for Scott. Harry E. Shaw writes of Scott's general practice of constructing his characters "from the skin out, not from the skin in," as it were.[14] The closeness with which *Rob Roy*'s first-person narration draws us to Frank's psyche is all the more remarkable given that, as critics frequently observe, our narrator is not a particularly self-aware character. The reader is frequently left to interpret motives, contradictions, and off-stage actions that Frank himself fails either to notice or understand.[15]

As Frank travels north to stay with his cousins, he is prepared to enter a region of exoticism and adventure. This is largely thanks to his Northumberland nurse, who regaled him with literally outlandish stories of the Scots on the other side of the border: "The inhabitants of the opposite frontier served in her narratives to fill up the parts which ogres and giants with seven-leagued boots occupy in the ordinary nursery tales."[16] Accordingly, Frank is taken aback by the first Scotsman he meets on the road, one Mr. Campbell, whose "shrewd, caustic, and somewhat satirical" bearing is off-putting, but hardly monstrous.[17] Other than "the national intonation" of his speech, and the "coarse" (but "decent") state of his dress, little marks Campbell as out of the ordinary; in particular, his political views are notably moderate despite the unsettled nature of the new Hanoverian dynasty.[18] Yet when Campbell reappears a few chapters later to vouch for Frank to the local magistrate, who is investigating the theft of a valuable briefcase from Morris, Frank's previous traveling companion, our narrator is increasingly struck by the various incongruities of Campbell's persona. Upon hearing his assertion that he declined to protect the victim during the robbery due to being "a man of pacific occupation," for example, Frank reports: "I looked at Campbell as he uttered these words, and never recollect to have seen a more singular contrast between the strong daring sternness expressed in his harsh features, and the air of composed meekness and simplicity which his language assumed."[19] Equally remarkable—although not to Frank, it seems, who fails to mention it—is that Campbell now shows as much facility speaking the language of English law, as he did playing the part of the honest Scots traveler in the roadside tavern.

Given the above, readers should be less surprised than Frank when the versatile Campbell turns up again, this time in Glasgow, where our Hero has traveled to assist in the recovery of the missing portmanteau. Morris' briefcase contained bills from Frank's father's firm, payable to a number of Highland chiefs, who in turn owe merchants in Glasgow and Edinburgh; the theft of these bills threatens not only to ruin the Osbaldistone business, but also to trigger unrest in the Highlands.[20] Campbell, meanwhile, changes identities almost as easily as the stolen bills are designed to change hands. First, he appears merely as a disembodied voice, whispering ominously in Frank's ear that "You are in danger in this city"[21]; soon after, he is the stranger who meets Frank at midnight on a bridge over the River Clyde. Now when Campbell speaks, his tone is formal, his language elevated and stripped of the Scotticisms that previously characterized it:

> But do you not fear the consequences of being found with one, whose very name whispered in this lonely street would make the stones themselves rise up to apprehend him – on whose head half the men in Glasgow would build their fortune as on a found treasure, had they the luck to grip him by the collar – the sound of whose apprehension were as welcome at the Cross of Edinburgh as ever the news of a field stricken and won in Flanders?[22]

Yet as he conducts Frank toward another nocturnal rendezvous, Campbell's Scottish accent begins to reappear, and soon he is even speaking in Gaelic. Not until Campbell is unexpectedly reunited with his cousin, a respectable Glasgow merchant named Nichol Jarvie, however, does Frank finally realize that this is the same man he previously met on the road: "I remained astonished at my own stupidity. . . . this man was Campbell himself."[23] Although he repeats the same physical description—"Rather beneath the middle size than above it"[24]—what most strikes Frank now is the extent to which Campbell's appearance suddenly corresponds to his nurse's stories: the Scotsman's broad shoulders and long, powerful arms "gave something wild, irregular, and as it were, unearthly to his appearance, and reminded me involuntarily, of the tales which Mabel used to tell of the old Picts who ravaged Northumberland in ancient times . . . distinguished, like this man, for courage, cunning, ferocity, the length of their arms, and the squareness of their shoulders."[25]

Ian Duncan writes perspicuously of the ways in which this description of Rob (which Scott repeats in the Magnum Opus edition's preface) foregrounds his simian qualities, accessing pre-Darwinian ideas and marking Rob Roy as simultaneously sub- and superhuman.[26] Rob consistently sutures in one body contending, not to say agonistic, parts and identities: he is half man and half beast; half wild Highlander and half cosmopolitan Briton; half residual element of the feudal past, and half opportunistic forerunner of a global future in which Britain will compete with its imperial rivals by any means necessary. Duncan refers to Rob as an embodiment of the liminal figure of "the primitive"; he is also an exemplary figure of what Bhabha terms "hybridity." The historical matrix from which Bhabha's theories emerge is largely the British Raj of the later nineteenth and early twentieth centuries; this is worth bearing in mind as I consider their relevance to Scott's representations of an earlier time and different place. Nevertheless, insofar as eighteenth-century English attitudes toward the Scots (especially Highlanders) anticipated Britain's later, fully imperial worldview, they arguably render Bhabha's insights applicable to this period.[27]

What is hybridity, when applied to the sociocultural realm? Although the term is widely associated with his analyses, Bhabha's own writings characteristically decline to provide a straightforward answer. Let us start, then, with a definition agreed upon by several other notable postcolonial theorists: "hybridity commonly refers to the creation of new transcultural forms within the contact zone produced by colonization."[28] This definition leaves unanswered the question of agency—who is creating these new "transcultural" forms?—but such ambiguity usefully underscores how one of hybridity's effects is precisely to complicate questions of power. Hybridity generally takes shape as a reaction formation by peoples in the process of being colonized. It is, thus, intimately related (although not identical) to what Bhabha calls "mimicry": the attempt by colonized subjects to emulate their colonizers. In some cases, this occurs through straightforward oppression; in others, it may be undertaken actively by the colonized to facilitate their own upward mobility; frequently, it is an uneasy mix of both. Regardless, mimicry threatens the colonized subject with social as well as self-alienation. From the colonizing power's point of view, moreover, mimicry is a double-edged sword whose ambiguous, unpredictable effects mirror the ambivalence of the colonizer's own desire for what Bhabha calls "*a subject of difference that is almost the same, but not quite.*"[29] Ironically, because "mimicry is at once resemblance and menace," the closer the colonized subject gets to a seamless impersonation of the colonizer, the more anxious the latter becomes.[30]

As we have seen, Rob Roy displays varying degrees of mimicry's dual orientation—submission and aggression—in a manner alternately natural and skilled, spontaneous and artful. The fact that, in protecting Frank and helping recover the stolen bills, he does the bidding of his patron, the Duke of Argyle, takes little away from the reader's impression of Rob's remarkable freedom of movement and identity. His ability to blend in wherever he goes—corresponding to Bhabha's designation of "hybridity as camouflage"[31]—combined with his knack for showing up when and where he is most needed, set him apart from most of the novel's other characters. Where Rob moves with ease between Highlands, Lowlands, and northern England, for example, his cousin Jarvie is made plainly uncomfortable by such border-crossings. When invited by Rob to visit him in the north, Jarvie at first declines: "Na, na, Robin . . . I seldom like to leave the Gorbals [an area on the south bank of the Clyde in Glasgow]; I have nae freedom to gang amang your wild hills, Robin, and you kilted red-shanks – it disna become my place, man."[32] The pun on "place" as both social standing (Jarvie is a respected member of Glasgow's merchant class) and home or base of operations, reinforces the restrictions that Jarvie, unlike Rob, feels even in his own country.

Nonetheless, after Jarvie agrees to accompany Frank into the Highlands, the modern businessman and the nominally primitive outlaw turn out to have more in common than either of them initially admits. Hybridity, in fact, is their common attribute, as Jarvie soon proves himself almost as comfortable in a Highland tavern (where he sets an opponent's tartan on fire during a brawl) as in his Glaswegian dining room, where he lectures Frank on "the opening which the Union had afforded between Glasgow and the British colonies in America and the West Indies, and on the facilities which Glasgow possessed of making up *sortable* cargoes for that market."[33] In the latter scene, Jarvie tries to help Frank comprehend the supposed divide between Highlands and Lowlands by asserting that "I maun hear naething about honour – we ken naething here [in the Lowlands] but about credit. Honour is a homicide and a bloodspiller, that gangs about making frays in the street; but Credit is a decent honest man, that sits at hame and makes the pat play [pot boil]."[34] Again, however, both Jarvie's subsequent actions and the novel's plot belie this attempt at strict demarcation: the civilized merchant proves he is still motivated by the supposedly primitive value of honor when he defends his kinsman Rob's reputation on several occasions; and the credit crisis sparked by the theft of the Osbaldistone bills is designed to spread northward until it provokes the supposedly primitive Highland clans to rise up and revolt (thereby effectively supporting the Jacobite rebellion, while actually protecting their financial interests). Under the multi-layered influences of modernity, in other words, Britain as a whole has become a hybrid nation, a productively unstable compound of the romantic and the prosaic, the atavistic and the contemporary.[35]

Although critics sometimes argue that he values diversity merely for its own sake, Bhabha stresses that his conception of hybridity always implies some degree of resistance to the homogenizing efforts of colonization: "hybridity as a . . . contesting, antagonistic agency."[36] In *Rob Roy*, the figure who most embodies this kind of resistance is neither Rob Roy nor Nichol Jarvie—both of whom ultimately put their mobility and subjective fluidity at the service of the modern British state—but rather Rob's imposing wife, Helen Campbell MacGregor. As readers generally recognize, Helen is a far more threatening character than either Rob or the novel's nominal villain, Rashleigh Osbaldistone (the man behind the bills' theft). She not only directs a deadly ambush of the government forces that take Frank and Jarvie prisoner after the tavern brawl, but also later has Morris, as an agent of the Hanoverians who have temporarily seized Rob, fatally thrown off a cliff. Helen undertakes these actions, moreover, with neither fear nor regret: as Morris' pleas for mercy go unheeded, Frank solemnly notes that "It is impossible to describe the scorn, loathing, and contempt, with which the wife of MacGregor regarded this wretched petitioner for the poor boon of existence."[37] Like her husband, she is a survivor; unlike him, she survives not by making her peace with modernity, but by defying it. In this sense, she is what Raymond Williams might call a "residual" element: "effectively formed in the past . . . but still active in the cultural process."[38] Helen's profound lack of contemporaneity manifests itself in the greater stasis of her person as well as her persona. Where Rob moves fluidly between borders and languages, his wife possesses neither his geographical nor linguistic mobility: she never moves beyond the bounds of the Highlands and speaks more in the register of an avenging angel than a Highland woman. Consider her final speech to Morris: "I could have bid you live . . . had life been to you the same weary and wasting burden that it is to me – that it is to every noble and generous mind. But you – wretch! you could creep through the world unaffected by its various disgraces, its ineffable miseries, its constantly accumulating masses of crime and sorrow . . . ."[39] Helen's elevated vocabulary and complex syntax recall the language of the King James Bible rather than the equally conventional Highland patois spoken by the novel's other characters in similar circumstances.

Add to this that, as Margaret Bruzelius has noted, Helen is repeatedly compared "to Deborah, Judith, and Jael – bloodthirsty Biblical heroines,"[40] and one quickly sees that Rob's wife forms a stark contrast to the fluid, mobile subjectivities and personae of Rob and Jarvie. Helen's only truly hybridic qualities are probably her "masculine" bravery and remorselessness; as a result, her virago-like intensity registers a compromised femininity (especially considered from Scott's Regency perspective) as the cost of her survivalist powers and instincts.[41] Later, Frank and Jarvie encounter Helen in a more sedate mood, appearing by her husband's side with "her dress studiously arranged in a more feminine taste than it had been the previous day," but one senses that this appearance of docile, traditional femininity is less authentic than the fierce, sword-wielding, blood-spattered figure she cut previously.[42] Attempting to domesticate her further, Frank now reflects that her "graceful, flowing, and declamatory" style of English is likely due to her acquisition of it as a second language. But even with these prosaic appearances and explanations—and even though Helen ultimately plays a role in the novel's resolution by gifting Frank a token from his love-interest—the reader is left far more impressed by the violence and bitterness implicit in Helen's final words, which recall rumors of her real-life sexual abuse at the hands of the Duke of Montrose's henchman: "All may be forgotten . . . all – but the sense of dishonor, and the desire of vengeance."[43]

As one of the novel's least hybrid characters, it may not be a coincidence that Helen MacGregor is also one of its most unhappy. It seems even less coincidental that, as the most threatening and anarchic figure in the novel, she is also one of its few women of any real importance. In general, the modern critical tradition has not been kind to Scott's Waverley heroines. Lukàcs pays almost no attention to them (with the exception of Jeanie Deans from *The Heart of Mid-Lothian*, about whom I will have more to say in the next chapter); Welsh, who helpfully identifies their frequently central roles in the novels' plots of (masculine) legitimation and inheritance, finds their psychology generally so oversimplified as to be essentially color-coded ("light" vs. "dark" heroines).[44] Yet especially considering the manifest weaknesses of many of Scott's less-than-impressive Waverley Heroes, I am generally convinced by Bruzelius' update on Welsh's argument that "competition [between men or masculine discourses in the Waverley Novels] creates gaps in which women can powerfully operate to substitute their own interests for those of the men who supposedly control them."[45] Nevertheless, these "wild women," as Bruzelius calls them, are the exceptions rather than the rule in Scott's corpus. Most Waverley Heroines, including Rose Bradwardine and Isabella Wardour, are as conventional as their eventual mates.

To Scott's credit, however, Diana Vernon, Frank's love interest in *Rob Roy*, does not fit easily into any of the aforementioned categories. Frank meets her almost immediately upon arriving at Osbaldistone Hall, the family seat of his Jacobite uncle and rugged cousins. He is immediately fascinated by her openness and wit as well as her beauty; she is more "frank" than Frank himself, and certainly more charismatic. Diana is participating in a fox chase when he first spies her: "It was a young lady, the loveliness of whose very striking features was enhanced by the animation of the chase and the glow of the exercise . . . She wore, what was then somewhat unusual, a coat, vest, and hat, resembling those of a man."[46] Scott's original readers, although equally taken with Die Vernon's breezy charms, were concerned by this and other anachronisms in her character, including her multiple solo interviews with Frank. Rather than read these quirks of dress and manner as errors on Scott's part, however, we may see them as infusions of hybridity— understood broadly as the subjective integration of difference—into his most dynamic heroine. Like Helen MacGregor, Die's forthrightness and intelligence sometimes manifest themselves as transgressions into masculinity; unlike Rob's wife, however, Diana never compromises her femininity with actual violence, and much of her mysterious conduct is eventually explained by the revelation that she has been protecting her presumed-dead father. (Here, *Rob Roy*'s plot takes its own generic turn toward hybridity, blending elements of Gothic along with its historical romance in the manner of *The Antiquary*.[47]) She also plays a more pivotal role than Helen in resolving the novel's primary conflict, helping recover Rashleigh's stolen bills and returning them to Frank. Once the 1715 Rebellion is snuffed out—taking with it, in the kind of black comedy that Scott enjoys more frequently than readers realize, all of Frank's northern cousins and his uncle too—Frank finds himself the inheritor of Osbaldistone Hall, and the path is cleared for him to marry Diana (despite her Catholicism, which is symbolically exorcised by the flight of her father in the novel's final pages).

Yet, *Rob Roy* ends on a more somber note than this synopsis suggests. As the first-person narration concludes, we are reminded we have been reading Frank's account at some years' remove from the events in question: "How I sped in my wooing, Will Tresham [Frank's longtime business partner], I need not tell you. You know, too, how long and happily I lived with Diana. You know how I lamented her. But you do not – cannot know, how much she deserved her husband's sorrow."[48] For understated pathos, there are few more effective passages in Scott's oeuvre. Most striking here is the absence of any mention by Frank of his and Diana's children, the basic guarantee of familial continuity associated with a fully happy conclusion. Readers can only assume that although the Union of England and Scotland once again proves fruitful in *Rob Roy*, Frank and Diana's union does not. Such personal infertility strongly implies that Diana's childlessness is related, symbolically if not directly, to her hybridic transgressions. Frank, loyal but uncomprehending to the end, is left to mourn her alone. He has survived, inherited his father's business, and prospered as a prudent Waverley Hero should, but his melancholy isolation at his narrative's conclusion ought to remind us of Žižek's account of the high price paid by the modern subject's emergence "through a violent abstraction from all its particular roots and determinations."

Performing the Crusades in *The Talisman*

The theme of transgression makes a natural segue to the theories of Judith Butler. Her landmark study, *Gender Trouble: Feminism and the Subversion of Identity*, ambitiously critiques assumptions about gender and sexuality in the works of a number of canonical philosophers and thinkers. Her influential conclusions are previewed in a series of rhetorical questions in the book's preface: "Is drag the imitation of gender, or does it dramatize the signifying gestures through which gender itself is established? Does being female, constitute a 'natural fact' or a cultural performance, or is 'naturalness' constituted through discursively constrained performative acts that produce the body through and within the categories of sex?"[49] Butler is of course well aware of Simone de Beauvoir's ground-breaking distinction between the categories of sex (as a function of biology) and gender (as a function of cultural norms). But, her interest is in how both of these categories are not only normatively constrained—our ideas regarding the "proper" usage of different body parts, for example, are no more "natural" than our ideas concerning "proper" masculine or feminine behavior—but also systematically overlapped to produce the body as recognizably "normal." Furthermore, as her first question suggests, by arguing that there is no natural connection between a sexed body and a given gender—by arguing, that is, that "If gender is the cultural meanings that the sexed body assumes, then a gender cannot be said to follow from sex in any one way"[50]—Butler recognizes that the practise of drag (dressing and behaving like someone of the "opposite" gender) is neither an idiosyncratic deviation nor a marginal cultural phenomenon, but an exemplary practise that highlights the radical performativity of all gender identities.[51]

As evidenced by its various appearances in the foregoing paragraph, the concept of performativity is central to Butler's theories. It turns out, however, to have two different (albeit related) valences in her work. In her early studies—that is, in *Gender Trouble* and its follow-up, *Bodies That Matter*—performativity generally connotes the method by which one "embodies" or performs one's gender by adhering to a set of more-or-less prescribed codes and norms in the domains of attire, behavior, and sexual orientation. Although Butler's critics sometimes accuse her of promoting a voluntaristic notion of gender identity—as if one could choose or swap one's gender on a daily basis, like changing clothes—in fact Butler is always clear that, if anything, the opposite dynamic is usually present: gender identity is normative and constraining, and one mostly performs one's gender not by consciously choosing it, but rather by automatically enacting it. Moreover, there is no "I" prior to engendering: the very possibility of being a social subject, a "body that matters," is entirely imbricated in one's assumption of a *gendered* subject position from which to speak and act.

Yet, Butler's theory of gender performativity is not all-constraining. Instead, the subject's necessarily recurring "acts of gender" introduce a potentially destabilizing temporal dimension to its operations:

> performativity cannot be understood outside of a process of iterability, a regularized and constrained repetition of norms. And this repetition is not performed by a subject; this repetition is what enables a subject and constitutes the temporal condition for the subject. This 'iterability' implies that 'performance' is not a single 'act' or event, but a ritualized production,

> a ritual reiterated under and through constraint, under and through the force of prohibition and taboo . . . but not, I will insist, determining it fully in advance.[52]

Gender performativity, we see again, does not follow subjectivity; it is what makes possible the constitution of a socially acceptable subject position. More, we can see that, *pace* Butler's critics, her point is not that gender identities are easy to construct or exchange. Rather, she is concerned to demonstrate that, social norms and expectations notwithstanding, gender performativity is consistently prone to "errors," diversions, and variations that may contribute to destabilizing the very norms most subjects try to approximate.

The key term in the above passage is "iterability," and it points to a second connotation of performativity that begins to take precedence in the second, more linguistically oriented phase of Butler's theoretical career.[53] Especially in *Excitable Speech: A Politics of the Performative*, Butler turns to the rhetorical tradition of "speech act theory," particularly as theorized by J. L. Austin. His well-known distinction between "constatives" (statements that merely describe the world) and "performatives" (statements that perform or otherwise produce certain effects in the world) has been taken up by earlier literary and critical theorists, most notably Jacques Derrida in his now-classic essay "Signature Event Context." There, Derrida questions (among other things) the viability of Austin's distinction, effectively demonstrating—although, famously, not to the satisfaction of Austin's philosophical heir, John Searle—that every constative is at some level also a performative insofar as, for example, the statement "the sky is blue" is always implicitly "[I assert that] the sky is blue."[54] In *Excitable Speech*, Butler explores points of contact between Austinian/Derridean performatives and Louis Althusser's notion of "interpellation," his term for the process by which an ideological discourse "hails" and so constitutes a subject in society.[55] Butler is well aware of their differences, noting that "For Austin, the subject who speaks precedes the speech in question. For Althusser, the speech act that brings the subject into linguistic existence precedes the subject in question."[56] In neither case, however, are speech acts entirely governed by the speaker's intentions. Butler's true interest in this conjunction again revolves around what she sees as the pressures and possibilities of the temporal features of performative and interpellative speech acts. Not only do such acts become most effective through repetition, but they also depend on implicit references to the previous contexts in which they have already been deployed:

> Just as for Austin the convention governing the institution of promise-making is verbally honored even in the case of a promise that no one intends to fulfill, so for Althusser one is entered into the "ritual" of ideology

regardless of whether there is a prior and authenticating belief in that ideology. . . . Who speaks when convention speaks? In what time does convention speak? In some sense, it is an inherited set of voices, an echo of others who speak as the "I."[57]

Butler's reading of Althusser's "ritual" of ideology chimes with Žižek's assertion that ideology resides in our behaviors as much if not more than in our thoughts or beliefs. Again, however, Butler is notably optimistic regarding the possibilities for resistance and subversion. As in the bodily performativity of gender, so also in the spoken performativity of discursive subjectivation: the very iterability (repetition) of the process that underwrites normative power introduces the potential emergence of challenges to that power.

At first glance, *The Talisman* would not appear to lend itself to such theoretical applications. Set during the unsuccessful Third Crusade of the late twelfth century, the novel mostly concerns the internal divisions roiling the Europeans' camp, and so predictably features an almost entirely male cast. Before turning to them, however, I want to note that the mere presence of a particular female character in *The Talisman* deeply irritated one of the book's most prominent original critics. Charles Mills, a contemporary of Scott's and the author of a multivolume history of the Crusades, complained that Scott erred in introducing Edith Plantagenet as a cousin of Richard the Lionheart and the love interest of the Scottish protagonist Sir Kenneth, since the historical record did not support her existence. Of course, Kenneth too is a fictional creation, and his unmasking near the novel's conclusion as the Earl of Huntingdon (a real historical personage who likely did not participate in the Third Crusade) is equally Scott's invention; but it seems telling that Mills was much more bothered by the fabrication of a *female* relative of Richard the Lionheart than by a fictionalized male nobleman.[58] In fact, both Edith and Berengaria of Navarre—the novel's only other female character of note—occupy plot positions that, thanks to Eve Kosofksy Sedgwick, we can recognize as confined "between men": the latter frequently mediates between her husband and other male characters, while the former is at one point offered in marriage to Saladin before eventually being allowed to marry Kenneth.[59] Yet, it was precisely this element of Scott's fiction-making to which Mills most strenuously objected, describing it as "carrying the jest a little too far; for the preservation of historical truth is really too important a principle to be idly violated."[60] One suspects that what really bothered Mills in this scenario was the possibility that Edith, a Christian woman, could be legitimately "violated" (in Mill's charged terminology) by Saladin, a Kurdish Muslim, through the legal institution of marriage.

This marriage, in fact, never occurs; as we will see, Scott's Saladin is far too honorable to agree to such an arrangement. My point, however, is that Edith herself has no say in the matter. Even more than the female characters in *Rob Roy*, the women in *The Talisman* are unable to exercise significant agency over their own lives. This is not to deny that they have plenty of opportunities to "perform" their expected gender roles; when Berengaria decides to supplicate for Kenneth's life after he faces execution for allowing the English camp's banner to be stolen, for example, Scott explains that

> Berengaria, such as we have described her, knew well – What woman knows not? – her own road to victory. . . . she rushed at once to the side of Richard's lowly couch, dropped on her knees, flung her mantle from her shoulders, showing, as they hung down at their full length, her beautiful golden tresses, and while her countenance seemed like a sun bursting through a cloud . . . she seized upon the right hand of the King . . . and gradually pulling it to her with a force which was resisted, though but faintly, she possessed herself of that arm, the prop of Christendom, and the dread of Heathenesse, and imprisoning its strength in both her little fairy hands, she bent it upon her brow, and united to it her lips.[61]

Everything about this passage highlights Berengaria's traditional femininity, and the contrast between her "little fairy hands" and Richard's muscular one, powerful even in repose, is especially pronounced. Citing a host of familiar assumptions about feminine beauty and weakness versus masculine ruggedness and power, it is the familiarity of Berengaria's performance that makes it effective. The near impossibility of imagining that Scott could reverse or scramble these gendered norms of dominance and subordination confirms Butler's assertion that "[gender] [p]erformativity is thus not a singular 'act,' for it is always a reiteration of a norm or set of norms, and to the extent that it acquires an act-like status in the present, it conceals or dissimulates the conventions of which it is a repetition."[62]

And yet numerous conventions are scrambled elsewhere in *The Talisman*, if not with regard to conventional distinctions between men and women, then with regard to those between the men themselves. Despite repeatedly being described in nominally heroic terms, for example, Richard (as in the above passage) spends much of the novel in his tent, ill and complaining of various maladies. Unlike the ever-adaptable Rob Roy, the English king literally never acclimatizes to his new environment, as Scott suggests in his introductory description: "even the iron frame of Coeur de Lion could not support, without injury, the alternations of the unwholesome climate, joined to ceaseless exertions of body and mind. He became afflicted with one of those slow and wasting fevers peculiar to Asia."[63] The climate is "unwholesome," of course, neither to its natives nor to those who understand how to adjust to it, but to those foreigners, like Richard, who prove unwilling or unable to modify their "iron frame[s]" to fit their new surroundings.

Richard is finally cured not by one of his own healers but by his arch-nemesis, Saladin, who wields the novel's titular amulet while disguised in one of his many guises (he is also the emir who battles Kenneth in the novel's opening chapter) as the doctor Hakim. As many critics have noted, Scott's depiction of Saladin is remarkably positive. In his dialogue with Kenneth following their duel, for example, Saladin is notably more tolerant and open-minded than the Christian knight; in his negotiations with Richard, he is more sagacious than the hot-headed King and his intolerant allies.[64] Indeed, Scott's frequently formulaic-sounding praise of Richard, Kenneth, and the novel's other Crusaders (some of whom are explicitly criticized by Scott for their rapacity and ignorance) makes the unconventionality of his portrait of the Muslim leader all the more noticeable. Most remarkable of all, perhaps, is the ease with which Saladin moves between his various disguises and roles. Bruzelius calls Saladin "a particularly attractive fantasy of masculine self-determination" because, unlike most of *The Talisman*'s other characters, he moves through its pages and plot with ease, grace, and purpose.[65] Seemingly aware of all the norms that might constrain him—including the Western literary convention of "the wily Oriental"—Saladin demonstrates an almost uncanny knack for turning them to his advantage.[66] In his initial encounter with Kenneth, when the Christian knight declares his horrified suspicion that "your blinded race had some descent from the foul fiend," Saladin replies "From whom should the bravest boast of descending, saving from him that is bravest? . . . from whom should the proudest race trace their line so well as from the Dark Spirit . . . ? Eblis may be hated, stranger, but he must be feared; and such as Eblis are his descendants of Kurdistan."[67] Taking Kenneth's insult, embracing it, and redeploying it, Saladin's strategy here anticipates Butler's insight that "in the ongoing interpellations of social life . . . these terms we never really choose are the occasion for something we might still call agency, the repetition of an originary subordination for another purpose, one whose future is partially open."[68] Butler acknowledges that such recontextualized citations are not without their dangers; still, as in the transformation of the epithet "queer" from insult to rallying cry, subversive citationality can convert subordination into contestation, and hence into agency.

Kenneth experiences an analogous transformation in *The Talisman*'s second half. After Hakim too pleads for the knight's life to be spared, Kenneth is given to the disguised Muslim leader as payment for his services to Richard, on one condition: "let him beware how he comes before the eyes of Richard . . . let him consult his own safety, and never appear in my presence more."[69] But Saladin, wishing to repay Kenneth for previously saving his life during an ambush, once more proves his moral superiority to the English monarch by returning the disguised knight to Richard's camp four days later. Only after he has prevented an assassination attempt on the English king do readers learn for certain that the mute African slave whom Saladin has provided is in fact Sir Kenneth himself, seemingly magically (albeit temporarily) transformed. Here is the initial description of the Kurdish ruler's "gift" to his adversary:

> The English knight accordingly introduced a person, apparently of no higher rank than a Nubian slave, whose appearance was nevertheless highly interesting. He was of superb stature and nobly formed, and his commanding features, although almost jet-black, showed nothing of negro descent. He wore over his coal-black locks a milk-white turban, and over his shoulders a short mantle of the same colour . . . The rest of his muscular limbs, both legs and arms, were bare, excepting that he had sandals on his feet, and wore a collar and bracelets of silver.[70]

The trope of performativity is literalized as Sir Kenneth stands, apparently changed beyond recognition, before his king. The decision to keep Sir Kenneth's features Caucasian may be charitably ascribed to Scott's desire to maintain a modicum of believability regarding the limits of Saladin's transformational powers; whatever its origins, it introduces a further element of hybridity into the knight's new appearance. His racialized transformation is nevertheless complete enough that, when he suffers from a poisoned blade intended for the king, no Christian knight will initially help him. The others' reluctance to suck the poison from the slave's arm spurs Richard to one of his few acts of real kindness: "And without farther ceremony, and in spite of the general expostulations of those around, and the respectful opposition of the Nubian himself, the King of England applied his lips to the wound of the black slave, treating with ridicule all remonstrances, and overpowering all resistance."[71]

In a skillful manipulation of the gap between narration and plot, only after this scene does Scott depict the events leading up to the thwarted assassination. Following in the disguised Saladin's retinue, Kenneth—now fully experiencing the abjection of his exile, "deprived at once of honour and of liberty"[72]—receives a series of lessons in tolerance and sympathy. First, he witnesses one of the novel's embedded literal performances, the description of which strikingly resembles the plot of The Talisman itself: "After this exordium, Hassan uplifted his voice, and began a tale of love and magic, intermixed with feats of warlike achievement, and ornamented with abundant quotations from the Persian poets, with whose compositions the orator seemed familiar."[73] This recitation is followed by a call to prayer that accomplishes what all Kenneth's previous experiences as a Crusader could not: it moves him to participate, however partially, in the foreign culture he has hitherto spurned.

> Even Kenneth, whose reason at once and prejudices were offended by seeing his companions in that which he considered as an act of idolatry, could not help respecting the sincerity of their misguided zeal, and being stimulated by their fervor to apply supplications to Heaven in a purer form, wondering, meanwhile, what new-born feelings could teach him to accompany in prayer, though with varied invocation, those very Saracens, whose heathenish worship he had conceived a crime dishonourable to the land in which high miracles had been wrought, and where the day-star of redemption had arisen.[74]

Kenneth may not be able fully to articulate his feelings here, but Scott leaves little doubt regarding the profundity of this transcultural epiphany.

The Crusader's inner transformation, then, is to some degree merely supplemented by his outer one when Saladin invites him to don the clothing and appearance of a North African slave. Although we neither see the actual blackening of Kenneth's skin nor hear most of his thoughts while in this "disguise," Scott implies that occupying the subject position of an abject Other alters Kenneth's psyche as well as his appearance; when he once again enters Edith's presence, we are told, "it was with humiliation, not of the posture only, but of the very inmost soul, that the unfortunate knight, thus strangely disguised, threw himself on one knee, with looks bent on the ground."[75] Momentarily "reduced" to the status of an African slave, chastened in the presence of a beloved to whom he has no access, Kenneth recognizes not only the parameters of his current disadvantaged condition, but also (at least potentially) the privilege that silently attends his usual status as a Crusader. At this moment, his experience reflects a basic tenet of Butler's work on ethics: "to take responsibility for oneself is to avow the limits of any self-understanding, and to establish these limits not only as a condition for the subject but as the predicament of the human community."[76]

It would be tempting to try to make *The Talisman*'s conclusion conform to Butler's iconoclastic ideas of personal and communal responsibility; it would also be false. After helping uncover the true thief of the English camp's missing banner and subsequently besting him in single combat, Kenneth reveals himself as the Crown Prince of Scotland, sent by his father to repair their relations with the English monarch. Restored to his rightful rank, Kenneth is simultaneously restored to the conventional Waverley Hero's path, free to marry whom he wishes and to inherit his own title and estate. Still, if it is unreasonable to expect Scott suddenly to alter significantly the narrative pattern that served him so well throughout most of his career—for this, we must look to a tragic Waverley Novel like *The Bride of Lammermoor* (1819), which I discuss in Chapter 5—it is nonetheless worth noting that Saladin looms larger than ever in *The Talisman*'s final pages. His beheading of the villainous Grand Master of the Templars is both a final flourish and a none-too-subtle reminder that, like Rob Roy before him, Saladin plays this novel's games more skillfully than its other participants. Furthermore, whereas *Rob Roy* ends with a proleptic summary of that adventurer's decline and death, Saladin not only exits *The Talisman* in full health and power, but also speaks its last lines of dialogue: "I may not yield you up that Jerusalem which you so much desire to hold. It is to us, as to you, a Holy City. But whatever other terms Richard demands of Saladin, shall be as willingly yielded as yonder fountain yields its waters."[77] Written in Scott's sentimentalized version of Eastern-inflected chivalric speech, Saladin's final declaration nonetheless essentially anticipates Butler's critical, ethicodiscursive insight that "To ask for recognition, or to offer it, is precisely not to ask for recognition for what one already is. It is to solicit a becoming, to instigate a transformation, to petition the future always in relation to the Other."[78] This sense of the transformative power of critical thought on the collective quality of our lived experience is, to my mind, one of the most valuable elements of contemporary theory; it is also arguably the guiding principle behind the best of Scott's fiction.

4

Governmentality, or *The Heart of Mid-Lothian* and *Quentin Durward* with Foucault and Agamben

In January 1818, Scott began writing what many critics agree is his most ambitious novel: *The Heart of Mid-Lothian*. In the four and a half years since *Waverley*'s publication, he had already achieved an unprecedented measure of critical and commercial success; both those novels published as straightforwardly anonymous texts (*Waverley*, *Guy Mannering*, *The Antiquary*, *Rob Roy*) and those presented in the new *Tales of My Landlord* series (*The Black Dwarf*, *The Tale of Old Mortality*) had been wildly successful. Already, too, they had spawned a vast secondary industry of "Waverleyana"; especially popular were the stage adaptations, which audiences were increasingly likely to encounter even before reading the books themselves.[1]

Having purchased riverfront property some 30 miles from Edinburgh in 1811, Scott had been steadily enlarging and building upon it. Abbotsford's construction was an expensive and drawn-out affair. As James Hogg remembers it, the Scott family became habituated to living in an unfinished manor/manner:

> The family being exceedingly hampered of room the architects finished always one part before another and the family took possession piecemeal and the peninsular war being then raging the everlasting aphorism began. Sir Walter showed his plan to every friend who came and always with this information in his broad Northumberland burr "We agh just like the Fghench in Saghagossa gaining foot by foot and ghoom by ghoom."[2]

Hogg implies, with characteristic irony, that the ongoing renovations forced the Scotts to become nomads in their own home. His cheeky portrayal of the Author of Waverley and his family, here and elsewhere, helps account for Lockhart's lasting anger with "the Ettrick Shepherd" in the wake of Scott's death in 1832. (Indeed, Hogg doubles down on his irreverence by subsequently insisting, with regard to his transcription of Scott's conversation, "I cannot spell it better to [Scott's] pronunciation but whoever has heard his daughter Anne's pronunciation has heard her father's.")

Hogg's sketch, although nominally about the prosaic trials of home building, also identifies two significant features of Scott's literary career: his consistent restlessness and his uncanny knack for using the medium of the historical novel to reflect on current as well as past events. Just as the Scott family continuously expanded their living quarters as more rooms in Abbotsford became available, so Scott continued to diversify his fictional repertoire as success gave him increasing freedom to experiment; thus, even John Sutherland (the least charitable of Scott's several biographers) admits that *The Heart of Mid-Lothian* "represents an impressive range of departures from the novels that precede it."[3] Furthermore, the comparison Hogg records of Scott likening Abbotsford's expansion to the slow advance of the French army in Spain, highlights his consistent interest in the parallels and relationships to be found, not just between the past and the present, but between the micromovements of everyday life and the macromovements of larger-scale cultural, social, and even political developments. Hogg's amusing anecdote, thus, not only sheds light on the workings of Scott's imagination, but also provides a convenient starting point for the connections I want to draw in this chapter between two of Scott's most politically oriented novels, *Mid-Lothian* and *Quentin Durward* (1823), and the provocative theoretical programs of Michel Foucault and Giorgio Agamben. Both theorists share a commitment to investigating the historical origins of modern liberalism; both are skeptical of the claims of "progress" usually made by its proponents and beneficiaries. Scott may not be as radical in his critique of modernity as either Foucault or Agamben; nevertheless, I hope to demonstrate that he has more in common with them than is usually allowed.

The biopolitics of *The Heart of Mid-Lothian*

Set in the decades between the first and second Jacobite Rebellions, *Mid-Lothian* features Scott's only central female protagonist, the humble but steadfast Jeanie Deans. It also reverses his favored plot trajectory: this time, a Scot travels south to England, experiences adventures, overcomes dangers, and returns triumphantly to Scotland. That the Waverley pattern can be reversed but still accomplish the same geopolitical goal—confirmation of Britain's essential unity—underscores Scott's commitment to representing post-Union Britain as a truly modern nation, connected through regular circulations of goods, finances, and people; as Penny Fielding notes, "Scott's novels . . . are increasingly busy with people travelling at various speeds up and down the nation between north and south."[4] *Mid-Lothian*'s frame narrative, which features Scott's newest authorial stand-in, Peter Pattieson, fittingly begins with an overturned mail coach, from whose *"insides* by a sort of summary and Caesarean process of delivery" emerge the lawyers whose stories of the old Edinburgh city jail (known as "the Heart of Mid-Lothian") inspire the ensuing narrative.[5] Scott subsequently extends this childbirth metaphor by describing "the womb of the leathern conveniency" from which the passengers are extricated.[6] He, thus, neatly brings together two of the novel's central insights regarding how the British state was consolidated over the course of the long eighteenth century: in the material sphere, through increasingly efficient and integrated state infrastructures (such as highways) and institutions (like the national postal service); and in the social sphere, through legal and cultural restrictions and norms that aimed to regulate and utilize its citizenry, especially women, for their productive *and* reproductive capacities.[7]

The material improvements that both accompanied and facilitated the modernization of the British nation-state have been well documented by historians; they have left concrete and archival traces that can be easily recovered. The formation and transformation of less material kinds of systems, by contrast, can be more difficult to recreate and track; nevertheless, Michel Foucault dedicated his career to demonstrating that they are of at least equal importance to our understanding of modernity. As Foucault observes near the end of the opening lecture of his 1979 series at the Collège de France, "Politics and the economy are not things that exist, or errors, or illusions, or ideologies. They are things that do not exist and yet which are inscribed in reality and fall under a regime of truth dividing the true and the false."[8] Because of their classical periodization and somewhat narrow focus, Foucault's final published books on the history of sexuality gave some commentators the impression he had turned away from the large-scale, systemic investigations that characterized the early ("archaeological") and middle ("genealogical") phases of his career. The ongoing posthumous publication of his annual Collège de France lectures, however, confirms that Foucault remained committed to what he calls, in *Discipline and Punish*'s introduction, "writing the history of the present."[9] As he explains in the lecture quoted above, he never saw himself as having laid such work aside:

The point of all these investigations concerning madness, disease, delinquency, sexuality, and what I am talking about now, is to show how the coupling of a set of practices and a regime of truth form an apparatus (*dispositif*) of knowledge-power that effectively marks out in reality that which does not exist and legitimately submits it to the division between true and false.[10]

The feedback loop of knowledge-power (*pouvoir-savoir*) will be familiar to readers of Foucault's best-known published texts. Nevertheless, as the centrality of the relatively unfamiliar term *dispositif* in the above quotation indicates, Foucault's Collège de France lectures introduce some substantively new concepts.[11]

According to Foucault, around the end of the eighteenth century, the overarching cognitive framework (*episteme*) of European thought underwent a significant shift. The transition from what he calls the Classical to the Modern ages involved a number of social, conceptual, and political mutations, many of which Foucault mapped over the course of his career. Several of his Collège de France lecture series track the emergence of a new form of social organization that receives relatively little attention *per se* in his books: governmentality. Emerging first at the level of the secular nation-state (itself a relatively new invention in eighteenth-century Europe, as we saw in Chapter 2 via Koselleck), the concept of governmentality is defined in detail a few weeks into Foucault's 1978 lectures. First, it concerns the means by which people come to be organized from above: "by 'governmentality' I understand the ensemble formed by institutions, procedures, analyses and reflections, calculations, and tactics that allows the exercise of this very specific, albeit very complex, power that has the population as its target, political economy as its major form of knowledge, and apparatuses of security as its essential technical instrument."[12] Second, it is a "tendency" or (borrowing vocabulary from Deleuze) a "line of force" that leads to the privileging of "the type of power we can call 'government'" over other forms of power, including "sovereignty" (which I will explore in more detail shortly) and even "discipline."[13] Third, it is as a historical phenomenon, the end-point or current phase of a process that began with the "state of justice" of the Middle Ages and proceeded through the European "administrative state" of the fifteenth and sixteenth centuries (about which, again, I will have more to say below).[14]

"Governmentality," then, is not identical to "government." Rather, it is a set of institutions, attitudes, and apparatuses that includes, but is not limited to, the more conventional elements of formal government. Governmentality, Foucault observes, is "at the same time both internal and external to the state," and to the extent that the latter becomes fully inhabited by the former, several precursor phenomena can be identified.[15] The first and most significant, for Foucault, is the long Judeo-Christian tradition of "pastoral" government, in which leaders both spiritual and secular are consistently figured as shepherds tending their flocks (subjects). For the Greeks, power was essentially territorial and site-specific: a Greek god would help found a city, for example. By contrast, Foucault speculates, the wanderings of the ancient Hebrew tribes led them to postulate a God whose power was focused on His people rather than on a specific location.[16] Eventually, this pastoral function was institutionalized by the Christian Church, where it "gave rise to an art of conducting, directing, leading, guiding, taking in hand, and manipulating men"—developments that Foucault sees as unique and decisive in Western history, since they are the "origin" and the "background" of the modern state insofar as the latter represents the moment "when governmentality became a calculated and reflected practice."[17] This moment, Foucault postulates, is roughly aligned with the late-sixteenth- and early seventeenth-centuries, which he identifies in *The Order of Things* as the hinge between the Medieval and the Classical *epistemes*. Just as nature becomes available for human classification and organization, so people become visible as essential resources of the state, over which not just sovereignty but also the principles of *raison d'État*, "the art of government," must be exercised. In concert with the historical decline of "the old forms of universality offered to and imposed on Europe throughout the Middle Ages practically since the Roman Empire," the new art of government is entirely self-referential: the modern state "seeks its own good and has no external purpose" other than to increase its own resources and forces.[18] Again, the "open time" and "multiple spatiality" that Foucault identifies with this modern geopolitical landscape—a world of competing states "not temporally oriented towards a final unity"—agree in their general terms with Koselleck's alignment of the mid-sixteenth-century with the decline of eschatology and the beginnings of modern politics.[19]

Keeping these developments in mind, when we turn to *The Heart of Mid-Lothian*, a number of points of contact and confirmation become visible. Borrowing once more from the annals of Scottish history, but now using relatively minor events to highlight major historical shifts, Scott crafts a compelling albeit tangled narrative. Impregnated by George Staunton, a well-to-do Englishman moonlighting as a Scottish smuggler, the beautiful peasant, Effie Deans, is accused of murder when the infant she has secretly delivered is kidnapped by Staunton's delusional former lover, Madge Murdockson. Effie's sister, Jeanie, merely needs to testify that Effie revealed her pregnancy to save her from a death sentence; but raised in the strict Presbyterian faith of their father, Jeanie refuses to perjure herself. Instead, with her sister awaiting execution, she sets off for London, alone and on foot, where she succeeds in kindling the interest of the Duke of Argyle in her sister's case. Argyle, in turn, helps petition Queen Caroline (wife of George II) for Effie's pardon, and later—having taken a liking to steadfast, earnest Jeanie—installs the extended Deans family on his "hobby farm" on the Highlands' verge.

The novel nonetheless concludes on a tragic note when Effie's long-lost son accidentally murders his father during a botched robbery.

Understandably, critics have often focused on the seemingly timeless issues of morality and the law raised by *Mid-Lothian*, from Dorothy Van Ghent's classic New Critical reading of Scott's investigation into "matters of conscience," to David Hewitt's recent chapter on the novel as an extended meditation on the nature of justice.[20] Seen through a critical historical optic, however, the novel also bears out several of Foucault's claims regarding key elements of the governmental reason that arose over the course of the long eighteenth century. The kind of theoretically informed, historicized reading I have in mind takes its cues from Charlotte Sussman's convincing argument that *The Heart of Mid-Lothian* should be read in the context of eighteenth-century theories of population.[21] Where Sussman focuses specifically on the novel's representations of the portability and potential deployment of various elements of Scotland's peoples—and thus draws implicitly on Foucault's work in *Discipline and Punish*—I propose to draw explicitly on Foucault's Collège de France lectures to highlight the novel's deployment of multiple modes of governmentality.

The Deans family's distinctive faith—specifically, their adherence to the Cameronian sect of Presbyterians—has frequently been noted by readers, as has Scott's "generally sympathetic representation" of their plight, especially in light of earlier criticism Scott bore for his portrayal of Cameronian fanaticism in *The Tale of Old Mortality*.[22] Cameronianism, however, is demonstrably not *Mid-Lothian*'s central concern. Jeanie's crucial decision not to perjure herself, for example, is imputed to her generally Christian morality; when Staunton tries to force her to promise that she will lie in court to save Effie's life, Jeanie simply responds that she "can promise nothing . . . which is unlawful for a Christian."[23] More, although Jeanie and Effie's father, Davie Deans, is mostly cast in a benevolent light, Scott consistently dissociates himself (through the thin veil of Pattieson's implied disapproval) from Deans' specific attitudes and beliefs.[24]

This is not to deny, however, that the novel is deeply interested in the role Christianity plays in informing the workings of the modern nation-state. When Jeanie's arduous journey to London is disrupted by the machinations of Meg Murdockson, Madge's conniving mother, Jeanie eventually finds herself before a country church. Here, Madge—having previously translated their adventures into the terms of John Bunyan's *Pilgrim's Progress* (1678)—tells her they will meet a man who can play another role in their story:

"But now we will gang to the Interpreter's house, for I ken a man that will play the Interpreter right weel; for he has eyes lifted up to heaven, the best of books in his hand, the law of truth written on his lips, and he stands as if he pleaded wi' men – O if I had minded what he had said to me, I had never been the cast-away creature that I am! – But it is all over now. – But we'll knock at the gate . . . ."[25]

Associated with the Holy Spirit, Bunyan's Interpreter offers his protagonist, Christian, both respite and wisdom in the early stages of his journey to spiritual redemption. Meg's "Interpreter" does something of the same for Jeanie, but with an important plot twist: he is not only a learned clergyman but also George Staunton's father. As a Presbyterian, Jeanie is initially reluctant even to enter an Anglican church. Scott informs us with a telling simile, however, that "in her present agitating and alarming situation, she looked for safety to this forbidden place of assembly, as the hunted animal will sometimes seek shelter from imminent danger in the human habitation, or in other places of refuge most alien to its nature and habits."[26] Jeanie's instinct is rewarded: after entering the church, she manages to behave with enough propriety that Mr. Staunton discerns her quality of character even from his position at the altar. Having just sermonized on "the practical doctrines of Christianity," the Rector subsequently places Jeanie under his pastoral care.[27]

The time Jeanie spends in Staunton's comfortable home not only allows her some measure of rest and recovery, but also facilitates her learning of George Staunton's history, since (conveniently enough) the latter is also currently under his father's care, having fallen from his horse in his haste to reach Edinburgh after receiving news of Effie's sentence. Equally importantly, Staunton Sr. furnishes Jeanie with a guide to a nearby town and a seat on a direct coach to London. The Rector does all this, moreover, without learning the details of Jeanie's situation or the nature of her connection to his wayward son. His purposeful ignorance of her motives ("I must not enquire into the cause of your journey, and so I cannot be fit to give you advice how to manage it"[28]), combined with his generous material assistance, reinforce Foucault's argument that the confessional elements of the Christian tradition became less important as its pastoral elements—that is, its mechanisms for shaping and "shepherding" subjects from without rather than from within—are promoted and subsequently absorbed into the broad machinery of governmentality.

The transition from "pastoral power" to "governmental reason" takes up most of Foucault's 1977–78 Collège lectures. Once the latter establishes itself in the seventeenth century as the basic rationale of the modern state, it needs to be deployed and realized. Managing the new, self-legitimizing state's growth—primarily by "manipulating, maintaining, distributing, and re-establishing [its] relations of force"—calls in turn for the creation of what Foucault identifies as the "two major assemblages of political technology" in the modern era: the police and the diplomatic-military apparatus. Each of these, I want now to suggest, is not only present in *The Heart of Mid-Lothian* but also, like the "pastoral power" of Reverend Staunton, identifiable with a particular character.

Foucault has relatively little to say about the diplomatic-military assemblage: it is the best-known development in his genealogical re-creation, and also the one that "has hardly changed since the eighteenth century."[29] *Mid-Lothian's* obvious candidate for this function is the Duke of Argyle, the Scottish nobleman whom Jeanie enlists to intercede on Effie's behalf. Scott famously likens Argyle to a "benevolent enchanter," a denomination that Duncan astutely links to Scott's repurposing of generic romance tropes for the modern novel.[30] Argyle's involvement in Effie's case is also highly overdetermined: he is intrigued by Jeanie's bravery and honesty, flattered by her appeal to their shared Scottishness, and not unwilling to use her sister's plight to repair his relationship with the royal family. Scott assures us soon after the Duke is introduced that "his mind was of that acute and penetrating character which discovers, with the glance of intuition, what facts bear on the particular point that chances to be subjected to consideration."[31] Thus, he is entirely suited to the bureaucratic operations that, beneath his noble exterior and romantic mannerisms, remain his true calling. Argyle's eventual installation of Davie Deans on his hobby farm, as well as his procurement of a nearby parish position for Jeanie's future husband, confirm that the Duke's central role in the novel is conservative: to reintegrate the Deans family into the social fabric from which they have been torn. Even Deans' ability to care for the Duke's highland cattle without undue fear of blackmail is guaranteed by Argyle's authority.[32] In other words, the Duke's patriarchal presence, especially throughout the last third of the novel, corresponds with the managerial role that Foucault sees the military-diplomatic apparatus playing in the regime of modern governmentality.

The function of the police in this regime, probably because it is less well understood, is of greater concern to Foucault in his lectures, and elicits a more complex representation from Scott in *Mid-Lothian*. Readers of *Discipline and Punish* will not be surprised that, for Foucault, law enforcement is probably the least significant function carried out by modern police institutions. Noting that an early meaning of the noun "police" was "a form of community or association governed by a public authority," Foucault describes a profound shift in the seventeenth century whereby, concurrent with the development of a governmental reason concerned above all with the management and manipulation of populations, "'police' begins to refer to the set of means by which the state's forces can be increased while preserving the state in good order."[33] As military-diplomatic apparatuses sought to align the internal growth of individual states with the external balance of power between them, increasingly sophisticated police forces attempted to maintain and regulate the array of productive forces within a given nation. For example, Foucault points to provisions in the Congress of Vienna, signed just a few years before the publication of *Mid-Lothian*, which effectively pledged the signees to maintain sufficient police presences within their respective nation-states.[34]

In *The Heart of Mid-Lothian*, representations of the police function are both pervasive and perturbing. The novel's opening chapters, for example, powerfully depict the Porteous Riots in Edinburgh, named after the Captain of the Guard found responsible for the deaths of multiple civilians who had become disorderly following the hanging of a popular smuggler. Although he is found guilty by a Scottish court, Porteous receives a stay of execution directly from Westminster. According to the historical record, when news of this order leaked, a mob gathered outside Edinburgh's city gates, made its way to the Tolbooth where Porteous was still imprisoned, and lynched him. In Scott's version of these events, however, there is a secondary, more personal motive behind this vigilante justice: led by George Staunton (the partner-in-crime of the deceased smuggler), the nocturnal raid on the Tolbooth is secretly designed to free Effie, who is awaiting her own trial. When she refuses to flee, however, Staunton has no choice but to rejoin the mob and reluctantly participate in Porteous' execution. Even by this early point in the novel, then, Scott has problematized any straightforward connection between police action and law enforcement; furthermore, both official and informal institutions of justice have been shown to be highly fallible if not downright corrupt.

Such complications are magnified with the introduction of one of the novel's most intriguing characters: the thief-turned-lawman James Ratcliffe. Imprisoned in the Tolbooth at the time of the Porteous riots, Ratcliffe nonetheless declines to use the ensuing chaos to escape. When questioned by the local magistrates, he admits his ulterior motive: "I would never have thought for a moment of staying in that auld gusty toom house . . . but that use and wont had just gien me a fancy to the place, and I'm just expecting a bit post in't."[35] Ratcliffe does not want to leave the sphere of law enforcement; he simply wishes to be promoted from prisoner to jailor. When asked why he should be trusted with that responsibility, especially since he has previously escaped from "half the jails in Scotland," his self-possessed response underscores the permeability of the line between police and criminal in the new dispensation of governmentality: "Wi' your honour's leave . . . if I kend sae weel how to wun out mysell, it's like I wad be a' the better a hand to keep other folk in."[36] Scott's intuition that law-breaking and law-enforcing are complementary activities, especially insofar as both hypostatize the social order, is further displayed in the scene where the policeman Sharpitlaw goes to visit Ratcliffe in prison to ascertain his intentions: the two men, we are told, "sate for five minutes silent, on opposite sides of a small table, and looked fixedly at each other, with a sharp, knowing, and alert cast of countenance, not unmingled with an inclination to laugh."[37] Unusually for Scott, the laughter evoked here is ironic rather than purely comic. It indicates both parties' shared awareness that, for all their apparent differences, their psychologies as well as their roles in the symbolic order are strikingly similar.

After his move to officialdom is accepted, Ratcliffe continues to display ambivalence regarding his new role, and especially how best to deploy his extensive knowledge of Britain's criminal underworld. When George Staunton summons Jeanie to a night-time rendezvous on the outskirts of Edinburgh to attempt to convince her that she must bear false witness to save Effie, for example, Ratcliffe skillfully warns him of the police's approach by tacitly encouraging Madge to resume singing loudly one of her many folk ballads. The resulting noise from "that mad yelling bitch," as Sharpitlaw angrily calls Madge, alerts Staunton to their presence in time for him to flee.[38] Later, however, Ratcliffe seems more committed to the cause of the police—so long as the latter is understood, again, not as a simple instrument of law enforcement, but rather in the broader Foucauldian sense of having as its object "[t]he good use of the state's forces."[39] Furnishing Jeanie with a handwritten "pass" designed to ensure her safe passage through potential dangers on her way to London, "Daddie Rat" (as Ratcliffe is still known in the criminal underworld) continues to exercise his previous criminal authority. When Jeanie is kidnapped by Meg's henchmen, his protection becomes invaluable: "'This is a jark from Jim Ratcliffe,' said the taller, having looked at the bit of paper. 'The wench must pass by our cutter's law.'"[40] Instead of stripping Jeanie and "send[ing] her begging back to her own beggarly country," as they have been ordered, the men bring her to Meg—a decision that leads directly to Jeanie's escape with Madge, her subsequent encounter with Rev. Staunton, and safe passage to London.

Although Daddie Rat never appears again directly in *Mid-Lothian*, his role in facilitating its more-or-less happy ending is, thus, simultaneously oblique and irreplaceable—much like the function of the police in general in the modern management of national populations. In the novel's final volume, this role is occupied by a new, almost equally shady (but more explicitly comic) figure: Duncan of Knockdunder. Duncan enforces the law on the Duke's northern property, but frequently turns a blind eye to criminal activity in exchange for a cut of the area's smuggling profits. He also echoes and embodies Ratcliffe's divided loyalties, inasmuch as Knockdunder's primary criminal rival in the Highlands—whom he eventually kills in the same skirmish in which Staunton is murdered—is also named Duncan. A Žižekian reading of this last detail would likely focus on its reflection of how the Law (of the Father) is frequently shadowed by its obscene underside. From within the Foucauldian vein that we have been mining in this chapter, however, the more salient point is how, within the purview of the governmental reason that extends from "civilized" London to the verge of the Highlands (the geographical scope of *The Heart of*

Mid-Lothian), policeman and criminal are equally imbricated in the processes by which effective ordering of the state's forces becomes the predominant goal of governmental assemblages.

Finally, no discussion of *Mid-Lothian*'s representations of the development of governmentality would be complete without a discussion of the role of the law itself. As several characters discuss and debate at length within the novel, Effie is condemned to die under a 1690 law designed to deter infanticide at a time when low birth rates and a shrinking population were still regarded as problems in Scotland. During Scott's career, by contrast, the so-called Highland Clearances were well under way, and the depopulation of the Highlands (in order to make more room for profitable sheep-farming) was frequently all but official policy. *Mid-Lothian*, of course, falls partway between these two moments, such that the law in question could be viewed by Scott's original readers as both inhumane and outdated. Alison Lumsden has recently argued that "Effie's trial . . . is a dramatization of the inadequacy of this particular law, but also of the legal system *in general* for dealing with human nature."[41] From the Foucauldian perspective in which I have been working, however, the "inadequacy" of the law that condemns Effie reveals something much more specific: the insufficiency of legal and judicial state apparatuses alone to make a nation's population not only docile and manageable, but also productive. To achieve these goals, other forms of coercion and control are needed: more precisely, the various forms of governmental reason, especially as embodied in diplomatic and police assemblages, that *Mid-Lothian* so effectively delineates. The ultimate aim of these assemblages, as Foucault makes clear in his next set of Collège lectures, is the creation and support of what he calls "biopolitics": a politics that attempts to exercise direct control over the lives and deaths of its subjects.[42] As I demonstrate below, the origins and inner workings of biopolitics are the explicit focus of one of Foucault's most influential theoretical heirs, Giorgio Agamben, as well as the implicit focal point of one of Scott's most innovative later novels, *Quentin Durward*.

Bare life and the origins of modern sovereignty in *Quentin Durward*

In a recently published collection of reflections on methodology, Agamben immediately makes no secret of the fact that Foucault is "a scholar from whom I have learned a great deal in recent years."[43] As they range from classical to contemporary sources, all of the pieces in Agamben's *The Signature of All Things: On Method* underscore the connections between his interests and methods, and those of Foucault. The collection's first essay, for example, focuses on their common deployment of "the paradigm" as that which, properly considered, "shows 'beside itself' (*para-deiknymi*) both its own intelligibility and that of the class it constitutes."[44] The paradigm is simultaneously historical and ahistorical, located "at the crossing of diachrony and synchrony."[45] Although the work of the philosophical historian—a valid description of both Foucault and Agamben—necessarily "require[s] an attention to documents and diachrony that cannot but follow the laws of historical philology," it is equally the case that "the *archē* they reach . . . is not an origin presupposed in time. Rather . . . it makes the inquirer's present intelligible as much as the past of his or her object."[46] Like Foucault's well-known paradigms of "the confession," "the examination," and "the care of the self," Agamben's paradigmatic critical concepts must also be understood, not only as simultaneously historical and contemporary, but also as actual (embodied and expressed through a variety of cultural and political institutions) and theoretical.

One of the most significant paradigms Agamben adopts from Foucault is the particular subject of a recent essay by the Italian philosopher. In "What is an Apparatus?" Agamben sets out to recover "a brief genealogy" of that concept in both Foucault's work and its wider historical context; in the process, he also explains his own understanding of this key term.[47] Describing the Foucauldian apparatus as a "network" that establishes linkages within "a heterogeneous set that includes virtually anything, linguistic and nonlinguistic, under the same heading: discourses, institutions, buildings, police measures, philosophical propositions, and so on," Agamben explains that "The apparatus always has a concrete strategic function and is always located in a power relation."[48] For most of modern human history, Agamben notes, such apparatuses have been used for the purposes of forming subjects; in today's hypercapitalist world, by contrast, Agamben posits that many of the most prevalent (including social media and other technologies of instant and ubiquitous communication and visibility) now contribute to the "desubjectification" of the average citizen. This unsettling development, Agamben explains, leads directly to a situation wherein "the harmless citizen of postindustrial democracies . . . who readily does everything he is asked to do, inasmuch as he leaves his everyday gestures and his health, his amusements and his occupations, his diet and his desires, to be commanded and controlled in the smallest detail by apparatuses, is also considered by power . . . as a potential terrorist."[49]

How did we come to this juncture, where—as evidenced by some of the rhetoric recently used to demonize the participants of the "Occupy Wall Street" movement—the seemingly clear distinction between "average citizen" and "threat to the social order" can quickly, even strategically, become blurry?[50] Agamben strives to illuminate this volatile situation via several further, linked paradigms that previous historians and philosophers have either overlooked or underestimated. In particular, I want to focus on three concepts in Agamben's critical program that together help delineate the particular contours of Western political modernity: *homo sacer*, the state of exception, and *oikonomia*. The fact that each of these phenomenon (as I will argue below) is also present in *Quentin Durward*, Scott's fictional meditation on the fifteenth-century formation of modern France, should not be misunderstood as indicating a historical originality that Agamben generally avoids positing. Nevertheless, its setting at the cusp of the early modern era not only makes *Durward* Scott's most direct fictional representation of the embryonic development of modern Europe, but also positions it in the space where Agamben locates every historicophilosophical *archē*: "between the moment of arising and becoming, between an archi-past and the present."[51]

In the study that established his reputation in Anglo-American circles, *Homo Sacer: Sovereign Power and Bare Life*, Agamben begins by observing that the ancient Greeks had two distinct terms for what we now call "life": *zoē*, "which expressed the simple fact of living common to all living beings," and *bios*, "which indicated the form or way of living proper to an individual or group."[52] His key insight is that, although this distinction superficially appears lost in today's West, it still functions in the political sphere, especially as concerns the operations of sovereign power. Keeping in mind Foucault's recognition that modern sovereignty is more oriented toward power over populations than territory, the stakes of Agamben's subsequent argument become clear. He claims, in effect, that sovereignty works by arrogating to itself the power of removing individuals under its authority from their place in the *bios* and returning them to an existence that is essentially bare: not inhuman, *per se*, but a-human; alive, but only in the most basic, "common" sense. It is here that, in critical dialogue with Carl Schmitt, Agamben locates the basis of sovereignty itself. For Schmitt, the sovereign is best defined as "he who decides on the exception."[53] The first or most fundamental exclusion that sovereign power characteristically makes, moreover, is for itself; the sovereign makes the laws, but is not himself or herself bound by them. This self-exclusion is complemented, Agamben observes, by the ability to exclude other subjects from the law's protection. The figure produced by this exclusion— best understood as a ban that captures the subject in an indeterminate zone, simultaneously inside and outside the law—is what, borrowing from Roman law, he calls *homo sacer*. Traditionally, this denominated a legal entity that could be killed without impunity, but whose life held no sacrificial value. For Agamben, however, *homo sacer* holds the key to unlocking the true nature of sovereignty:

> The life caught in the sovereign ban is the life that is originarily sacred – that is, that may be killed but not sacrificed – and, in this sense, the production of bare life is the originary activity of sovereignty. The sacredness of life,

which is invoked today as an absolutely fundamental right in opposition to sovereign power, in fact originally expresses precisely both life's subjection to a power over death and life's irreparable exposure in the relation of abandonment.[54]

Overturning several centuries of Enlightened political theory—including the liberal tradition with which Scott, via the Scottish Enlighteners, was familiar— Agamben here reveals modernity's fundamental juridico-ontological framework to be anything but progressive.

The most immediate figure of "bare life" in modern history is the concentration camp victim, whose plight Agamben explores at the end of *Homo Sacer* and in even more harrowing detail in *Remnants of Auschwitz: The Witness and the Archive*, which focuses at length on the most abject figure of all, the so-called *Muselmann* (the camp inmate who has become so traumatized as to appear barren of any subjectivity whatsoever). The refugee, the political prisoner, and the dispossessed or homeless person are further types of real-life *homines sacri*: all are victims of the contemporary political regime of modern sovereignty, falling between zones of subjectivation and into the indeterminacy that reveals their "bare life." But, the most far-reaching, and consequently the most troubling revelation of Agamben's philosophical archeology of modern political subjectivity, does not arrive until late in *Homo Sacer*:

> If it is true that the figure proposed by our age is that of an unsacrificeable life that has nevertheless become capable of being killed to an unprecedented degree, then the bare life of *homo sacer* concerns us in a special way. Sacredness is a line of flight still present in contemporary politics, a line that is as such moving into zones increasingly vast and dark, to the point of ultimately coinciding with the biological life itself of citizens. If today there is no longer any one clear figure of the sacred man, it is perhaps because we are all virtually *homines sacri*.[55]

In the figure of the citizen whose sociopolitical presence is apprehended by state power as merely essential existence, Agamben's analysis of the development of sovereign power coincides entirely with Foucault's account of governmentality's rise to ubiquity. In the eyes of modern sovereign authority, Agamben grimly concludes, we have all been reduced to "bare life" and nothing more.[56]

To understand this fatal overlap, we need to know its history. Foucault, as we have seen, traces the paradigmatic origins of modern biopolitics back to the "state of justice" of the Middle Ages. Agamben links the metastasizing of *homo sacer*'s domain to the rise of another feature of political life: the normalization of the "state of exception." Historically, the state of exception—in which all normal laws and rights are temporarily suspended—has been a political state's response to "the most extreme internal conditions," like civil wars and sieges.[57] Building on Schmitt's assertion that the state of exception necessarily precedes, and therefore founds, any normative liberal or democratic political regime,[58] Agamben unfolds an archeology of the West's juridico-political system that exposes its essential dualism: it is a "double structure, formed by two heterogeneous yet coordinated elements: one that is normative and juridical in the strict sense . . . and one that is anomic and metajuridical."[59] The state of exception, in this critical exposition, normally acts as a hinge between these two, dialectically related elements (embodied for example in the distinction between the republican Roman Senate and the people). When they are allowed to come together in the figure of a single person or party, however, then "the state of exception . . . becomes the rule, [and] then the juridico-political system transforms itself into a killing machine."[60] This deadly scenario reveals an important truth: since it is precisely the state of exception that both articulates and blends "life and law, anomie and nomos," its regular appearance throughout history reveals that "bare life" is not something that precedes governmentality; rather, it is a product of the very "biopolitical machine" that claims authority to protect or destroy it at will.[61]

There is more to Agamben's analysis of our modern political condition. Before exploring these developments in more detail, however, let me begin to apply what has already been unpacked to identify the critical stakes of *Quentin Durward*. Its fifteenth-century French setting indexes Scott's long-standing interest in European history; the epigraph on its title page, written in French and probably composed by Scott himself, translates literally as "War is my country,/ My armor is my house,/ And in any season/ Combat is my life."[62] Despite this martial opening note, however, most of the novel's violence—at least until the battle for Liege with which it closes—is perpetrated on civilians by government forces. What Max Weber identifies as the state's monopoly on legitimate violence is still just being consolidated in *Quentin Durward*, but Scott is clear that most of the responsibility for that development in Europe belongs to Louis XI.

"Machiavellian" is the adjective most often used to describe Scott's portrait of this monarch, and with good reason, since Scott explicitly compares him to the infamous Renaissance statesman in the novel's Magnum Opus introduction: "Even an author of works of mere amusement may be permitted to be serious for a moment, in order to reprobate all policy, whether of a public or private character, which rests upon the principles of Machiavel, or the practice of Louis XI."[63] Yet even as Scott condemns Louis for being a tyrant, coward, and pleasure seeker, he also admits that "the little love intrigue of Quentin is only employed as the means of bringing out the story" of Louis' remarkable introduction into fifteenth-century France of what was called "statecraft" in Scott's era. This term, I want to suggest, is essentially synonymous with governmentality, especially insofar as Louis XI's signature accomplishments include professionalizing France's army, stripping power from feudal barons like Charles of Burgundy (whose ambitions form Louis' main obstacle in *Quentin Durward*), and gathering reliable information about his people (frequently by employing bands of gypsies, at least in Scott's telling). Calling Louis "the most crafty Sovereign of his time" in the novel's first main chapter, Scott compares him to a doctor "engaged, like an unfeeling but able physician, in curing the wound of the body politic."[64] "[U]nfeeling but able" is an apt description of the sovereign attitude, especially in its exceptional disposition. If the gypsy whom Quentin finds hanging from a tree in Chapter 6 is an embodiment of the subject reduced to "bare life"—his hanging, via the king's authority, is both perfectly legal and devoid of any sacrificial value[65]— then Louis' authority, perennially threatened by the rebellious French nobility, is substantially constructed through such death-dealing acts.

Frequently attended by his Provost-Marshal, Louis also enjoys surveilling his domains at firsthand by roaming the countryside in disguise. One of these excursions leads to his first meeting with Quentin, who has just arrived from war-torn Scotland seeking mercenary work. Not knowing to whom he speaks, the young Scot initially declines an invitation to apply to the Scottish Guard, Louis' elite corps of personal archers, on two grounds: first, that he "love[s] the open air better than being shut up in a cage or a swallow's nest yonder"—a disparaging reference to the heavily fortified castle at Plessis where Louis and his Guard reside; and second, that Quentin is not happy with the sight of a nearby hanged man. The following dialogue ensues:

> "Ay and indeed!" said [the King] . . . "But what then? – they are so many banners displayed to scare knaves; and for each rogue that hangs there, an honest man may reckon that there is a thief, a traitor, a robber on the highway, a pillour and oppressor of the people, the fewer in France – these, young man, are signs of our Sovereign's justice."
>
> "I would have them further from my palace though, were I King Louis," said the youth. "In my country, we hang up dead corbies [crows] where living corbies haunt, but not in our gardens or pigeon-houses. The very scent of the carrion – fough – reaches my nostrils at the distance where we stood."
>
> "If you live to be an honest and loyal servant of your Prince, my good youth," answered the Frenchman, "you will know there is no perfume to match the scent of a dead traitor."[66]

Although readers might expect a Waverley Hero to object to the sight of a dead body, the sixteenth-century Scotsman is accustomed to the sight of executed corpses displayed as deterrents. What puzzles him in this case is why the king displays them so near his castle, which is already heavily fortified, rather than in a location more likely to witness actual criminal activity. Louis' response is revealing: the corpses hanging within sight of his castle are not meant to deter would-be criminals, but rather to inscribe and confirm his royal authority to assign the identities of the "honest" man versus the "traitor." As "signs of our Sovereign's justice," they corroborate Louis' power to preside over the life and death of his subjects, a biopower that effectively reduces all of his subjects to bare lives while placing Louis himself in what Agamben would call a "zone of indistinction." The above passage illustrates perfectly Agamben's insight that the sovereign and his most oppressed subjects exist in a relation that is simultaneously antagonistic and mutually constitutive. Each is included in the politicojuridical order by virtue of being excluded from it: "*The sovereign sphere is the sphere in which it is permitted to kill without committing homicide and without celebrating a sacrifice, and sacred life – that is, life that may be killed but not sacrificed – is the life that has been captured in this sphere.*"[67]

This perverse logic is confirmed when Quentin subsequently cuts down the body of a recently executed gypsy. The "bohemians," as Scott calls them, are precisely caught in the double exception of the sovereign ban, since they can be killed with impunity but their deaths hold no sacrificial value. When Quentin asks why none of the onlookers has taken down the corpse, one of them points to the fleur-de-lys carved into the trunk of the tree from which the body hangs. The message is clear: the hanged man is the property of the king, in death as much as (or perhaps more than) in life. Quentin quickly discovers the consequences of his trespass when he is surrounded by a party of French soldiers who immediately take him prisoner. Literalizing the "capture" of an individual life by sovereign power, Quentin is rapidly reduced to the status of the *homo sacer* whom, only minutes before, he had attempted to aid. It matters little that the hanged man was already dead when Quentin released him; by touching the banned corpse, Quentin has "interfere[d] with the King's justice"—with the performance of sovereign power—and now is threatened with a similar punishment.[68] He is saved only by the last-minute appearance of members of the Scottish Guard, including his uncle, who assert that Quentin cannot be hanged by Louis' henchmen because he belongs to them. When Quentin avers that, in fact, he has "not yet determined whether to take service with you or no," his uncle warns him to decide quickly "whether you choose to do so, or be hanged – for I promise you that, nephew of mine as you are, I see no other chance of your 'scaping the withie [noose]."[69] Quentin's immediate decision to join the Guard is, thus, not merely a submission to necessity (although it certainly is what Žižek would call a "forced choice"); it also neatly embodies what Agamben calls the state of exception's "specific contribution" to laying bare the biopower at the core of sovereignty: "the separation of 'force of law' from the law."[70] There is no juridical necessity for Quentin to resign his freedom and join the King's bodyguard; but the threat of death under which he is placed—and which places him in a "zone of indistinction" precisely obverse to that of Louis' authority above the law—carries the force of law insofar as it compels him to act despite his inclination to the contrary. As Agamben observes, even when this force of law is revealed to be essentially fictional, it merely highlights the state of exception's ultimate purpose: to create a "force of law without law" which it is subsequently sovereign power's prerogative to claim for itself.[71]

Agamben's analysis of the structure of sovereign power, as carried out in *Homo Sacer* and *State of Exception*, is profoundly troubling. More recently, he has undertaken another significant genealogical investigation of that structure's "origin" and dissemination. The concept of *oikonomia*—roughly translatable as "economy," but with connotations and an etymological history that Agamben skillfully unearths, beginning with its Aristotelian meaning of "administration of the house"—is in fact present even in his pre-*Homo Sacer* work,[72] but it takes on a greatly expanded role in his latest major text, *The Kingdom and the Glory: For a Theological Genealogy of Economy and Government*.[73] Here, Agamben presents the case for understanding modern sovereignty as deriving from two apparently opposed, but in fact deeply complementary, religious paradigms: "political theology, which founds the transcendence of sovereign power on the single God," and "economic theology, which replaces this transcendence with the idea of an *oikonomia*, conceived as an imminent ordering . . . of both divine and human life."[74] With the rise of Pauline Christianity, says Agamben, a shift occurs whereby the Judaic focus on monotheistic authority—an authority that is inherently political—is replaced, to a large degree, by a consensus that the "mystery" of salvation through Christ's intercession must be disseminated via "the members of the messianic community."[75] As Agamben notes, the terms Paul uses to describe this community (e.g. *doulos* ["slave"], *diakonos* ["servant"], *oikonomos* ["administrator"]) are all drawn from the vocabulary of "domestic administration." The Aristotelian language of household management, in other words, is absorbed and repurposed for early Christian evangelicalism—an apolitical "origin" with great implications for "the history of Western politics," says Agamben, since Aristotle's domestic *oikos* implicitly repudiates the politics of the Platonic *polis*.[76]

The administrative connotations of *oikonomia* were subsequently applied to the dogma of the Trinity, which arises in the second and third centuries A.D. largely as a counter to various Gnostic heresies. The Pauline phrase "the economy of the mystery" turns into its catachrestic counterpart, "the mystery of the economy," in order to describe (without really explaining) the activity by which God orders His tripartite nature, such that it is simultaneously "articulated" and "'harmonize[d]' . . . into a unity."[77] This is especially important given that the "mystery of the economy" retains its power long after Trinitarian debates give way to notions of God's providential ordering of the world. In turn, providence and its individualized variation, fate, become associated with the two sides or faces of modern statehood, "Kingdom" and "Government," that together represent "both aspects of the theological machine"—that is to say, the transcendent and the immanent—even as they transmogrify into their modern forms (sovereign/ legislative and executive/ governmental).[78] But when, in the modern era, the explicitly transcendent side of what Agamben calls "the bipolar theological machine" begins to recede, both sides increasingly identify themselves with "the figure of the modern rule of law, in which the law regulates the administration and the administrative apparatus applies and implements the law."[79] As the circularity of this last clause suggests, the explicit abandonment of the theological paradigm masks its ultimate triumph: the order that *oikonomia* promotes and establishes continues to claim an essentially apolitical basis in the natural order of things even, or perhaps especially, when that order is mandated by force. Agamben concludes *The Kingdom and Glory* with an appendix that first aligns his project with Foucault's Collège de France lectures and then illuminates the providential dimension of Adam Smith's famous "invisible hand."[80] This not only confirms the essential compatibility of Agamben's ideas and methods with those of Foucault regarding governmentality, but also points to potential connections between Scott's fictions and the "theological machine" tradition, since Scott would have absorbed Smith's economic views through the courses he took at the University of Edinburgh with Smith's protégé, Dugald Stewart.

Given Agamben's uncovering of the theological origins of modern governmentality, it is fitting that King Louis, in his favorite disguise as a merchant, takes Quentin to a chapel soon after meeting him. In fact, the king's devotion is repeatedly emphasized by Scott, beginning with his description of Louis' entrance to this humble church "with a step and manner expressive of the most heartfelt contrition and humility."[81] Nevertheless, Scott leaves no doubt that such piety is not to be admired, since Louis is just as enthralled by superstition as by religious rituals; although he pays "the most rigid and scrupulous attention" to the Catholic service, he is also "prone to be deceived by soothsayers, astrologers, diviners, and all that race of pretenders to occult science."[82] But although Scott consistently denigrates Louis' predilection for a variety of supernaturalisms, Agamben's genealogy provides an alternative explanation: Louis' deep investment in spiritualisms both sacred and profane is symptomatic of his sovereign authority's original theological dependence. Louis' repeated recourse to metaphysical methods of attempting to descry and influence the shape of worldly things, that is, signals that in the early stages of modern Europe's formation, the economies of belief and governmentality are not yet explicitly disarticulated. Even while Scott consistently contrasts Louis' worldly ambitions with his demonstrations of piety, the underlying insight regarding their intimate connection supports Agamben's thesis that "The *oikonomia* of the moderns . . . in truth maintains the theological model of the government of the world."[83] Louis' ultimate triumph over his rival Charles the Bold is accomplished, thanks to luck as much as to wise planning, but there can be little doubt that, even if neither Scott nor his Machiavellian monarch is aware of the connection, the latter's ability to direct the political tide of modernity away from feudalism and toward the centralized nation-state is securely, if obliquely, knotted to his reliance on a wide variety of metaphysical rituals.

In this light, a crucial moment occurs when Louis faces death at the hands of Charles' soldiers. Having become a "guest" of his rival with the intent to lull Charles into inaction after the arranged murder of his brother-in-law, the Bishop of Liege, Louis finds himself a virtual prisoner when the Duke's suspicions are nonetheless aroused. As Charles' soldiers bolt the doors and Louis' few loyal followers prepare to defend him to the death, the King quickly realizes that strategy, not chivalry, holds the key to his survival. Accordingly, when the senior Scottish Guardsman Lord Crawford (previously described as "one of the last reliques of the gallant band of Scottish lords and knights who had so long and so truly served Charles VII")[84] places himself between Louis and Burgundy with sword unsheathed, Louis talks him down: "stand back, Crawford – were it my last word, I speak as a King to his officer, and demand obedience – stand back and, if it is required, yield up your sword. I command you to do so, and your oath obliges you to obey."[85] This command is given by a monarch canny enough to recognize that good governance is increasingly becoming a matter of effective management rather than old-fashioned valor; indeed, this is precisely the modern conception of politics as *oikonomia* to which Quentin objects when, during his first meeting with Louis, his "mountain chivalry" leads him to chide the French king for his seeming cowardice: "he lies here in his Castle, or only rides from one fortified town to another; and gains cities and provinces by politic embassies, and not in fair fighting."[86] Yet though he is indeed guilty of arranging the Bishop's death, Louis' order to Crawford successfully buys enough time to allow for Charles' rage to subside, and the King is merely placed under house arrest rather than killed.

There is yet another striking element of Louis' gambit to be illuminated via Agamben's discerning analyses. When the King compels Crawford to overrule his own sense of injured honor and give up his weapon, he does so by explicitly reminding the Scotsman of his oath of allegiance. According to Agamben, the oath is a "sacrament of language" that marks humanity's performative ability to put itself at stake in language: to swear *by* something or *on* something is effectively to "express the demand . . . to bind together in an ethical and political connection words, things, and actions."[87] The oath, as one of the most ancient of human expressions, is, thus, simultaneously part of the "anthropogenic machine" that differentiates man ("the speaking animal") from beast, and also a prototypical expression of that same force of law that becomes separated from the actual juridico-political domain during every state of exception.[88] By having Louis paradoxically invoke Crawford's oath of feudal loyalty for the express purpose of negating the chivalric ethos that motivates it, Scott bears out Agamben's insight that the force of law is an essentially immanent construction: generated by humans, it can also be manipulated by them to maintain authority over their fellow "speaking animals."

As modern politics becomes increasingly indistinguishable from *oikonomia*—"that is, of a governance of empty speech over bare life"—so, Agamben asserts, philosophy (or theory) must remember its vocation as "a critique of the oath: that is, it calls into question the sacramental bond that links the human being to language."[89] By contrast, oaths are repeatedly honored over the course of *Quentin Durward*: not only Crawford's oath to obey Louis, but also Quentin's swearing of loyalty to the Burgundian Countess Isabelle, and later his promise to care for the horse of the condemned gypsy Hayraddin Maugrabin, who has just imparted to Quentin both the knowledge and the treasure he will need to help defeat Louis' brutal ally William De la Marck and claim his beloved's hand in marriage.[90] *Quentin Durward*, thus, cannot be said to offer a critique of the oath, in the sense that Agamben calls for greater scrutiny of the politico-anthropogenic machine of modernity; rather, Scott presents an extended exemplification of its historical dissemination. Nevertheless, it bears keeping in mind that the novel's conventionally happy ending, which concludes with one of Charles' advisors declaring that "it is Sense, Firmness, and Gallantry, which have put [Quentin] in possession of Wealth, Rank, and Beauty,"[91] is preceded by the gruesome display of De la Marck's severed head, recognizable by its animal-like jaws (which helped earn him the nickname "the Wild Boar of Ardennes"). The upshot of this juxtaposition is unmistakable: although Quentin's triumph—and, by extension, that of every Waverley Hero—might appear to be of his own making, it is facilitated by the same processes of modernity that systematically create the conditions whereby man and animal, civilized hero and "wild" villain, protected member of society and *homo sacer*, are alternately distinguished and conflated.

Scott, as we have seen, generally focuses his novels' conclusions on the "winners" of these processes. By contrast, Agamben (like Foucault) repeatedly draws our attention to the "losers": a category that, at their most pessimistic, potentially encompasses all citizens of all modern states, as well as those who lack even the partial protections of citizenship. But surely these differences are primarily matters of convention, discretion, and disposition. On the essential ethico-political (in)consistency of modernity, Scott is just as prescient as today's contemporary theorists.

5

Hospitality and community, or *The Bride of Lammermoor* and *Chronicles of the Canongate* with Habermas, Derrida, and a multitude of theorists

L et us enter the scene of Scott writing in his heyday. It is 1819, five years after the publication of *Waverley*. Since then, the Great Unknown has published almost a half-dozen more best-selling, critically acclaimed novels; two additional metrical romances, of the kind that won him his initial literary fame and fortune; and a variety of nonfiction prose pieces, including the first substantial review of Austen's fiction. In 1818, he is offered and accepts a baronetcy. By most measures, Scott is at the zenith of his career.

Composing *The Bride of Lammermoor* (1819), however, proved surprisingly difficult. Despite his official anonymity, the Author of Waverley was beset with visitors at Abbotsford, each of whom demanded his attention and potentially disrupted his rigorous writing regimen. More troubling still was the severe, as-yet-undiagnosed gallstones that left Scott dependent on large quantities of painkillers for protracted periods. From these conditions emerged the myth, popularized by Lockhart in his *Memoirs of Sir Walter Scott*, that Scott dictated nearly all of *Bride* in a pain- and drug-induced haze. As Jane Millgate and others have definitively demonstrated, this account is simply false; four-fifths of the novel exists in manuscript in Scott's handwriting, and the final portion that he dictated was likely composed after the worst of the gallstones (and the heaviest doses of laudanum) had passed. Nevertheless, although the Romantic myth of *Bride*'s tortured composition has been mostly exploded, the novel is undeniably one of Scott's most pessimistic. Published with the one-volume *A Legend of the Wars of Montrose* to constitute the third series of *Tales of my Landlord, Bride* seems to go out of its way to resist readers' expectations of a happy ending. It may be said, then, to have less in common with the Waverley Novels that preceded and directly succeeded it, than with the three stories that make up Scott's late collection of shorter fiction, *Chronicles of the Canongate* (1827). Although ranging in location from Scotland to India, each of its tales—"The Highland Widow," "The Two Drovers," and "The Surgeon's Daughter"—delineates the disintegration of multiple planes of social cohesion. As in *The Bride of Lammermoor*, but perhaps with even greater force due to their more compact formats, the bonds of family, friendship, professional, and even national identities are repeatedly torn asunder.[1] Furthermore, the causes of these breakdowns are common to both texts: the failure of hospitality, and the loss or sacrifice of community.

It may be no coincidence that hospitality and community have lately become some of the most-discussed concepts in contemporary theory. As Roberto Esposito has recently asserted, "Nothing seems more appropriate today than thinking community: nothing more necessary, demanded, and heralded by a situation that joins in a unique epochal knot the failure of all communisms with the misery of new individualisms."[2] But as Esposito subsequently notes, the concept of community has also proven remarkably difficult either to theorize or to practice; indeed, the twentieth century bore witness to the destructive potentials of large-scale communities (whether fascist or communist) imposed from above.[3] More recently, however, the return of largely horizontal mobilizations of collective, public action—from the worldwide demonstrations in 2002–03 against the American-led invasion of Iraq, to the recent protests in Europe against so-called austerity measures, to the "Occupy Wall Street" movement in America—seems to indicate a widespread unwillingness to accept "the misery of the new individualisms" that Esposito fears may characterize the twenty-first century.

Scott's novels and tales, of course, reflect and represent historical eras significantly earlier than the twentieth-century movements in relation to which many contemporary critical theorists position their writings on hospitality and community. Nevertheless, the fact that, as Badiou observes, some thinkers extend the "totalitarian century" back as far as 1793 (i.e. to Robespierre's short-lived, bloody leadership of the French Revolution), should remind us that Scott's era witnessed the formal birth of many of today's mass political movements: modern liberalism can certainly be traced to the principles laid down by the architects of the French Revolution; conservatism to Edmund Burke's *Reflections on the Revolution in France* (1790); feminism to Mary Wollstonecraft's *Vindication of the Rights of Woman* (1792); anarchism to William Godwin's *Enquiry Concerning Political Justice* (1793); and socialism to the ideas of utopian reformers like Saint-Simon, Fourier, and Robert Owen. Hospitality, for its part, is a key component of Immanuel Kant's famously enlightened formulation of an ideal world community.[4] Accordingly, this chapter brings a number of contemporary theorists' ideas regarding hospitality and community to critical readings of several of Scott's most tragic narratives. In doing so, I aim to show not only how those fictions exhibit many of the theorists' concerns, but also how, especially in *Chronicles*, Scott marshals the resources of fiction to present a vision of community that at least partially redeems the concept from its manifest difficulties.

A bridge too far: Inauthentic hospitality in *The Bride of Lammermoor*

The theme of community's inevitable failure, if not its utter impossibility, runs like a red thread through much of the modern critical writing on this subject. For Max Horkheimer and Theodor Adorno, the combination of the Enlightenment's privileging of instrumental reason with the twentieth-century culture industry's standardization of tastes and values has created a situation wherein "Individuals shrink to the nodal points of conventional reactions and the modes of operation objectively expected of them. Animism had endowed things with souls; industrialism makes souls into things."[5] Likewise, in the face of society's increasingly sophisticated and omnipresent disciplinary apparatuses, Foucault generally imagines that resistance to such forms of subjectivation (insofar as it was even possible) would come, not via coordinated movements of communal action, but rather from a variety of short-lived, more-or- less spontaneous "'reverse' discourse[s]" and "tactical reversal[s]."[6] This line of thinking finds its most extreme expression in the writings of Jean Baudrillard, whose early critiques of Marxian theory give way to a series of oracular texts that ironically celebrate the solipsistic virtualities of postmodernity even as they foreclose the possibility of resistance other than through a series of "fatal strategies" located beyond or beneath human agency.[7]

Not all contemporary theorists, however, have abandoned the possibility of meaningful communal action. Among the most influential to maintain it is Jürgen Habermas, whose formulation of "the bourgeois public sphere" as a milestone in the development of Western civil society remains attractive even if its existence in eighteenth-century England, where Habermas argued it originated, has been questioned.[8] In *The Philosophical Discourse of Modernity*, Habermas asserts that, contrary to Baudrillard's ironic celebration of postmodernity as well as to Horkheimer and Adorno's condemnation of modernity, the project of Enlightened modernity—understood broadly as the elaboration of "an *inclusive* concept of reason"—is neither deluded nor concluded, but simply incomplete.[9] After the terrorist attacks on the United States of 11 September 2001, some expected Habermas finally to renounce his belief in "communicative action," his term for the efficacy of intersubjective rationality conducted along consensual lines.[10] Instead, Habermas reiterated the necessity of engaging in reasoned dialogue on both national and international levels:

> Struggling with the difficulties of understanding, people must, step by step, widen their original perspectives and ultimately bring them together. And they can succeed in such a "fusion of horizons" by virtue of their peculiar capacity to take up the roles of "speaker" and "hearer." Taking up these roles in a dialogue, they engage in a fundamental symmetry which, at bottom, all speech situations require. . . . And in the course of mutual perspective-taking there can develop a common horizon of background assumptions in which both sides accomplish an interpretation that is not ethnocentrically adopted or converted but, rather, *intersubjectively* shared.[11]

Far from abandoning communicative action in the shadow of 9/11, Habermas calls for more of it. Although he acknowledges the vast material inequalities between peoples that often contribute to mutual incomprehension, he nevertheless holds out hope for a concept of community based on the ideals "of the legal and moral foundation of a liberal order," on the grounds that "Membership in this inclusive moral community . . . promises not only solidarity and a nondiscriminatory inclusion, but at the same time equal rights for the protection of everybody's individuality and otherness."[12] In this view, the basic linguistic, juridical, and ethical norms established by the bourgeois public sphere allow alternative modes of existence to flourish within a shared "life-world," Habermas' term (adapted from the phenomenological tradition) for the knowledges and practices that form the common horizon of a given community's lived experiences. For Habermas, Western modernity does not need to be replaced or subverted; it just needs to be held accountable to its own, frequently self-advertised ideals of freedom, equality, and justice.

Those ideals are certainly at stake in *The Bride of Lammermoor*, which initially appears to present, in starker terms than any other Waverley Novel, a conflict between the forces of feudalism and those of the emerging liberal-democratic order. As it opens, Edgar Ravenswood is attending the funeral of his father, whose untimely death seems to have been hastened by the failure of his lengthy legal bid to recover his hereditary estate. While the Ravenswoods have traditionally aligned themselves with Tory causes, moreover, the Ashtons—the *nouveau riche* family who have purchased Ravenswood Castle and its domains—align themselves with the more progressive Whig party. Since the novel is focalized primarily through Edgar Ravenswood, readers might expect to be encouraged to sympathize unproblematically with him. Early on, however, Scott undercuts this assumption when his omniscient narrator explains that the Ravenswoods are notoriously backward, even atavistic, in their outlook and attitudes. Here, for example, he describes the elder Ravenswood's dying moments:

> The thread of life, which had been long wasting, gave way during a fit of violent and impotent fury, with which he was assailed on receiving the news of the loss of a cause, founded, perhaps, rather in equity than in law, the last which he had maintained against his powerful antagonist. His son witnessed his dying agonies, and heard the curses which he breathed against his adversary, as if they had conveyed to him a legacy of vengeance. Other circumstances happened to exasperate a passion, which was, and had long been, a prevalent vice in the Scottish disposition.[13]

The Ravenswoods, with their apparently heritable disposition to anger, clearly represent Scotland's feudal past; alongside the Jacobites and Highlanders of Scott's previous Waverley Novels, they exist on the wrong side of history. Nevertheless, the cause in which Lord Ravenswood has been engaged— attempting to reclaim his family estate—is admittedly just; it is simply not legally feasible. The very starting point of the novel's plot, thus, complicates Habermas' normative notion of justice as "what is equally good for all," and which can in theory always be "extended step by step to the 'right' [that] forms a bridge between justice and solidarity."[14] But in *The Bride*, the originary misalignment of the juridical and the ethical means that Habermas' imagined "bridge," whose construction is imperative for "relations of reciprocal recognition" to be established, is impassable if not illusory.

As it happens, the only material bridge to feature in the novel is equally unusable. When Edgar, having spontaneously saved William Ashton and his daughter Lucy from being gored by a wild bull, reluctantly brings his temporary companion Bucklaw to the dilapidated seaside tower that is the sole remainder of his family's property, they see the following:

> The pale moon, which had hitherto been contending with flitting clouds, now shone out, and gave them a view of the solitary and naked tower, situated on a projecting cliff that beetled over the German ocean. On three sides the rock was precipitous; on the fourth, which was that towards the land, it had been originally fenced by an artificial ditch and drawbridge, but the latter was broken down and ruinous, and the former had been in part filled up . . . .[15]

Located at the far end of "a kind of isthmus," Wolfscrag is a "wild hold" accessible only via a "cautious mode of approach"[16]; its location, thus, mirrors the precarious social and historical isolation in which Ravenswood finds himself in the novel's opening chapters. Moreover, no matter how much Edgar struggles to build symbolic bridges to the novel's other characters—and, in the cases of both William Ashton and Bucklaw, it's never clear whether Ravenswood's heart is entirely in such endeavors—he is consistently prevented from doing so.

Andrew Lincoln proposes that what sets *The Bride* apart from most of Scott's other fictions is its rejection of those very devices and vehicles of social cohesion that normally triumph in the Waverley Novels.[17] As I (and others) have argued elsewhere, Scott generally shared with his Scottish Enlightenment mentors an interest in promoting the discourse of sympathy—the ability to feel other's feelings—as a kind of social glue, capable of bonding the diverse members of their nation. This program took on added intensity in the period surrounding the 1707 Act of Union with England.[18] *The Bride of Lammermoor* is in fact set in this era, but with a twist: while the original edition is clearly situated before the Union, several alterations in the Magnum Opus edition suggest a post-Union setting.[19] Scholars continue to debate Scott's motives for making these changes, but for our purposes it is enough to note the anxiety that clearly surrounds all attempts at community building, whether on the level of the nation or the family, in *The Bride.*

Ironically, the novel's central proposed union—the marriage of Edgar Ravenswood and Lucy Ashton, and hence the symbolic union of Scotland's Tory past and Whig future—is even in both parties' best interests: the Ashtons would gain respectability and political clout by matching their daughter with a Ravenswood, and Edward would regain his family lands by marrying Lucy. Although modern readers may balk at the obviously patriarchal nature of this arrangement, Scott makes clear that the two young people at *The Bride's* center genuinely care about each other.[20] Furthermore, as we have seen, in most other Waverley Novels, the kind of gender-normative courtship in which Edgar and Lucy engage (he is all masculine strength and vigor, she is all feminine grace and modesty) would seem to offer both the literal and symbolic union around which the rest of the novel's social order would coalesce.

So, what is different about *The Bride*? The manifest failure of communal regeneration in this novel can be traced, I think, to its concerns regarding questions of hospitality. This concept is a touchstone for many contemporary theorists, especially as theory underwent an "ethical (re)turn" in the later 1990s and 2000s.[21] In particular, hospitality emerges as a key piece of Jacques Derrida's late-career deconstructive project. Arguably, there was always a latent "ethics of deconstruction": a 1977 interview, for example, finds Derrida insisting that "a deconstructive practice which did not bear on 'institutional apparatuses and historical processes' . . . would [merely] reproduce, whatever its originality, the self-critical movement of philosophy in its internal tradition."[22] But with the publication of *Specters of Marx: The State of the Debt, the Work of Mourning, and the New International* in 1994, Derrida's thinking—which had hitherto been primarily focused on philosophical, literary, linguistic, and artistic subjects – moved decisively, or at least more explicitly, into the conjoined realms of politics and ethics.[23] In this context, the question of hospitality—of openness to the Other, but also of what we owe to others without obligation— becomes paramount. Among his many writings on the subject, the following long quotation from Derrida occurs, not uncharacteristically, as a parenthetical aside that is nonetheless arguably central to his theoretical priorities:

> For to be what it "must" be, hospitality must not pay a debt, or be governed by a duty: it is gracious, and "must" not open itself to the guest [invited or visitor], either "conforming to duty" or even, to use the Kantian distinction again, "out of duty." This unconditional law of hospitality, if such a thing is thinkable, would then be a law without imperative, without order, and without duty. A law without law, in short. For if I practice hospitality "*out of duty*" . . . this hospitality of paying up is no longer an absolute hospitality, it is no longer graciously offered beyond debt and economy, offered to the other, a hospitality invented for the singularity of the new arrival, of the unexpected visitor.[24]

Hospitality (from the Latin *hospitalitem*, "friendliness to guests") is for Derrida a fundamental ethical principle, one that by definition must exceed all sense of obligation or indebtedness in order to be genuine. As opposed to Agamben's "force of law," in which extralegal imperatives operate as if legitimized by the power of juridical decree, Derridean hospitality must be offered freely, without official direction or even sanction. It is the spontaneous opening of the self to others that makes hospitality an essential component, if not also the fundamental driver, of community. Accordingly, in a slightly earlier essay, Derrida makes clear that "hospitality is not simply some region of ethics . . . [I]t is ethicity itself, the whole and the principle of ethics. . . . This interruption of the self by the self, if such a thing is possible . . . this is ethical discourse – and it is also, as the limit of thematization, hospitality. Is not hospitality an interruption of the self?"[25]

Let's now examine how such hospitality fails to take hold in *The Bride of Lammermoor*. After Ravenswood offers what meager welcome he can to the prodigal fortune-hunter Bucklaw—over the comic objections and machinations of the family's sole remaining manservant, Caleb Balderstone—the reader sees firsthand that Edgar has few resources left to satisfy his old-fashioned sense of *noblesse oblige*. We are, thus, primed to be alarmed by Ashton's subsequent exploitation of Ravenswood's aristocratic instincts, in order to place his daughter once more in Edgar's path. Everything about their second meeting is meant to appear spontaneous, yet thanks to dramatic irony, readers can see that Ashton has carefully arranged for himself and Lucy to come within range of Wolfscrag.[26] When at the conclusion of a hunt that Edgar has only been able to observe (due to his lack of funds and much to his chagrin) a cloaked older man begins to flatter Ravenswood with his attentions, we are not surprised when the stranger turns out to be Ashton. Before revealing himself, however, he takes advantage of the sudden inclement weather to put Edgar in the awkward position of being obligated to offer him and his daughter shelter. Scott's diction here is telling:

> The horse of the fair huntress shewed symptoms of impatience and restiveness, and it became impossible for Ravenswood, as a man or a gentleman, to leave her abruptly . . . He was, or believed himself, *obliged* in courtesy to take hold of her bridle, and assist her . . . While he was thus engaged, the old gentleman observed that the storm seemed to increase . . . and that he would be *obliged* to the Master of Ravenswood to point him the way to the nearest place of refuge from the storm. At the same time he cast a wistful and embarrassed look toward the Tower of Wolfscrag, which seemed to render it almost impossible for the owner to avoid offering an old man and a lady, in such an emergency, the temporary use of his house.[27]

This is clearly nothing like Derrida's ideal hospitality; the stiff language of obligation is simply too palpable to allow for the development of authentic sympathy. Compounded with Ashton's willingness to use his daughter instrumentally, such artificiality causes the rapprochement between the Ashtons and Ravenswood to be brittle and precarious from its inception.

Ashton's coercion of Edgar's hospitality initiates a series of ultimately tragic events. Balderstone is thrown into such panic by the arrival of these unexpected guests that he refuses to allow Bucklaw to return to Wolfscrag, precipitating the latter's anger against Ravenswood, and providing fodder for Lady Ashton when she later encourages Bucklaw to marry Lucy himself.[28] The Ashtons' sudden appearance also forces Caleb to hunt for provisions in the nearby hamlet of Wolfshope, where a number of semicomic mishaps help historicize the novel's theme of community's dissolution. Most of the villagers have already earned the right to own their land and possessions, Scott explains: they are "emancipated from the chains of feudal dependence . . . They might be, on the whole, termed independent."[29] The majority of Waverley Novels, as we have seen, portray the transition from feudal to modern social arrangements in generally positive terms (even when matters are ultimately more complicated). By contrast, in *The Bride*, although we are invited to chuckle at Caleb's nostalgia for the days when the villagers surrendered whatever was demanded of them to the estate, there is little sense that any compensatory bonds between the ranks have arisen to replace these now-decayed feudal connections. Indeed, Caleb's attempts to extort continued tributes from the villagers have been permanently thwarted by the arrival of "a shrewd country attorney" who uses his legal prowess to combat successfully "all arguments arising from antique custom and hereditary respect."[30] Subsequently, Caleb can scavenge provisions from Wolfshope for the Ashtons only via thievery. He manages to keep his ill-gotten gains, moreover, only by successfully convincing the cooper and his wife that Edgar and Lucy's marriage is imminent, and that they will personally benefit from the Ravenswood family's revived fortunes.

Yet, any return to such traditional associations—what Marx famously calls "the motley feudal ties that bound man to his 'natural superiors',", and to which Caleb refers (without Marx's irony) as "that due and fitting connection betwixt superior and vassal"[31]—is short-circuited by Lady Ashton's pride and ambition. Described from the novel's start as a domineering mother and overbearing wife, Lady Ashton condemns Edgar as "a beggarly jacobite bankrupt" as well as "the inveterate enemy of [our] family," and leaves Sir William little choice but to sever his (and his daughter's) ties with the moody Master.[32] Although she claims to be protecting her family by forcing this break, the self-interest guiding Lady Ashton's machinations is obvious. On matters of decorum, Scott even makes an early point of describing her as "a severe and strict observer of the external forms, at least, of devotion" whose "hospitality was splendid, even to ostentation."[33] The influence she wields over her husband by force of personality and strength of rhetoric, moreover, is frequently characterized as unfeminine and therefore unnatural. As Ian Duncan notes, Lady Ashton is part of the "demonic matriarchy"—which also includes Blind Alice the fortune-teller, the grotesque witch/nursemaid Ailsie Gourlay, and the fatal mermaid of the Ravenswood fountain—that presides over the characters' fates in *The Bride of Lammermoor*.[34] This "obscene" community of *femmes fatale* ultimately succeeds in turning Lucy Ashton into one of their own, provoking the madness that leads her to stab Bucklaw on their wedding night and then feverishly expire.

Lucy's frantic, belated burst of feminine violence is matched by Edgar's Hamlet-like inability to act decisively. Despite his initial rescue of Lucy and her father, Edgar is subsequently capable neither of averting Lucy's marriage to Bucklaw, nor of avenging her untimely death, nor even of saving his family's good name. Prevented from courting Lucy and humiliated by Lady Ashton, Edgar allows his kinsman, the Marquis of A—, to send him overseas on a mysterious political mission (presumably an early Jacobite plot). By the time Edgar returns to Scotland, the ephemeral Tory ascendancy that had temporarily empowered the Marquis has passed, and Lady Ashton has pushed through

Lucy's engagement to Bucklaw. This is not to say that Edgar has not shown at least the desire to adapt to the changing times. In fact, when his courtship of Lucy still appears to have a future, Edgar tries to reconcile himself to an accommodation with the new, bourgeois regime represented by the Ashtons: in his words to himself, "We sink under the force of the law, now too powerful for the Scottish chivalry. Let us parley with the victors of the day, as if we had been besieged in our fortress without hope of relief."[35] Yet, the very simile that articulates Ravenswood's logic here is drawn from the vocabulary of feudal warfare, not the language of Derridean hospitality. Like Helen MacGregor, Edgar is at best a residual cultural element. Once the impossibility of his courtship with Lucy becomes evident, he quickly reverts to the atavistic attitudes and habits of his chivalric forefathers. During his violent interruption of Lucy and Bucklaw as they sign their marriage articles, Edgar is described as already belonging more to the past than the present: "Ravenswood had more the appearance of one returned from the dead, than of a living visitor."[36] Because of a fateful combination of birth and breeding, in other words, the Master of Ravenswood seems simply incapable of heeding Derrida's plea: "Let us say yes *to who or what turns up*, before any determination, before any anticipation, before any *identification* . . . ."[37] Here, we may also recall Koselleck's observation that the "unknown quality" of the future is a hallmark of modernity's new historical sense: a sense that Edgar clearly lacks.

There is more to *The Bride*'s relentless depiction of the failures of hospitality and community than simple failures of character. Although these are certainly present, they are heightened and exaggerated by a host of supernatural omens and ominous legends, including not only the members of the above-mentioned "demonic matriarchy," but also the raven accidentally shot by Lucy's little brother, and Edgar's uncanny resemblance to the portrait of his vengeful ancestor.[38] Furthermore, references to "fate" abound in *The Bride*: the "book of fate" that is said to record Edgar's initial curses against the Ashtons is at least as damning as the "fatal" wedding registry in which Lucy reluctantly (and, in fact, incompletely) signs her name.[39] This sense of tragic inevitability is realized most completely by Edgar's involuntary fulfillment of his family's prophecy:

> When the last Laird of Ravenswood to Ravenswood shall ride,
> And wooe a dead maiden to be his bride,
> He shall stable his steed on the Kelpie's flow,
> And his name shall be lost for evermoe![40]

Edgar's disappearance in the dangerous tidewaters between Wolfscrag and Wolfshope while on his way to duel Lucy's brother in the wake of her death, precisely meets this curse's several conditions. The novel's final paragraphs fulfill the prophecy and more: not only Edgar and Lucy, but also his manservant Caleb and all of her male relatives are summarily dispatched by Scott. Lady Ashton alone lives to old age, we are told, "the only survivor of the group of unhappy persons, whose misfortunes were in a great degree owing to her implacability. . . . A splendid marble monument records her name, titles, and virtues, while her victims remain undistinguished by tomb or epitaph."[41] *The Bride of Lammermoor* opens with a funeral and concludes with a tomb. In between, hospitality is repeatedly abused and abandoned, and all possibility of communal solidarity or regeneration is lost.

No entrance: The impossibility of community in "The Highland Widow" and "The Two Drovers"

The concept or thought of death, so omnipresent in *The Bride of Lammermoor*, is central to another contemporary theorist's writings on community. In his essay, "The Inoperative Community," Jean-Luc Nancy—who, like Derrida, frequently advances his ideas through extended engagements with the writings of others—begins with the observation that "The gravest and most painful testimony of the modern world . . . is the testimony of the dissolution, the dislocation, or the conflagration of community."[42] Unlike Horkheimer, Adorno, or Baudrillard, Nancy attributes modernity's failures not to the malign influences of Enlightened reason or Western capitalism, but rather to a constitutive misunderstanding regarding the nature of the communal itself. We are used to thinking of community as something that has been lost, fragmented, or dissolved, and which therefore can only be approximated at best; for the most part, we tend to mourn its passing or disappearance, recall it with hazy nostalgia, or (like Edgar Ravenswood) even try to avenge its loss. The conceptual framework for this attitude is provided by the late-nineteenth-century German sociologist Alfred Tönnies, who formulated the distinction between *gemeinschaft* (traditional community, with its authentic, unmediated social interactions) and *gesellschaft* (modern society or the State, with its artificial, instrumental social relations).[43] Ever since, social and critical theorists have been considering the implications of Tönnies' dichotomy.

Habermas questions the logic of the opposition itself, stating that the principles of his theory of communicative action are designed to account for "the relational structure of otherness and difference . . . in such a way that they reveal the possibility of conditions of life that escape the false opposition between '*Gemeinschaft*' and '*Gesellschaft*'."[44] Nancy takes an even more radical approach. In his view, the opposition between community and society is not to be overcome or escaped as much as recognized to be phantasmatic:

> *Community has not taken place*, or rather, if it is indeed certain that humanity has known (or still knows, outside of the industrial world) social ties quite different from those familiar to us, community has never taken place along the lines of our projections of it . . . No *Gesellschaft* has come along to help the State, industry, and capital dissolve a prior *Gemeinschaft*. . . . *Society* was not built on the ruins of a *community*. It emerged from the disappearance or the conservation of something – tribes or empires – perhaps just as unrelated to what we call "community" as to what we call "society." So that community, far from being what society has crushed or lost, is *what happens to us* – question, waiting, event, imperative – *in the wake of* society.[45]

Despite the prophetic tone of this passage, Nancy's basic point is quite concrete: the sense that some prior social arrangement was more immanent, egalitarian, or authentically human not only seems to be a historical constant, but also consistently illusory. Any actual community—and here we should note that, for Nancy, this could take a variety of forms—will come about only after society as we currently know it has been radically transformed. (Agamben suggests something similar with the title of his own reflections on the subject, *The Coming Community*.[46]) By contrast, the widespread conviction that community has always already been lost can (and frequently does, as the twentieth century demonstrated) lead to regressive, oppressive, even fascistic social formations. Hence the necessity, says Nancy, "of realizing that the nostalgia for a communal being was at the same time the desire for a work of death."[47]

The fatal danger of imagining that a prior social arrangement was necessarily superior to the current one is amply illustrated, as we have seen, in *The Bride of Lammermoor*. It is also a main theme of the first story in Scott's *Chronicles of the Canongate*. In "The Highland Widow," a well-to-do Lowland lady recalls a tour she took of the Highlands in the years following the 1745 Jacobite Rebellion. Although her Highland guide excels at locating picturesque stopping points for her carriage, Mrs. Baliol frequently notes the countryside's many signs of loss and death: the multiple cairns marking the graves of Robert the Bruce's defeated enemies; the deforested flanks of Ben Cruachan; even the very roads that make her tour possible, since they were engineered by first Roman and later British occupiers.[48] A practical-minded Lowlander, Mrs. Baliol is able to see some good in these changes; with regard to the repurposing of General Wade's military roads for commercial and touristic purposes, for example, she observes that "the traces of war are sometimes happily accommodated to the purposes of peace."[49]

This open attitude toward the new, however, is countered by the tragic tale that ensues. A closer view of a magnificent oak standing by the banks of the Awe River reveals a dilapidated cottage belonging to the widow of the story's title. Like Edgar at Lucy's signing of her marriage articles, Elspat MacTavish is already spectral: "as indifferent to my gaze," Mrs. Baliol observes, "as if she had been a dead corpse or a marble statue."[50] Elspat's piteous history, also like Ravenswood's, is a tale of decline: her husband, once a largely prosperous Highland raider, sided with Bonnie Prince Charlie and the Jacobites, and was subsequently hounded to death by the victorious British forces. Their only child, Hamish Bean, becomes the repository of Elspat's shattered ambitions: "such were her imaginations, [that he might] emulate one day the fame of his father, and command the same influence which he had exerted."[51] Elspat is so committed to her rose-colored vision of the past, when she and her husband lived by their wits and deeds in the "romantick" Scotland of authentic experience (to use Matthew Wickman's evocative orthography),[52] that she fails to see how the post-1745 world, with its "substitution of civil order for military violence," is largely a different place.[53] Scott's description of how Elspat can only "anticipat[e] the future from recollections of the past"[54] agrees with Koselleck's description of the limitations of a premodern sense of historicity, and her ornate rhetoric (like Helen MacGregor's) is characterized by a timeless combination of biblical and Ossianic diction and syntax.

Hamish is a dutiful, even devoted son. But, his adjustment to the new British order—he wears a "long-skirted Lowland coat" (as required by law), for example, instead of the traditional Highland tartan[55]—disappoints Elspat deeply. Tired of her disapproval, Hamish eventually enlists in one of the newly formed Highland regiments bound for America. Although he explains his motivations primarily in terms of wishing to provide for his mother, we infer that he also wants to assert his independence from her and, by extension, the past she represents. When Elspat discovers this "betrayal," she drugs Hamish to prevent him from meeting his regiment on time, knowing that the punishment for such laxness—a public flogging—will be too humiliating for him to bear. After a tense standoff with the soldiers who come to retrieve him, Hamish fatally shoots one of them (with Elspat's deluded encouragement) and is subsequently executed the following day by a firing squad. The fact that his victim was a fellow Highlander, albeit from a rival clan, is a grim irony: the victims of conservative nostalgia, Scott intuits, are often also the most vulnerable to exploitation or oppression. Although Elspat long survives her son, she soon descends into the grief-stricken, isolated delirium in which the narrator finds her some years later.

A brief coda adds a final twist to the story as it details Elspat's final evening. Seemingly paralyzed by old age, word of her imminent death brings two younger women to oversee her final hours. When they wake in the night, she has disappeared. Scott leaves us with conflicting explanations for this mystery, ranging from the supernatural (some villagers believe Elspat was claimed by an evil spirit) to the mundane (in her delirium, she may have wandered off and died of exposure). But, the explanation given by a Highland clergyman is the most resonant: "He thought, that impatient of the watch which was placed over her, this unhappy woman's instinct had taught her, as it directs various domestic animals, to withdraw herself from the sight of her own race, that the death struggle might take place in some secret den, where, in all probability, her mortal remains would never meet the eyes of mortals."[56] Self-exile unto death, in other words, is the only possible endgame for a subject like Elspat who, trapped by the nostalgic logic of "the lost community," must become as isolated and unmourned in death as she was dismissive of modern society in life.

In "The Highland Widow," Hamish's fate is sealed as soon as he shoots the British officer who comes to retrieve him; pleas for clemency from his pastor are turned back with the explanation that the commanding general, who is "half a Lowlander, half an Englishman," has already ruled out any defense of Hamish's actions along cultural lines as "Highland visions . . . as unsatisfactory and vain as those of the Second Sight."[57] The second tale in *Chronicles*, "The Two Drovers," extends this theme of clashing cultural norms, while delineating another version of the failure of community. The story—probably Scott's most frequently anthologized prose piece—concerns an unlikely friendship between two cattle herders, the Englishman Harry Wakefield and the Highlander Robin Oig. The events take place two decades or so later than those related in the first tale: relations between the Highlands and the rest of Britain have now normalized enough to permit a high degree of cross-border commerce and even intercultural familiarity. Because Britain undertook the consolidation of its various peoples into a single nation earlier than the rest of Europe,[58] the situation of "The Two Drovers" arguably approximates the conditions outlined by Habermas when he describes "the double-sided national consciousness" (simultaneously elite and popular) that began to permeate nineteenth-century Western Europe:

> the idea of the nation also contributed to the creation of a mode of solidarity between persons who had until then remained strangers to one another. The universalistic reformulation of inherited loyalties to village and clan, landscape and dynasty was a difficult and protracted process . . . By expanding the parameters for the implementation of human rights and

democracy, the nation-state made possible a new, more abstract form of social integration beyond the borders of ancestry and dialect.[59]

Influenced by the Scottish Enlightenment, many of Scott's Waverley Novels support Habermas' general schema. But, the stories in *The Chronicles of the Canongate*—perhaps because they were written near the end of Scott's career, after the double blows of bankruptcy and his wife's death—demonstrate far less faith in the possibility of communities (or nations) extended and made mutually open and habitable through rational communication.[60]

The Habermasian ideal of the modern, democratic nation, in which the public sphere of civil society exists in constructive tension with a juridico-political state framework, is not intended to impose homogeneity on its various participants. Instead, it is meant to sustain, even nurture, their differences: "collective identities are made, not found. But they can only unify the heterogeneous. Citizens who share a common political life also are others to one another, and each is entitled to *remain* an Other."[61] As "The Two Drovers" opens with descriptions of its protagonists and their friendship, Scott initially seems to have anticipated Habermas' vision:

> It is difficult to say how Henry Wakefield and Robin Oig first became intimates; but it is certain a close acquaintance had taken place betwixt them . . . Thus, though Robin could hardly have comprehended his companion's stories about horse-racing, cock-fighting, or fox-hunting, and although his own legends of clan-fights and *creaghs*, varied with talk of Highland goblins and fairy folk, would have been caviar to his companion, they contrived nevertheless to find a degree of pleasure in each other's company . . . when the direction of their journey permitted.[62]

Tolerating each other's differences even when they are unable truly to understand them, often "find[ing] a degree of pleasure" in their differing knowledges and worldviews, Harry and Robin seem model citizens of the post-'45 British nation-state. The final clause of the above passage, however, contains a subtle but significant qualification: "when the direction of their journey permitted." In other words, Harry and Robin's seemingly robust cross-cultural friendship is maintained within a framework of converging interests, specifically their parallel cattle-driving ventures. As long as their commercial pursuits run parallel, their intranational differences can be put aside or even used to strengthen their partnership. But as soon as their interests diverge or conflict, those same differences become increasingly awkward stumbling blocks.

The process by which their friendship unravels in a series of culturally overdetermined misapprehensions has already been well documented.[63]

Dwelt upon less frequently, however, is the event that sets in motion its destruction: competition for the scant available pasture land. The ease and speed with which their friendship is not only undone but also rendered lethal by the sudden introduction of competing commercial motives—as happens when Robin accidentally pastures his cattle on land that Harry had thought was reserved for his use—suggests, at the very least, the fragility of that relation.[64] But, it may also indicate a weakness in Habermas' conjoined concepts of communicative action and the lifeworld. In the middle book of their recent theoretical trilogy on globalization and its discontents, Michael Hardt and Antonio Negri place Habermas in a tradition of theorists of civil society in order to censure him for making the same error as his predecessors:

> There is, of course, a rationalist and moralist echo that runs throughout this effort to divide the world of free and ethical communication from the system of instrumentality and domination[,] a sense of indignation against the capitalist colonization of the lifeworld. This is where Habermas' conception of ethical communication in a democratic public sphere appears completely utopian and unrealizable, however, because it is impossible to isolate ourselves, our relationships, and our communication outside the instrumentality of capital and the mass media. We are all already inside, contaminated.[65]

For Hardt and Negri, Habermas' vision of a public sphere or lifeworld whose existence may be considered apart from the political, economic, and institutional contexts in which it necessarily exists is naïve at best. From their neo-Marxist perspective, no prophylactic of mutual tolerance or respect is strong enough to protect against the corrosive effects of capitalist dehumanization; indeed, the very idea of "separate spheres" for culture, politics, law, and economics is from their point of view not only false but also dangerous.[66]

This skepticism is borne out by the tragic denouement of "The Two Drovers," in which Harry, thinking he is solving their dispute amicably—that is to say, in the English style—boxes the unprepared Robin into unconsciousness. The humiliated Highlander returns some hours later, having retrieved his traditional dagger, and restores his sense of personal honor by fatally stabbing his friend and then turning himself over to the authorities. The sudden, bloody demise of Robin and Harry's friendship vividly realizes Hardt and Negri's concern that no lifeworld, however practically and even hospitably constructed, is immune to corruption by the tensions, contradictions, and systemic injustices of the economic and political realities in which it is always fully imbricated. Yet, "The Two Drovers" does not end here. Instead, Scott effectively turns the narrative over to a new character: the English judge who presides at Robin's trial. After the narrator observes that "when the rooted national prejudices of the prisoner had been explained . . . the generosity of the English audience was inclined to regard his crime as the wayward aberration," readers seem encouraged to hope that Robin will be forgiven for his crime, or at least receive a lightened sentence.[67] Instead, the judge is given a three-and-a-half-page monologue in which he makes it abundantly clear that, far from exonerating Robin, an Enlightened ability to appreciate the foreign context of Robin's Highland value system—in which an insult to personal honor demands violent retribution— actually confers greater responsibility to ensure that justice is carried out "impartially." After reviewing all of the case's mitigating factors, the judge concludes:

> But though all this may be granted . . . it cannot, and ought not, even in this most painful case, to alter the administration of the law . . . The first object of civilization is to place the general protection of the law, equally administered, in the room of that wild justice, which every man cut and carved for himself, according to the length of his sword and the strength of his arm. . . . should this man's action remain unpunished, you may unsheath, under various pretences, a thousand daggers betwixt the Land's-end and the Orkneys.[68]

Since Robin's fatal attack on his friend occurred in a tavern south of the Anglo-Scottish border, it makes sense that he be tried in an English court. But, the geographical scope of the judge's final address—from the southernmost tip of England to the northern islands of Scotland—clearly establishes what Agamben would call its "force of law" over the entire United Kingdom.[69]

This absolute authority, moreover, is reinforced stylistically by the fact that the judge's voice is almost the only one heard during the tale's concluding pages. Replacing his previous, richly differentiated representations of the characters' regionally various dialects with the standard English of the nameless judge, Scott also moves from what M. M. Bakhtin has taught us to call a dialogic mode—in which multiple worldviews are represented linguistically— to a literally monological speech by a presiding authority whose legitimacy is underscored by his institutionally sanctioned anonymity.[70] (He is simply "the venerable Judge.") Even so, if he were either to misunderstand or outrightly condemn the role played by Robin's Highland background in Harry's murder, the finale of "The Two Drovers" might be less disturbing, since we could then conclude that the Habermasian ideal of communicative rationality is still intact, but merely unrealized. The judge's painstaking demonstration of his full understanding of Robin's Otherness, however, paints a darker picture: mutual understanding does not necessarily produce the fine balance of heterogeneity and communalism that Habermas celebrates as one of modernity's greatest political achievements (or potentials, at least). The true tragedy of "The Two

Drovers" is not that Harry and Robin cannot prevent their atavistic national prejudices from destroying their friendship and ultimately their lives; it is, rather, that neither they nor the judge can prevent the simultaneously normalizing and divisive pressures of modernity from turning them all against each other, despite their Habermasian commitments to shared understanding. Harry and Robin, we must conclude, would have been better off had they never struck up their democratic friendship in the first place.

Community lost and found in "The Surgeon's Daughter" and Chrystal Croftangry's narrative

If "The Two Drovers" is still the best-known text within *Chronicles*, then "The Surgeon's Daughter" has in recent years become the most critically acclaimed. It follows two young men—a born Scotsman, Adam Hartley, and an adopted one, Richard Middlemas—who attempt to make their fortunes in 1770s India while competing for the affections of the same woman: Menie Grey, the eponymous heroine. The exotic subject matter of this novella (it is significantly longer than "The Highland Widow" and "The Two Drovers" combined) was originally seen as little more than a selling point for curious readers, but thanks to the rise of postcolonial theory and, more recently, globalization studies, is now taken seriously in its own right. Accordingly, "The Surgeon's Daughter" has been praised for Scott's deft dismantling of orientalist clichés and salutary focus on "the ramifications of cultural contact and exchange."[71] These are undoubtedly important reasons for paying it renewed attention, especially in tandem with other so-called orientalist productions of Scott's day (including *The Talisman*, discussed in Chapter 3).[72]

Here, however, I want to focus on how "The Surgeon's Daughter" takes up many of the same themes as the two tales that precede it in *Chronicles*. Certainly, they share plots that revolve around Scottish exports, be they animals or people.[73] But, the themes of abused hospitality and failed community are again paramount in "The Surgeon's Daughter." The story opens with the unexpected arrival of a heavily pregnant foreigner in the Scottish Borders village of Middlemas: the introduction, that is, of a foreign element into an apparent *gemeinschaft*, a tight-knit community. The subsequent disappearance of the child's father, followed by the young mother's forced return to her father's care, leaves the infant in the hospitable care of Dr. Grey, who attempts to bring Richard up in as sober a fashion as that of his other protégé, Adam Hartley. Initially cast as friends, their rivalry over Grey's daughter—not unlike Robin Oig's and Harry Wakefield's competition for fertile pasturage—leads inevitably to animosity. Although Hartley receives official paternal permission to court

Menie, as well as to inherit the doctor's medical practice, he soon discovers that she and Richard Middlemas—who has always been the more ambitious (and unstable) of the two young men—have long been secretly engaged. Each man subsequently determines to seek his fortune in India: Middlemas, because he cannot bear the thought of "feel[ing] like a mill-horse, walking my daily round in this dull country, while other gay rovers are trying how the world will receive them"[74]; and Hartley, because he hopes for a chance to prove himself abroad as well as recover from his romantic disappointment.

Having left the original, albeit always already compromised society of the Scottish village (its quiet imbrication in larger networks of travel and trade render it a *gesellschaft* despite itself), neither Middlemas nor Hartley—the latter most closely resembling the typical Waverley Hero of Scott's earlier fictions—finds happiness in India. As complications ensue, several more plot devices from previous *Chronicles*' tales reappear, albeit in altered forms befitting their increasingly exotic settings. In a scenario reminiscent of Elspat's ill-fated drugging of Hamish, Middlemas is betrayed by the con artist who had promised him a military commission, left for dead in a soldiers' hospital on the Isle of Wight, and only rescued thanks to Hartley's professional intervention. Yet, this escape is shadowed by tragedy when, in one of the more melodramatic episodes of Scott's oeuvre, Middlemas accidentally precipitates his long-lost mother's death during a chance encounter. More determined than ever to make his fortune as a colonial adventurer, he quickly departs Britain, but once arrived in India, despite experiencing "that warm hospitality which distinguished the British character in the East,"[75] he soon falls out with his commanding officer and slays him. Unlike Robin, however, Middlemas does not stay to receive his punishment, but flees Fort St. George into the south-east Asian interior.

Three years later, when Scott's narrative picks up again, Middlemas has insinuated himself into a very different community: the close, erotically charged circle surrounding the trouser- and turban-wearing adventuress Mrs. Montreville. This "unsexed women, who can no longer be termed a European,"[76] as Hartley indignantly describes her, might seem a good fit Middlemas, who has proven himself perennially unhappy in more traditional social arrangements. Once again, however, his ambition outruns his common sense, and Hartley learns that his former friend plots a series of complicated transactions: having lured Menie to India and put her under Montreville's protection, while disguising himself as the latter's dark-skinned manservant (a device recycled from *The Talisman*), Middlemas plans to offer his fiancé to Tipu Sultan, son of the powerful Muslim leader Haider Ali, in exchange for the governorship of Bangalore. (A rawer version of the exchange of a woman between men is hard to imagine.) Simultaneously, Middlemas—again playing the "middle" man, as his name implies—has remade contact with the

British, to whom he hopes to betray Tipu, in order to retrieve Menie at the last moment and thereby regain his place in British society. Almost needless to say, Middlemas' machinations go awry: his planned treachery is exposed by a humble Fakir to whom Hartley has confided his suspicions, and who turns out to be none other than Haider Ali himself.

Besides displaying his facility for creating intricate plots, Scott accomplishes much via the sheer narrative restlessness of "The Surgeon's Daughter." Above and beyond feeding readers' appetites for stories of oriental adventure, the incessant geographic movement of Richard Middlemas highlights the difficulty, perhaps even the impossibility, of maintaining a sense of communal belonging in an era of ever-expanding global capitalism. At every potential resting point of Middlemas' career—every node in the web of global networks where he could come to rest—his desire for wealth and status goads him onward. Even as he mourns his mother's death, he counts the money she has left him "with mercantile accuracy" and deems it enough to launch his Indian adventures; earlier, when describing to Hartley all the "lacs and crores of rupees" that potentially await them in India, he unselfconsciously portrays Menie as "in herself a gem – a diamond – I admit it."[77] This latter comment suggests that we can best shed light on the origins of Middlemas' insatiable ambition and ultimately fatal restlessness, neither via Bhabha's hybridity nor even Žižek's concept of desire (although both are relevant), but by recognizing how completely Middlemas has internalized the restless, competitive ethic of modern capitalism, which from at least Marx onward has been recognized as antithetical to the spirit of hospitality and community. Unwilling to resign himself to life in a Scottish village on the peripheries of British society, but unable to secure a stable niche within the ever-shifting alliances and rivalries of pre-Raj India, Middlemas ends his career under an elephant that stamps him to death at Haider's command.

Importantly, Hardt and Negri offer a potential solution to the problem of capitalism's seemingly inherent antagonism to horizontal relations of social cohesion (a solution that also implicitly addresses Nancy's insight that community is what comes in the wake of society). Rather than continue to imagine that resistance to capitalism's atomizing imperatives must take the form of homogenizing or nostalgic common identities such as "the people" or "the masses," Hardt and Negri propose an alternative: the multitude.

> The multitude designates an active social subject, which acts on the basis of what the singularities share in common. The multitude is an internally different, multiple social subject whose constitution and action is based not on identity or unity (or, much less, indifference) but on what it has in common. . . . From the socioeconomic perspective, the multitude is the common subject of labor, that is, the real flesh of postmodern production,

and at the same time the object from which collective capital tries to make the body of its global development. . . . The biopolitical production of the multitude, however, tends to mobilize what it shares in common and what it produces in common against the imperial power of global capital.[78]

Hardt and Negri freely admit that their conception of the multitude as "the only social subject capable of realizing democracy, that is, the rule of everybody by everybody" is imperfect: it "raises numerous conceptual and practical problems," which they try, not always with total success, to address throughout the three volumes of their theoretico-political trilogy.[79] The significance of their position, as the above passage demonstrates, is how they conceive of "multitude" as immanent to the global regime of capitalism (the new form of Empire, in their view). Just as Marx predicted the bourgeoisie will be brought down by the same underclass of exploited workers they necessarily produce, so Hardt and Negri believe that the biopolitical production of exploited populations worldwide is creating the very multitude—brought together by their common oppression, as well as by the technologies and networks that facilitate their exploitation, but nevertheless remaining "singularities"—that will eventually overtake Empire itself.[80]

For some theorists, the totality of global capital's hold on the everyday lives of most world citizens (including those *homini sacer*, to invoke Agamben's phrase, captured by global capital precisely by their exclusion from its benefits) is cause for despair; for Hardt and Negri, by contrast, it is also cause for optimism inasmuch as it makes the multitude's formation possible, indeed inevitable. To be sure, Hardt and Negri's concept of multitude is specific to our historical moment of "postmodern production," when much of the most profitable labor in the so-called developed world has become largely knowledge- and service-based, and when the circuits of global capital exchange have become nearly instantaneous and ubiquitous (albeit unevenly distributed). Accordingly, it would be a mistake to read directly the potential of multitude back into the era of "The Surgeon's Daughter," which significantly precedes the historical zenith of the British Empire: "Our story took place at a period, when the Directors of the East India Company, with that hardy and persevering policy which has raised to such a height the British Empire in the East, had determined to send a large reinforcement of European troops to the support of their power in India, then threatened by the kingdom of the Mysore."[81] Although this concluding aside by Scott's narrator celebrates British overseas resolve, it also makes clear that their grip on the Indian subcontinent at the time of Middlemas' and Hartley's adventures is far from secure. The old, indigenous sociopolitical structures are falling; the new, imperial ones have not yet coalesced. Caught in the middle—literally crushed—is Richard Middlemas. Yet, Hartley, the assumed hero of Scott's novella, does little better: despite his good intentions, he survives his nemesis by less than two years before dying of a fever caught from a patient. Furthermore, the narrator accurately reveals that both Tipu and Haider will die in battle with the British in the coming years; as for the fictional Mrs. Montreville, rumor reports her eventual poisoning. The only survivor of "The Surgeon's Daughter" is Menie Grey herself, who returns to her native Scottish village to perform acts of charity, but never to marry nor fully to reintegrate into her community of origin. Like *The Bride of Lammermoor*, "The Surgeon's Daughter" concludes with a description of a tomb.

Yet, *Chronicles of the Canongate* does not end here, for the three tales I have now discussed (and on which critics traditionally focus) are embedded in a substantial frame narrative. Indeed, it is the down-market Edinburgh neighborhood of the tales' narrator and compiler, Chrystal Croftangry, which lends the volume its title. ("The Highland Widow" is technically a transcription of a narrative told to him by a friend.) Croftangry is a retired gentleman who, having lost his fortune and eventually regained most of it overseas, has returned to Edinburgh to realize his long-held dream of becoming a published author. *Chronicles* was the first Waverley Novel to which Scott, having publicly revealed his authorship just months before, added an introduction under his own name. As the first chapter begins, then, readers could be expected to see the humor in the most celebrated writer of his day impersonating a would-be first-time author. Certainly, Croftangry's description of himself as "a Scottish gentleman of the old school, with a fortune, temper, and person, rather the worse for wear" reflects Scott's own, habitually self-deprecating image, as well as his recent financial woes.[82] But beyond creating another authorial stand-in, I want to argue that Croftangry allows Scott to craft a frame narrative that both reflects and at least partially resolves several of his internal stories' concerns.

In *Chronicles*' opening chapter, Croftangry seeks out a former friend and benefactor, only to find him physically and mentally incapacitated. Much affected by this *memento mori*-like reunion, Croftangry knows that "according to the ordinary rule of Edinburgh hospitality," he would be "a welcome guest in several respectable families," but chooses not to seek out other old acquaintances on the grounds that "all community of ties between us had ceased to exist."[83] In other words, Croftangry experiences the same questions and anxieties—under what conditions is the promise of hospitality rendered insufficient? At what point, if ever, does or should a past community give way to something newer?—that shape the fates of his subsequent tales' characters. Significantly, Croftangry decides to forego all attempts to renew the high-ranking bonds of his previous life and instead takes lodgings with a humble Highlander, Janet MacEvoy, with whom he had lodged before his adventures abroad. This decision follows another unusual choice: despite having the chance to repurchase part of his family's estate—which would have been in keeping with the established "romance" plot of *Waverley* and many of its successors—Croftangry instead spends the majority of his capital repaying a long-forgotten debt to a former family servant. More specifically, he buys and then transfers the lease of the country inn that she manages. Perhaps not coincidentally, the inn or tavern is a traditional figure (or chronotope, in Bakhtin's terminology)[84] of a place designed for the convergence of strangers: that is, a place that facilitates both traditional hospitality and the formation of new communities. Croftangry's decision to invest his capital in maintaining a hospitable nexus for travelers to mingle and form new social bonds, rather than to repurchase his family estate, indicates an admirably Derridean openness to the unknowable future.

If this virtual community occupies Croftangry's moral imagination, then another potential community sustains his authorial ambitions: the readers he hopes to reach with his stories. His interpolated audience is initially small, comprising little more than Janet—who "wept most bitterly," Croftangry reports, upon hearing "The Highland Widow"—and Mr. Fairscribe, who helped Croftangry out of his legal troubles and now proves a reliable, if conventionally minded, source of literary advice.[85] But, Croftangry's ambitions extend beyond this immediate circle, so that readers who finish "The Surgeon's Daughter" find a final chapter that relieves the preceding narratives' gloom by bringing us up to date on Croftangry's latest literary success: his recent reading of the tale we have just completed to a gathering of local ladies. His reception is warm: "At length my task was ended, and the fair circle rained odours upon me, as they pelt beaux at the Carnival with sugar-plums, and drench them with scented spices."[86] Scott's typical self-deprecation is fully evident here, as is his sly (and equally typical) mockery of the women who comprised an ever-larger portion of the British reading public in the early nineteenth century. Nevertheless, even as the audience's discussion digresses from the literary merits of Croftangry's writing to more stereotypically domestic concerns, the women's concluding focus on textiles is not as irrelevant as it appears. For as they debate the relative merits of "the imitation shawls now made at Paisley, out of real Thibetan wool," it becomes clear that Scott is not only identifying the increasingly global nature of British commercial goods, but also providing an apt metaphor for the possibility of an increasingly hybridized literature; in Croftangry's words, writing "The Surgeon's Daughter" was like "compos[ing] my shawl by incorporating into the woof a little Thibet wool."[87] Published near the end of the Romantic era, "The Surgeon's Daughter" thus anticipates the increasingly global British literature (and global literature written in English) of the Victorian period and beyond.

Scott's original readers did not have to wait long for confirmation of Croftangry's (fictional) successes, both at establishing himself as a *bona fide* author and at embedding himself within a supportive community of readers and critics. The year after *Chronicles*, Scott published another full-length novel, *The Fair Maid of Perth* (1828), as the second series of *Chronicles of the Canongate*, with an introductory chapter in which Croftangry relates the events that led him to pen this narrative of fourteenth-century Scotland. Unlike the pathos-laden circumstances described in the framing chapters of the first *Chronicles*, these now involve Croftangry's semicomic "rescue" of a historical bloodstain from the labors of an overly zealous Englishman eager to show off his "unequalled Detergent Elixir."[88] Croftangry's new introduction, that is, thematizes not only the work of historical preservation and recovery undertaken by most of the Waverley Novels, but also the frequently quotidian circumstances from which they derive, and in which Scott always carefully anchors his narratives.

On this note, I'd like to conclude this chapter by returning to a fuller consideration of Jacques Rancière's suggestion, first mentioned in my introduction, that literature can be regarded as "a symptomatology of society." For Rancière, we can now add, literature is a historical artifact, which comes into being at the turn of the nineteenth century in a mutually empowering relationship with the equally emergent concept of democracy in its most profound sense:

> On the one hand, [the "new literature"] marks the collapse of the system of differences that allowed the social hierarchies to be represented. It achieves the democratic logic of writing without a master and without a purpose, the great law of the equality of all subjects and of the availability of all expressions . . . But, on the other hand, it opposes the democracy of writing with a new poetics that invents other rules of appropriateness between the significance of words and the visibility of things. . . . This is indeed what literature does by leaving the great racket of the democratic stage to the orators in order to tunnel into the depths of society; by inventing their hermeneutics of the social body, this reading of the laws of a world on the body of mundane things and in words of no importance whose history and sociology will be shared as a legacy by Marxist science and Freudian science.[89]

The "new literature" of the nineteenth century works simultaneously on two levels. Externally, it becomes the voice and vehicle of the people; this is not unlike Lukàcs' interpretation of Scott as the first novelist to capture accurately the mass movements of history. But crucially, Rancière also sees this new literature—especially the nineteenth-century European novel, which arguably could not have come into existence without Scott's example—quietly articulating society's inner processes by speaking of mundane, everyday things, events, and people at least as often as the fall of kings or other world-historical events.[90] By thus "tunnel[ing] into the depths of society," literature effectively anticipates the hermeneutics of suspicion that informs Freudian and Marxian theory and, by extension, the work of most of the theorists discussed in this book. It accomplishes this quietly, moreover, via a kind of "mute speech" whose power resides in its indirection and even indecision regarding its political and social commitments.[91]

Ultimately, Rancière believes strongly in literature's ability to affect what he calls "the distribution of the sensible," a phrase that captures not only how our perceptions of the world are inevitably shaped by our aesthetic and political assumptions, but also how our very abilities to act and think are (over)determined by our allotted social roles and arenas. If, as Rancière argues, "Politics revolves around what is seen and what can be said about it, around who has the ability to see and the talent to speak, around the properties of space and the possibilities of time," then it follows that every artistic practice with the potential "to intervene in the general distribution of ways of doing and making as well as in the relationships they maintain to modes of being and forms of visibility" is, at least potentially, an agent of democratic change.[92]

The various communities represented in *The Bride of Lammermoor* and *Chronicles of the Canongate* all end in failure; their would-be members, with the notable exception of Crystal Croftangry, are reduced to mere memories, at best, by their narratives' conclusions.[93] Even so, the striving for what Hardt and Negri call "the rule of everybody by everybody" is kept alive, not by the mimetic qualities of these narratives, but rather by the interpretive agencies they facilitate. It may be, as Rancière claims, that "there will never be, under the name of politics, a single principle of the community, legitimating the acts of government based on laws inherent to the coming together of human communities."[94] But, this does not mean that we should abandon all hope of true, communitarian democracy—the admittedly utopian horizon of much contemporary theory. Rather, it means that we must continue forging new understandings of "the political" as a space in which ideals of open, hospitable communities can continue to be produced, interrogated, contested, and hopefully enacted. Seen in this critical light, there is no more thoroughly democratic set of literary texts than Walter Scott's Waverley Novels.

Conclusion

Posthuman Scott?

Walter Scott is an extraordinarily insightful, inventive, and prescient author. Although the odds seem long that his fictions will ever recover the popularity they once enjoyed—even the author of a recent popular book on Scott begins by conceding as much[1]—I hope I have succeeded in demonstrating that the Waverley Novels heartily repay close attention from literary critics, historians, and especially theorists. Since I began this book's introduction by focusing on Scott, however, I want to begin my conclusion by focusing on theory. This is not just for the sake of balance, but also because I strongly believe it is in and through theory that scholars in the humanities and social sciences have some of the best chances of making an impact, not only on our own particular fields, but also on our students, peers, and even the general public.[2]

Certainly, all of the theorists whom I discuss in *Walter Scott and Contemporary Theory* consider their work to be relevant far beyond the spheres of literary and even cultural production. Returning to Rancière, one of the thinkers with whom I began this book, would, thus, make a fitting conclusion; it would also be a little too neat. For alongside the theorists on whom I've focused —whose interests and methodologies can be said, roughly, to issue from a combination of Nietzschean, Freudian, and Marxian influences—there exists another set of contemporary theorists. These latter thinkers generally share the progressive politics of their counterparts, but take their cues from a substantially (albeit not entirely) different set of theoretical starting points. For the purposes of briefly surveying some of their central ideas—and making a few, even more brief gestures toward their possible applications to Scott's fictions—I propose to group them together under the banner of "posthumanism." Some may not agree that these theorists can all be discussed effectively under the same rubric; some may object that, under close analysis, they turn out not to participate in the same style of left-wing politics as many of their more mainstream theoretical counterparts. Undoubtedly, their collective position here in my conclusion is misleading, since some of these posthumanists are of the same generation (more or less) as Derrida, Foucault, and the other major figures of later-twentieth-century high theory.

These risks are worth running, however, because a growing consensus is emerging that a new theoretical direction has begun to be forged in recent years: one that seeks, albeit in a variety of ways, to move beyond the twin pillars of discourse analysis and ideology critique that support the methodologies of most of those theorists previously discussed.[3] That older methodological orientation, which almost entirely dominated theory until recently, stems largely from the so-called linguistic turn, codified in the early twentieth-century linguistic theories of Ferdinand de Saussure, but announced as a critical project even earlier by (among others) Friedrich Nietzsche when he declared that what was formerly assumed to be "truth" is really "A movable host of metonymies, metaphors, and anthropomorphisms; in short, a sum of human relations which have been poetically and rhetorically intensified, transferred, and embellished, and which, after long usage, seem to a people to be fixed, canonical, and binding."[4] Nietzsche's pronouncement is no less provocative today than it was when he first wrote it in 1873, and his insight that what passes for "truth" in discourse is really the effect of "a sum of human relations" is in many ways the operative kernel of the Marxian, psychoanalytic, and deconstructive traditions alike. But for some theorists, that intense focus on "human relations" has come to seem narrow and limiting. According to these thinkers, the anthropocentric bias of the linguistic turn—a result of the assumption that since the only access we can have to "truth" is through language, then we can only critically concern ourselves with the products of discourse—is preventing us from asking a host of new, potentially pressing questions.[5] What have been the consequences, for example, of the distinctions and hierarchies we have drawn up to regulate relations between ourselves and the other living (and even nonliving) inhabitants of this planet? What should we make of the fact that humanity has now become so dependent on various forms of technology (including biotechnologies) that it might be a misnomer to call ourselves "human" at all?

These kinds of questions are being raised by the contemporary theorists whose work, broadly speaking, falls under the heading of "posthumanism." Certainly, some of their questions seem specific to the parameters and features our own historical moment: a moment of late capitalism, post-postmodernism, cybernetics, the World Wide Web 2.0, smart phones, genetic decoding and manipulation, environmental degradation, and globalization. With some adjustments of terms or technologies, however, many of the issues they raise are perfectly relevant to Scott's own era—an era which, as I have argued already, sees the introduction of many of the industrial, political, and social developments that characterize modernity in general. In his aptly titled book, *What is Posthumanism?*, Cary Wolfe begins by asserting that "when we talk about posthumanism, we are not just talking about a thematic of the decentering of the human in relation to either evolutionary, ecological, or technological coordinates . . . we are also talking about *how* thinking confronts that thematics, what thought has to become in the face of those challenges."[6] For a genealogy of posthumanism, Wolfe cites Foucault's prophetic insight that the name and figure of "man" is a historically contingent formation, "probably no more than a kind of rift in the order of things," that is likely to change as our understanding of ourselves and our world enters new intellectual epochs and epistemes.[7] Like many writers on posthumanism, Wolfe tends to treat it as an almost completely contemporary phenomenon, underestimating the long durational evolution of many posthuman developments. Nevertheless, his return to Foucault is a salutary reminder that the roots of posthumanism go back at least to the 1960s.[8]

Indeed, Foucault is not the only theorist I have already discussed who has written on posthuman subjects in one way or another. Derrida clearly recognized the artificiality, and often damaging consequences, of the conceptual binarism between "the human" and "the animal" that has informed Western philosophy almost from its origins; Agamben has traced the genealogy of what he calls "the anthropological machine" that does the intellectual work of this separation; Baudrillard long viewed "humanity" as purely human in little but name only; and Habermas has written extensively about the ethical and political stakes of our growing ability to manipulate human lives at the genetic level.[9] Nevertheless, many of the new (or newly prominent) posthumanists take much of their critical inspirations from sources other than the poststructuralist tradition. In particular, many are indebted to the ideas of Gilles Deleuze and his sometime collaborator, Félix Guattari, the philosophers on whom, as we saw in Chapter 2, Manuel DeLanda draws frequently. To see how Deleuze and Guattari make available a radically different theoretical apparatus, we can begin by remembering that DeLanda is openly indebted to what he helpfully calls their "process ontology": a philosophical worldview in which "something else" besides transcendental essences (and also, although DeLanda does not say this explicitly, besides human-created discourses) "is needed to explain what gives objects their identity and what preserves this identity through time. Briefly, this something else is *dynamical processes.*" As DeLanda explains, although all "dynamical processes" are entirely "*immanent* to the world of matter and energy," they are far from random or inchoate.[10] Yet, they are neither essentially controlled nor produced by human action, perception, or discourse; on the contrary, we are intimately caught up in, even formed by, these processes.

This process-oriented ontology, to which DeLanda gives clarifying definitions and dimensions, admittedly remains somewhat obscure, or at least purposefully fluid in the two volumes of *Capitalism and Schizophrenia* that Deleuze and Guattari produced together in the 1970s and 80s. Nevertheless, as Jane Bennett points out, their philosophy contains the seeds of much of today's posthumanist renaissance (an oxymoronic term, to be sure), especially its focus on the "material vitalism" that imbues all things, organic as well as inorganic, with various properties and, by extension, varying degrees of agency.[11] Deleuze and Guattari's asubjective notion of agency, as well as their insistence that what we usually take to be autonomous individuals or entities are really better understood as "multiplicities"—in turn made up of "singularities"—looks back (as do Hardt and Negri) to the materialist philosophy of Spinoza, as well as to other figures of the "radical Enlightenment."[12] It also finds at least partial expression in some of the best-known poetry of Scott's Romantic-era contemporaries, such as William Wordsworth's "Lines written a few miles above Tintern Abbey," with its famous evocation of "A motion and a spirit that impels/All thinking things, all objects of all thought,/And rolls through all things."[13]

Despite the pantheism of these lines, however, Wordsworth clearly still believes in drawing a line between "thinking things" and "objects of thought." But for posthumanists, even this distinction creates and naturalizes a gap between humanity and the world at large, subordinating the latter to the former in ways that have lead, more or less directly, to various forms of alienation and exploitation. Tracing the modern roots of this habit of mind to the Romantics, Timothy Morton argues that we need to develop a concept of "ecology without nature," that is, an ecological mode thinking that does not reflexively make nature something "out there" (even if it does so in the name of protection or conservation rather than exploitation).[14] Another contemporary theorist who writes at length about this destructive intellectual convention is Michel Serres, whose highly poetic style simultaneously advances and conceals a rigorous philosophical undertaking, the core of which may be his concept of "the quasi-object." According to Serres, "the quasi-object" problematizes the artificial difference between "being" and "relating" that quietly informs the Western tradition's long-standing illusion of human autonomy and exceptionalism. Taking advantage of the French pun on "furet," which is both an animal (a ferret) and a thing (an object, hidden behind one's back or on one's person, to be searched for in a game of "hunt-the-slipper or button"), Serres embeds his definition in a characteristically playful example:

> This quasi-object is not an object, but it is one nevertheless, since it is not a subject, since it is in the world; it is also a quasi-subject, since it marks or designates a subject who, without it, would not be a subject. . . . Who are we? Those who pass the furet; those who don't have it. This quasi-object, when being passed, makes the collective, if it stops, it makes the individual. . . . Who is the subject, who is an "I," or who am I? The moving furet weaves the "we," the collective; if it stops, it marks the "I."[15]

In Serres' account, subjects and objects are not separate categories, with humans in the former camp and all other earthly entities in the latter; instead, they are intimately, dynamically interconnected. In *The Five Senses: A Philosophy of Mingled Bodies*, Serres demonstrates how various bodies of organic matter—including our human bodies—are far less permanent or impermeable than we have generally understood:

> The variety of sight, basted with large tacking stitches on to the variety of hearing, these sewn temporarily to each other, and each one separately and both together tacked on to those of taste, smell, and touch, piece by piece and in no particular order . . . This is how we originate and how we are formed: a slapdash piece of work, subject to the vagaries of time and the blunders of brief opportunities. . . . Our upbringing or environment, the chain formed by the chance assembly of our genes, makes weird half-breeds of us, variables on a globally stable pattern.[16]

Serres again radically destabilizes our conventionally fixed sense of the autonomy and distinctiveness of being human, challenging us to see ourselves as part of a larger, steadily fluctuating organic (dis)order.

There is little in Scott's novelistic oeuvre that reflects such drastically dislocational posthumanism with such explicit verve; even his poetry, despite its many memorable phrases and passages, rarely approaches the sense of deep, organic interconnectedness articulated by Wordsworth and other Romantic poets.[17] Nevertheless, on a less exalted level, there are plenty of moments in Scott's prose that anticipate at least some of the spirit of posthumanism as it regards human-animal relations. Animals—especially horses and dogs, both of which Scott was known to hold in high regard—feature regularly and often prominently in the Waverley Novels. To take only one example, in *The Talisman* a dog not only plays a central role in resolving the plot (by literally sniffing out the perpetrator of the theft for which Sir Kenneth has been blamed), but also receives a ringing encomium still popular with dog lovers today.[18] Outside the fiction, Lockhart records many tales of Scott's close relations with both kinds of animals, including a horsey anecdote in which Scott opines that "these creatures have many thoughts of their own, no doubt, that we can never penetrate."[19] Not for nothing does the great gothic spire of the Scott Monument in Edinburgh shelter a marble statue of Scott's dog, Maida, seated at her owner's feet. Would it be going too far to see in these aspects of Scott's life and work evidence of what Donna Haraway calls the ever-present "knot of species co-shaping one another in layers of reciprocating complexity all the way down"?[20]

There is another strand of posthumanism, however, which takes its cues from a different source in the work of Deleuze and Guattari. Their concept of the machine is introduced in the *Anti-Oedipus: Capitalism and Schizophrenia*, a critique of what they see as the implicit collaboration of psychoanalysis and capitalism to channel desire into normative, socially productive directions. By redescribing the human body as an "assemblage" of parts, each with its own capacities for production and consumption, rather than as a totalizing (and therefore implicitly dualistic or transcendent) organism, Deleuze and Guattari show that its capabilities outrun what either psychoanalysis or capitalism presumes and allows. The body as a "desiring machine," in turn, becomes one node in any number of larger networks of body-machines. Although these networks are not random, neither can they be known in advance: "Desiring-machines are binary machines, obeying a binary law or set of rules governing associations: one machine is always coupled with another. The productive synthesis, the production of production, is inherently connective in nature . . . Every 'object' presupposes the continuity of a flow; every flow, the fragmentation of the object."[21] Furthermore, in the "third stage" between flow and fragmentation, Deleuze and Guattari see the possibility of what they famously call the "body without organs": an internally undifferentiated body, which is, therefore, profoundly "unproductive" by the normative standards of psychoanalysis and capitalism.[22] The body without organs, in other words, is the ultimate desiring-machine whose productions and consumptions can be neither regulated nor canalized; hence, Deleuze and Guattari associate it with the figure of the schizophrenic, the subject whose unruly, even unknowable desires (whether by design or impulse) resist smooth insertion into the circuits of capital and vital exploitation that Deleuze and Guattari identify with the State.

Thanks to its highly poetic style as well as its profusion of ideas, *Anti-Oedipus* (like its theoretical "sequel," *A Thousand Plateaus*) provides posthumanists with a rich variety of critical directions to explore. As humanity's reliance on technological prostheses (from artificial limbs and pacemakers to cell phones, GPS, and beyond) becomes ever greater, Deleuze and Guattari's concept of the body-as-machine has come to seem more literal than metaphorical. In this vein, Haraway's "Cyborg Manifesto" is probably still the best-known re-envisioning of how our increasingly technologized bodies can, by their very "unnaturalness," become sites of resistance to the hegemonic values and forces of Western patriarchy.[23] In truth, the melding and, by extension, the blurring of the lines between man and machine has been going on for several centuries; indeed, the Enlightened era that produced the Cartesian dualism which, Haraway argues, is deeply threatened by the figure of the cyborg, also made possible many of the scientific, technological, and theoretical advances which, in turn, have facilitated our current posthuman moment. Not only such paradigm-shifting technologies as the spinning jenny (invented in 1764) and the steam engine (first produced in 1775), but also Charles

Babbage's early nineteenth-century prototypes of the earliest programmable computers ("difference" and "analytical engines") and the concurrent vogue for automata of various sizes, shapes, and dispositions have their roots in the Enlightenment.[24]

Of course, robots, computers, and cybernetic technology all fail to appear in the Waverley Novels; given their mostly historical settings, even the cutting-edge technologies of Scott's own day are also largely absent from his fictions. But, Scott clearly shared his era's interest in technological progress, as he had his outwardly baronial mansion, Abbotsford, equipped with state-of-the-art gas lighting and a pneumatic bell system.[25] Furthermore, his characters frequently make use of a variety of historically appropriate technologies that significantly enhance, augment, or otherwise alter their "natural" human senses, especially optical devices such as eyeglasses, magnifying glasses, and telescopes. One of the early scenes in Scott's novel of early seventeenth-century London, *The Fortunes of Nigel* (1822), even features the two young apprentices of the king's watchmaker, David Ramsay, enticing customers to his booth with cries of "What d'ye lack, sir? What d'ye lack, madam? – Barnacles [i.e. spectacles], watches, clocks?"[26] Although space forbids a fuller exposition, this moment is arguably emblematic of the novel's broader interest in differentiating between initial or surface appearances and deeper or more magnified ones, a theme worked out through the fates of both its eponymous hero and its primary historical personage, James I. Such an approach would acquire additional dimensions in light of media theorist Friedrich Kittler's description of "the results of this arming of the eye with glasses and lenses, telescopes and microscopes in the seventeenth century: the postulate of the visibility of all things collapsed under the evidence of the invisibly small under the microscope – like spermatozoa – and the invisibly large through the telescope – like the phases of Venus or the rings of Saturn."[27]

Elsewhere, Scott demonstrates his familiarity with one of the most popular contrivances of his day, the automaton, when two mechanical lions appear to menace the eponymous hero of his late novel, *Count Robert of Paris* (1831). As Ian Duncan notes, this remarkable scene at the emperor's palace in eleventh-century Constantinople begins with Count Robert smashing an automated lion he has mistaken for a live animal, continues with him encountering and eventually killing a real tiger, and concludes with the introduction of an orangutan named Sylvan who (like Rob Roy) displays an unsettling mixture of human and simian characteristics.[28] Moreover, in a telling detail that dovetails with my earlier discussion of the antianthropocentrism of posthumanist theory, it is Sylvan, not the Count, who lingers over the dead tiger: "Meantime the creature . . . at length discovered the body of the tiger, – touched it, stirred it, with many strange motions, and seemed to lament and wonder at its death."[29] When an animal displays more visible grief than a human at the death of another creature, we are clearly approaching the "open" realm of the posthuman described by Agamben as the "zone of indeterminacy" where "the two terms collapse upon each other . . . and in [their] place something appears for which we seem to lack even a name."[30]

There is at least one more branch of posthumanism that deserves our attention, which we can briefly access by returning to my earlier discussion of Deleuze and Guattari's concept of the body as desiring-machine. Even as the body without organs resists normative demands for production and consumption, it is simultaneously "plugged into" those circuits such that "a connection with another machine is always established, along a transverse path."[31] By the time of *A Thousand Plateaus*, this idea of the machine-system has both fragmented and metastasized, creating a cluster of related concepts. (This is fitting, given that Deleuze and Guattari elsewhere assert that the philosopher's primary task is to create concepts that can be developed in various unexpected ways.[32]) One of their best known is the rhizome, a model for the kind of decentralized network in which "any point . . . can be connected to anything other, and must be," and that "ceaselessly establishes connections between semiotic chains, organizations of power, and circumstances relative to the arts, sciences, and social struggles."[33] Another is the related idea of "smooth space" (which also recalls the body without organs of *Anti-Oedipus*), a space not of homogeneity but rather of "the smallest deviation, the minimum excess . . . Smooth space is a field without conduits or channels. . . . [It] is wedded to a very particular type of multiplicity: nonmetric, acentered, rhizomatic multiplicities that occupy space without 'counting' it."[34] Smooth space is qualitatively different from striated space—segmented, regulated, hierarchical—that lends itself to (and is in turn produced by) relations of exploitation and oppression. As Gerald Raunig observes, especially in smooth spaces, the very distinction between human and machine begins productively to collapse:

> It is no longer a matter of confronting man with machine to estimate possible or impossible correspondences, extensions, and substitutions of the one or the other . . . but rather of concatenations, of how man becomes a piece with the machine or with other things in order to constitute a machine. The "other things" may be animals, tools, other people, statements, signs or desires, but they only become machines in a process of exchange, not in the paradigm of substitution.[35]

In other words, a machinic relation need not involve actual machines or technologies: whenever an individual enters into a relationship of exchange with something or someone else, a "machine" has in effect been created.

This insight is one way to bridge the gap between Deleuze and Guattari's thought, and the superficially quite different work of Bruno Latour. Although he is probably still best known to Anglo-American scholars for his revisionist histories of science, in recent years Latour's sociophilosophical theories, in particular, Actor-Network-Theory (ANT), have begun to receive increased attention. Eschewing psychoanalysis' interest in the desires of the actors involved in a given relation, as well as high theory's focus on the language in and through which actions are conducted or described, ANT aims to avoid either overestimating the importance of individual motivation or denying any meaningful "external referent."[36] Instead, it pays attention first and foremost to the associations or connections between any kind of actor, human or otherwise, in the social sphere: in short, anything that can have an effect on anything else. Latour's term for these entities, "actants" (borrowed from formalist literary theory), thus purposefully includes immaterial entities such as values and fictions, as well as material things such as people, animals, ideas, and institutions. By seeking to trace and uncover the networks that link various actants, rather than "to marginalize them or segment them into three distinct sets: facts, power, and discourse," ANT aims to describe, and thus to understand, the real complexity of the world in which we live and act.[37] By refusing preemptively to grant humans more agency than nonhuman actants in a given network, moreover, ANT bears both ontological and epistemological similarities to the "object oriented ontology," "flat ontology," or "speculative realism"—all three terms are currently in use—of such innovative and increasingly influential philosophers as Levi Bryant, Graham Harman, and Quentin Meillassoux, as well as to the work of fellow "science studies" scholars like Isabelle Stengers.[38]

What would it entail, were we to take seriously the machine-like qualities and capabilities of human communities, the agency of objects, or the networks of both people and things in Scott's Waverley Novels? It might mean revisiting the mob at the start of *The Heart of Mid-Lothian*, to see what traits emerge when a human mass becomes more than the sum of its parts; or reconsidering the relations between (inorganic) memorials and other kinds of bearers of history, animate and inanimate, in *The Tale of Old Morality*; or revising our view of the significance of seemingly extrinsic scenes of spectacle, like the series of historical pageants performed for Queen Elizabeth in *Kenilworth* (1821). It might even mean revaluing a work like *Reliquiae Trotcosienses*, Scott's quasifictionalized account of the contents of Abbotsford's halls and bookshelves, written during the series of strokes he suffered in 1830–31, but suppressed and lost until recently. Some of this work has already been started by other critics; I hope the kinds of attempts I have made in this book to connect Scott's fiction with contemporary theoretical tools and insights will facilitate and spur much more.[39]

Latour's ANT, along with several other similarly oriented approaches—DeLanda's process philosophy, Niklas Luhmann's systems theory, and Immanuel Wallerstein's world-systems analysis, for example—represent a significant departure from the linguistically oriented, hermeneutics of suspicion-based theories that continue to hold sway.[40] My brief consideration of the contemporary theory that is emerging on the other side of the linguistic turn would not be complete, however, without some discussion of the increasingly influential philosophical writings of Alain Badiou. More than any other theorist surveyed in this book, Badiou unabashedly positions himself on the side of universal truths, even calling himself a neo-Platonist in some respects; as he asserts in a virtual rejoinder to the majority of contemporary theorists (although not to speculative realists like his protégé Meillassoux): "There are only bodies and languages, except that there are truths."[41] Without going deeply into the complex and provocative details of Badiou's mathematically supported ontology, laid out in his two major treatises *Being and Event* and *Logics of Worlds*, it must suffice here to note that for Badiou, the proper work of philosophy is neither more nor less than to explain how "truths" enter the world in one of four "domains": art, politics, science, and love.[42] Unlike Plato's Ideas, Badiou's truths are not ahistorical, transcendent, or self-sufficient; instead, they emerge from (although they cannot by derived from) specific situations, are thoroughly immanent, and require individuals to commit themselves to them in order to be made manifest.[43] Indeed, for Badiou, subjectivity is something that one discovers, or assumes, precisely by becoming militantly faithful to the event of a truth's appearance in the world—an appearance, moreover, that both supplements and renders infinitely open the situation from which it emerges.[44]

What might happen, were we to test Badiou's theories (even merely as I have sketched them) against the picture of subjectivity with which this book began, that is, against the narrative development of Edward Waverley, Scott's first novelistic protagonist? I suspect that, seen from Badiou's perspective, Waverley's well-known awakening from the "romance" of the Jacobite past into the "reality" of Hanoverian present would appear more as an act of cowardice than of maturity: a rejection of the alternative truths opened by the possibility of a new dispensation, and a flight back to the coordinates of the present situation as it is already constructed. But, would the 1745 Rebellion even qualify as an authentic "Event" in Badiou's philosophy? For Badiou, the authentic political Event must hold out the possibility of radical freedom through the egalitarian restructuring of the previous situation (or State, taken in both its historico-political and mathematical connotations). To achieve this, says Badiou, several further criteria must be met: the political Event must be "ontologically collective to the extent that it provides a virtual vehicle for a virtual summoning of all"; it must take the measure of the existing State (thus demystifying its appearance of uncountable/unaccountable power); and it must be oriented toward infinity, that is, toward "deliberation about the possible."[45] The 1745 Jacobite uprising, as Scott depicts it in *Waverley*, arguably fulfills the first and third of these criteria—theoretically, anyone can join it; it certainly reveals the potential weakness of the Hanoverian regime—but as an attempt to restore the Stuarts to the British throne, it falls far short of Badiou's lofty requirement that the authentic political Event be oriented toward the new. It fails to rend open—or, in even more Badiouian terms, to render infinitely open—the artificial closure of its contemporary situation. Of course, as we saw in Chapter 1, *Waverley* lacks the courage even to remain faithful to this inauthentic Event, abandoning the Jacobites at an opportune moment that ironically allows him to triumph even as their rebellion fails. It is hard to imagine a protagonist less authentically committed (or "militantly faithful," to use one of Badiou's favored expressions) to a cause than Waverley.

Let me conclude this admittedly inconclusive—or in a more affirmative Badouvian register, this self-consciously "open"—conclusion by focusing on an oft-overlooked moment in *Waverley*: the end of the novel's penultimate chapter. Following the near-magical recovery of the Baron's traditional wine cup, which he fills to offer his teary toast to the "Prosperity of the united houses of Waverley-Honour and Bradwardine," Scott's narrator draws the proverbial curtain with a fond farewell: "It only remains for me to say, that as no wish was ever uttered with more affectionate sincerity, there are few which, allowing for the necessary mobility of human events, have been, upon the whole, more happily fulfilled."[46] Scott joins his own character, in other words, in completing the novel's "happily ever after" conclusion. Yet, there is something odd about this unnecessarily doubled moment: given that the romance of Waverley's story was said to have ended, and his real life to have begun, back on the shores of Ulswater, it seems surprising for Scott to condone such a notably generic, "romantic"-sounding final sentiment. But perhaps that is precisely the point. Perhaps Scott is well aware that it is far easier to make one's peace with the status quo than to attempt the Badiouian task of "punch[ing] a 'hole' in [the] knowledges" that constitute the present situation.[47] Far from being the misty-eyed idealist he was for too long accused of being—but equally far from being the calculating opportunist that some less generous recent critics have claimed—it seems to me that Scott here shows himself characteristically, equally attuned to human folly and (post)human aspirations.

As I hope I have demonstrated in the foregoing chapters, the Waverley Novels continue to offer us—indeed, to challenge us with—a richly diverse archive of ways of thinking about ourselves, our history, and our collective modernity. To take up that offer and that challenge—a challenge that, I hope I've also demonstrated, can be productively met through the critical insights afforded by contemporary theory—is a uniquely pleasurable responsibility.[48] It means becoming part of the extended "critical generation" that Scott prophetically (albeit ironically) hails at the end of *Waverley*'s introductory chapter: an introduction that is a gateway to the future as well as to the past.[49]

Notes

Introduction

1 William St Clair's research confirms what many Scott scholars and admirers have long suspected: by sales figures alone, Scott was easily the most popular author, not only of his lifetime (1771–1832), but also of much of the Victorian era. See St Clair, *The Reading Nation in the Romantic Period* (Cambridge: Cambridge University Press, 2004).

2 Walter Scott, *The Journal of Sir Walter Scott*, ed. W. E. K. Anderson (Edinburgh: Canongate Books, 1998b), 3.

3 Ibid., 132.

4 Sir Leslie Stephen, *Hours in a Library*, Vol. 1 (London: Smith, Elder, and Co., 1892), 137–68; E. M. Forster, *Aspects of the Novel* (New York: Houghton Mifflin Harcourt, 1985), 30.

5 Northrop Frye, *The Secular Scripture: A Study of the Structure of Romance* (Boston: Harvard University Press, 1976), 5. Daiches' contributions to Scott studies are more substantial; see especially his two-part article, "Scott's Achievement as a Novelist," *Nineteenth Century Fiction* 6.2 and 6.3 (1951): 81–95 and 153–73.

6 Georg Lukács, *The Historical Novel*, trans. Hannah and Stanley Mitchell (London: Merlin Press, 1962), 36.

7 Alexander Welsh, *The Hero of the Waverley Novels: With New Essays on Scott* (Princeton: Princeton Press, 1992). The original edition of Welsh's book was published by Yale University Press in 1962. The other major Scott studies from the 1960s are Francis R. Hart, *Scott's Novels: The Plotting of Historical Survival* (Charlottesville: University of Virginia Press, 1966) and A. O. J. Cockshut, *The Achievement of Sir Walter Scott* (New York: New York University Press, 1969).

8 See, in chronological order, Graham McMaster, *Scott and Society* (Cambridge: Cambridge University Press, 1981); Harry E. Shaw, *The Forms of Historical Fiction: Sir Walter Scott and His Successors* (Ithaca: Cornell University Press, 1983); Jane Millgate, *Walter Scott: The Making of the Novelist* (Toronto: University of Toronto Press, 1984); Judith Wilt, *Secret Leaves: The Novels of Sir Walter Scott* (Chicago: University of Chicago Press, 1985); James Kerr, *Fiction against History: Scott as Storyteller* (Cambridge: Cambridge University Press, 1989).

9 Of the many books that could be cited here, a good recent starting point is *The Age of Cultural Revolutions: Britain and France, 1750–1820*, eds Colin Jones and Dror Wahrman (Berkeley: University of California Press, 2002). I also continue to find valuable Marilyn Butler's *Romantics, Rebels, and Reactionaries: English Literature and its Background, 1760–1830* (Oxford and London: Oxford University Press, 1981). On the financial transformations of the period, including Britain's 24-year experiment with an inconvertible paper currency from 1797 to 1821, see Matthew Rowlinson, *Real Money and Romanticism* (Cambridge: Cambridge University Press, 2010).

10 Ina Ferris, *The Achievement of Literary Authority: Gender, History, and the Waverley Novels* (Ithaca: Cornell University Press, 1991); Ian Duncan, *Modern Romance and Transformations of the Novel* (Cambridge: Cambridge University Press, 1992); Robert Crawford, *Devolving English Literature* (Oxford: Oxford University Press, 1992); Fiona Robertson, *Legitimate Histories: Scott, Gothic, and the Authorities of Fiction* (Oxford: Clarendon, 1994); Katie Trumpener, *Bardic Nationalism: The Romantic Novel and the British Empire* (Princeton: Princeton University Press, 1997); James Chandler, *England in 1819: The Politics of Literary Culture and the Case of Romantic Historicism* (Chicago: University of Chicago Press, 1998).

11 Catherine Jones, *Literary Memory: Scott's Waverley Novels and the Psychology of Narrative* (Lewisburg, PA: Bucknell University Press, 2003); Caroline McCracken-Flesher, *Possible Scotlands: Walter Scott and the Story of Tomorrow* (Oxford: Oxford University Press, 2005); Julian Meldon D'Arcy, *Subversive Scott: The Waverley Novels and Scottish Nationalism* (Reykjavik: Vigdís Finbogádottir Institute and University of Iceland Press, 2005); Andrew Lincoln, *Walter Scott and Modernity* (Edinburgh: University of Edinburgh Press, 2007). The outlier among the studies of the 1990s that returned Scott to critical prominence, ironically, is John Sutherland's *The Life of Walter Scott: A Critical Biography* (Oxford: Blackwell, 1995), which seems determined to perpetuate the Modernist myth of Scott as little better than a hack writer.

12 Ian Duncan, *Scott's Shadow: The Novel in Romantic Edinburgh* (Princeton: University of Princeton Press, 2007). See also Penny Fielding, *Scotland and the Fictions of Geography: North Britain, 1760–1830* (Cambridge: Cambridge University Press, 2008); Evan Gottlieb, *Feeling British: Sympathy and National Identity in Scottish and English Writing, 1707–1832* (Lewisburg, PA: Bucknell University Press, 2007); Yoon Sun Lee, *Nationalism and Irony: Burke, Scott, Carlyle* (Oxford: Oxford University Press, 2004); Kenneth McNeil, *Scotland, Britain, Empire: Writing the Highlands, 1760–1860* (Columbus: Ohio State University Press, 2007); Matthew Wickman, *The Ruins of Experience: Scotland's 'Romantick' Highlands and the Birth of the Modern Witness* (Philadelphia: University of Pennsylvania Press, 2007).

13 See *Scott, Scotland, and Romantic Nationalism*, eds Ian Duncan, Ann Weirda Rowland, and Charles Snodgrass, special issue of *Studies in Romanticism* 40.1 (2001): 3–168; *Romantic Enlightenment: Sir Walter Scott and the Politics of History*, ed. Bruce Beiderwell, special issue of *European*

Romantic Review 13.3 (2002): 223–324; *Approaches to Teaching Scott's Waverley Novels*, eds Evan Gottlieb and Ian Duncan (New York: Modern Language Association of America, 2009); *Romancing Scotland*, ed. Marshall Brown, special issue of *Modern Language Quarterly* 70.4 (December 2009): 403–525.

14 I refer especially to Richard Hill, *Picturing Scotland through the Waverley Novels: Walter Scott and the Origins of the Victorian Illustrated Novel* (Burlington, VA: Ashgate, 2010); Alison Lumsden, *Walter Scott and the Limits of Language* (Edinburgh: Edinburgh University Press, 2010); Ann Rigney, *The Afterlives of Walter Scott: Memory on the Move* (Oxford and New York: Oxford University Press, 2012); and *The Edinburgh Companion to Sir Walter Scott*, ed. Fiona Robertson (Edinburgh: Edinburgh University Press, 2012).

15 Slavoj Žižek, *Looking Awry: An Introduction to Jacques Lacan through Popular Culture* (Cambridge, MA: The MIT Press, 1991), vii–viii. The title of my introduction also echoes that of Žižek's edited volume *Everything You Always Wanted to Know about Lacan . . . But were Afraid to Ask Hitchcock* (London: Verso, 1992b).

16 See St Clair, *Reading Nation in the Romantic Period*, esp. 172–5.

17 Robert Miles, *Romantic Misfits* (Basingstoke and New York: Palgrave Macmillan, 2008), 134.

18 For other important recent considerations of the Romantic novel, see for example, Miranda Burgess, *British Fiction and the Production of Social Order, 1740–1830* (Cambridge: Cambridge University Press, 2000); Gary Kelly, *English Fiction of the Romantic Period, 1789–1830* (London and New York: Longman, 1989); Deidre Shauna Lynch, *The Economy of Character: Novels, Market Culture, and the Business of Inner Meaning* (Chicago and London: University of Chicago Press, 1998); Trumpener, *Bardic Nationalism*; *Recognizing the Romantic Novel: New Histories of British Fiction, 1780–1830*, eds Jill Heydt-Stevenson and Charlotte Sussman (Liverpool: University of Liverpool Press, 2008); *The Cambridge Companion to Fiction in the Romantic Period*, eds Richard Maxwell and Katie Trumpener (Cambridge and New York: Cambridge University Press, 2008).

19 For more on these and other developments that made Britain uniquely capable of achieving a large measure of global dominance in the century following 1815, see John Belich, *Replenishing the Earth: The Settler Revolution and the Rise of the Anglo-World, 1783–1939* (Oxford and New York: Oxford University Press, 2009), esp. 51–8.

20 Jacques Rancière, "The Distribution of the Sensible," in *The Politics of Aesthetics*, trans. Gabriel Rockhill (London and New York: Continuum, 2004a), 33.

21 Often reluctant to acknowledge his literary debts to female novelists, Scott was nevertheless preceded to some degree in the genre of the historical novel by, for example, Maria Edgeworth's *Castle Rackrent* (1800), which he openly admired, and Jane Porter's *The Scottish Chiefs* (1810), which he did not.

22 Scott, *The Betrothed*, ed. J. B. Ellis (Edinburgh: Edinburgh University Press, 2009), 4.

23 The classic modern exposition of Scott's views of creative labor is Kathryn Sutherland's "Fictional Economies: Adam Smith, Walter Scott and the Nineteenth-century Novel," *ELH* 54 (1987): 97–127. Scott's ties to and knowledge of the ideas of the previous generation of Scottish Enlighteners have been well established; see, for example, Peter Garside, "Scott and the 'Philosophical Historians'," *Journal of the History of Ideas* 36 (1975): 497–512. On the subject of Scott and philosophy, see also Richard Maxwell, "Inundations of Time: A Definition of Scott's Originality," *ELH* 68.2 (2001): 419–68. As Richard Hill has recently demonstrated, the material production of any given Waverley Novel—especially after they began to be illustrated— required a small army of illustrators, engravers, printers, and publishers (see *Picturing Scotland*, esp. Chapters 1–4).

24 Jerome McGann, "Walter Scott's Romantic postmodernity," in *Scotland and the Borders of Romanticism*, eds Leith Davis, Ian Duncan, and Janet Sorensen (Cambridge: Cambridge University Press, 2004), 116.

25 Jonathan Culler, *Literary Theory: A Very Short Introduction* (Oxford: Oxford University Press, 2000), 5.

26 Peter Wagner, *Modernity: Understanding the Present* (Oxford and Malden, MA: Polity, 2012), 22.

27 Cf. Andrew Piper's description of the historical novel genre, especially in Scott's hands, as the literary place "where the intersection of fictionality and facticity common to all novels was most intensely compressed": *Dreaming in Books: The Making of the Bibliographic Imagination in the Romantic Age* (Chicago and London: University of Chicago Press, 2009), 109.

28 For thorough introductions to the importance of the events of 1968 for French thought and culture, see Julian Bourg, *From Revolution to Ethics: May 1968 and Contemporary French Thought* (Montreal and Kingston, Ontario: McGill-Queens University Press, 2007); Kristin Ross, *May '68 and its Afterlives* (Chicago: University of Chicago Press, 2002). On the decline of "high theory," see, for example, Peter Osborne, "Philosophy after Theory: Transdisciplinarity and the New," in *Theory After 'Theory,'* eds Jane Elliott and Derek Attridge (London and New York: Routledge, 2011), 19–33.

29 Peter Dews' *Logics of Disintegration: Post-Structuralist Thought and the Claims of Critical Theory* remains one of the best critical surveys of "high theory" (London and New York: Verso, 1987). For a more beginner-friendly text, I continue to recommend Madan Sarup, *An Introduction to Post-Structuralism and Postmodernism*, 2nd edn (Athens, GA: University of Georgia Press, 1993).

30 François Cusset's *French Theory: How Foucault, Derrida, Deleuze, & Co. Transformed the Intellectual Life of the United States* (trans. Jeff Fort [Minneapolis and London: University of Minnesota Press, 2008]) provides an accessible but detailed account of the "rise and fall" of "[High] French Theory" in America.

31 Other contemporary theoretical topics that I considered when planning this book include globality, mediality, sexuality, (dis)ability, and transversality. The relative absence of such important Waverley Novels as *Guy Mannering* and *The Tale of Old Mortality* is not meant to be significant; interested readers may consult recent interpretations of them in, for example, McCracken-Flesher, *Possible Scotlands*, 23–5 and 46–50; Lincoln, *Walter Scott and Modernity*, 91–105 and 155–69; and the essays by Antony J. Hasler and Tara Ghoshal Wallace in *Approaches to Teaching Scott's Waverley Novels*, eds Gottlieb and Duncan, 140–9 and 170–6.

32 In this way, I avoid the common errors of generalizing about Scott on the basis of a single novel (usually *Waverley*) and of paying critical attention only to the Scottish-themed Waverley Novels.

Chapter 1

1 Welsh, *The Hero of the Waverley Novels*, xiv.

2 As Michael Hardt and Antonio Negri point out in *Empire*, the political visions of Rousseau and Hobbes converge in their shared commitment to a vision of modern sovereignty as "the alienation of . . . single wills toward the sovereignty of the state" (Cambridge, MA and London: Harvard University Press, 2000, 85). I discuss their ideas at more length in Chapter 5.

3 The phrase "Sixty years since" indicates that the novel's main events take place before and during the outbreak of the 1745 Jacobite Rebellion. This dating, in turn, relies on Scott's account of initially having begun the novel in 1805, only to put it aside for close to a decade before serendipitously finding it again. This highly Romantic story of creative impulse, stasis, and renewal has been questioned by literary historians; see, for example, Peter Garside, "Hidden Origins of Scott's *Waverley*," *Nineteenth Century Literature* 46.1 (June 1991): 30–53.

4 A succinct but thorough account of the most significant historical events informing Scott's "Scottish" Waverley Novels is provided by Douglas Mack and Suzanne Gilbert, "Scottish history in the Waverley Novels," in *Approaches to Teaching Scott's Waverley Novels*, eds Gottlieb and Duncan, 26–37.

5 Walter Scott, *Waverley*, ed. Claire Lamont (New York: Oxford University Press, 1986), 10. Wherever possible, I cite widely available, scholarly paperback editions of Scott's novels; in all other cases, I cite the hardcover volumes of the Edinburgh Edition of the Waverley Novels (EEWN), an invaluable resource for Scott scholars. Casual readers should be aware, however, that the EEWN reconstructs Scott's novels as he (may have) originally intended them, rather than as they were actually published. Prior to the EEWN (and the Penguin Classics paperbacks based on them), most modern reprints of Scott's novels were based on the "Magnum Opus" editions that Scott began to publish near the end of his career.

6 See Ronald L. Meek, "The Scottish Contribution to Marxist Sociology," in *"Economics and Ideology" and Other Essays* (London: Chapman and Hall, 1967), 34–66.

7 Scott, *Waverley*, 4.

8 Ibid., 4.

9 Cf. Franco Moretti's tendentious claim that the "English [sic] . . . culture of stability and conformity" mitigates against an authentic *bildungsroman* tradition, in *The Way of the World: The Bildungsroman in European Culture*, new edn (London and New York: Verso, 2000), 181.

10 See Slavoj Žižek, *The Sublime Object of Ideology* (New York and London: Verso, 1989), 11–53 and also, for example, *Enjoy Your Symptom! Jacques Lacan in Hollywood and Out* (New York and London: Routledge, 1992a).

11 See, for example, Žižek, *Welcome to the Desert of the Real: Five Essays on September 11 and Related Dates* (London and New York: Verso, 2002b), 31–2.

12 For one of Žižek's most complete discussions of the ideological valences of psychoanalytic theories of fantasy, see his "Between Symbolic Fiction and Phantasmatic Spectre: Toward a Lacanian Theory of Ideology," in *Interrogating the Real*, eds Rex Butler and Scott Stephens (London and New York: Continuum, 2005), 229–48.

13 Scott, *Waverley*, 14–15.

14 Ibid., 15. The danger of indiscriminate reading, especially for women and children, was a consistent theme in eighteenth-century literary criticism; see, for example, William B. Warner, *Licensing Entertainment: The Elevation of Novel Reading in Britain, 1684–1750* (Berkeley and Los Angeles: University of California Press, 1998).

15 Cf. Duncan's influential observation that "The old commonplace of an antithetical relation between romance and reality, invoked by the novel in its own apologies of origin, produces a new, dialectical figure of romance as the fulcrum against which – positioned on its edge, between inside and out – reality can be turned around" (*Modern Romance* 2).

16 In a literary vein, M. M. Bakhtin's concept of the chronotope (space-time image) is very pertinent here; see his *The Dialogic Imagination*, ed. and trans. Caryl Emerson and Michael Holquist (Austin: University of Texas Press, 1981), 84.

17 Scott, *Waverley*, 32.

18 Ibid., 33.

19 Ibid, 33.

20 Ibid., 80.

21 Žižek, *Sublime Object of Ideology*, 49.

22 Scott, *Waverley*, 105.

23 Ibid., 192.

24 Ibid., 193.

25 Žižek, *For They Know Not What They Do: Enjoyment as a Political Factor*, 2nd edn (London and New York: Verso, 2002a), 11.

26 Scott, *Waverley*, 156.

27 Ibid., 221.

28 Žižek, "Connections of the Freudian Field to Philosophy and Popular Culture," in *Interrogating the Real*, eds Butler and Stephens, 59.

29 For a helpful discussion of the "unreality" of the Big Other, see Alenka Zupançiç, *The Odd One In: On Comedy* (Cambridge, MA and London: The MIT Press, 2008), 15–18.

30 On this point, see Žižek, "'The Most Sublime of Hysterics': Hegel with Lacan," in *Interrogating the Real*, eds Butler and Stephens, 47.

31 Scott, *Waverley*, 283.

32 Celeste Langan, "'The Poetry of Pure Memory': Teaching Scott's Novels in the Context of Romanticism," in *Approaches to Teaching Scott's Waverley Novels*, eds Gottlieb and Duncan, 69.

33 Žižek, *In Defense of Lost Causes* (London and New York: Verso, 2008), 25.

34 Žižek, *Tarrying with the Negative: Kant, Hegel, and the Critique of Ideology* (Durham, NC and London: Duke University Press, 1993), 23.

35 There are notable similarities between this formulation and Giorgio Agamben's "state of exception," which I explore in Chapter 4.

36 Žižek, *Tarrying with the Negative*, 23.

37 Žižek, *In Defense of Lost Causes*, 100.

38 See, for example, Paul Hamilton, *Metaromanticism: Aesthetics, Literature, Theory* (Chicago and London: University of Chicago Press, 2003), 115–38.

39 Scott, *Waverley*, 325, 332.

40 Ibid., 338.

41 Žižek, *Sublime Object of Ideology*, 29. See also Peter Sloterdijk, *Critique of Cynical Reason*, trans. Michael Eldred (Minneapolis: University of Minnesota Press, 1987).

42 Scott, *Waverley*, 309.

43 Ibid., 338.

44 Žižek, "Hegel with Lacan," 43.

45 For a literalization of such mapping, see Franco Moretti, *Atlas of the European Novel, 1800–1900* (London and New York: Verso, 1998), 37–41.

46 Scott, *Ivanhoe*, ed. Ian Duncan (New York: Oxford University Press, 1996), 14.

47 Ibid., 25. See Dror Warhman, *The Making of the Modern Self: Identity and Culture in Eighteenth-Century England* (New Haven and London: Yale University Press, 2004).

48 Scott, *Ivanhoe*, 17–18.

49 See, for example, Jones, *Literary Memory*; Lincoln, *Scott and Modernity*; Lumsden, *Scott and the Limits of Language*; McCracken-Flesher, *Possible Scotlands*.

50 Joan Copjec, "Introduction," *Supposing the Subject*, ed. Copjec (London and New York: Verso, 1994b), ix. See also Copjec, *Read my Desire: Lacan against the Historicists* (Cambridge, MA: MIT Press, 1994a).

51 Scott, *Ivanhoe*, 52.

52 Ibid., 39, 498. For these and other matters of historical accuracy (or lack thereof) in the novel, see Graham Tulloch's Introduction and Notes to the Edinburgh Edition of *Ivanhoe* (London and New York: Penguin, 2000a), xi–xxix, 403–86.

53   Scott, *Ivanhoe*, 498.

54   Ibid., 77.

55   Ibid., 98.

56   Ibid., 433.

57   David Simpson, "'Which is the merchant here? and which the Jew?': Friends and Enemies in Walter Scott's Crusader Novels," *Studies in Romanticism* 47 (Winter 2008): 441.

58   Scott, *Ivanhoe*, ed. Duncan, 81–2.

59   Ibid., 433.

60   Žižek, *Sublime Object*, 125.

61   Ibid., 95.

62   Ibid., 127.

63   Scott, *Ivanhoe*, 431.

64   Žižek, *Welcome to the Desert of the Real*, 152.

65   Ibid., 153.

66   Žižek, *The Fragile Absolute: or, Why is the Christian legacy worth fighting for?* (London and New York: Verso, 2000), 150. Filmic examples cited by Žižek include when Keanu Reeves' character in *Speed* (1994; dir. De Bont) shoots his partner in the leg to free him from the villain's grasp and when (in a flashback) Kevin Spacey's character in *The Usual Suspects* (1995; dir. Singer) shoots his wife and child when they are being held hostage by rival mob members, so that he can then ruthlessly pursue his enemies.

67   Žižek, "Heiner Müller out of joint," in *The Universal Exception: Selected Writings, Volume Two*, eds Rex Butler and Scott Stephens (New York and London: Continuum, 2006b), 50. For Žižek's criticism of the theories of political resistance in the writings of his fellow contemporary theorists Badiou, Rancière, and Etienne Balibar, see *The Ticklish Subject: The Absent Centre of Political Ontology* (New York and London: Verso, 1999), 171–244.

68   Scott, *Ivanhoe*, 431.

69   See Duncan, Introduction to *Ivanhoe*, xxvi.

70   See Žižek, *The Parallax View* (Cambridge, MA and London: The MIT Press, 2006a), esp. 20–4.

71   Scott, *Ivanhoe*, 502.

72   See Duncan, "Introduction" to *Ivanhoe*, xxv–xxvi n. 28; Rigney, *Afterlives of Walter Scott*, 98–104.

73   Žižek, *Parallax View*, 8.

Chapter 2

1   John Gibson Lockhart, *The Life of Sir Walter Scott* (London: J. M. Dent & Sons, 1906). This Everyman edition reprints the abridgement Lockhart himself prepared for publication in 1848.

2 Quoted in Lamont, Introduction to *Waverley*, ed. Lamont, vii.

3 Ferris, *Achievement of Literary Authority*, 80.

4 Quoted in Ferris, *Achievement of Literary Authority*, 83.

5 William Hazlitt, "Scott and the spirit of the age in *New Monthly Magazine* 1825," in John O. Hayden, *Sir Walter Scott: The Critical Heritage* (London: Routledge, 1995), 284.

6 Julia Wedgwood, "'The romantic reaction,' *Contemporary Review* 1878," in Hayden, 502.

7 Lukàcs, *Historical Novel*, 40.

8 In addition to many of the articles in the special issues of *Studies in Romanticism*, *European Romantic Review*, and *Modern Language Quarterly* devoted to Scott, see also Mike Goode, "Dryasdust Antiquarianism and Soppy Masculinity: The Waverley Novels and the Gender of History," *Representations* 82 (2003): 52–86. For a brief introduction to the Romantic-era historical novel as a genre, see Richard Maxwell, "The historical novel," in *The Cambridge Companion to Fiction in the Romantic Period*, eds Maxwell and Trumpener, 65–87. On Scott's relation to Romantic historicism, see Ann Rigney, *Imperfect Histories: The Elusive Past and the Legacy of Romantic Historicism* (Ithaca, NY: Cornell University Press, 2001), esp. 13–58.

9 Quoted in David West, *Continental Philosophy: An Introduction*, 2nd edn (Cambridge and Malden, MA: Polity, 2010), 41.

10 Michel de Certeau, *The Writing of History*, trans. Tom Conley (New York: Columbia University Press, 1988), 2; Michel Foucault, *The Order of Things: An Archaeology of the Human Sciences* (New York: Random House, 1970), xxiii; Hayden White, *Metahistory: The Historical Imagination in Nineteenth-Century Europe* (Baltimore and London: The Johns Hopkins University Press, 1973), ix.

11 Ruth Mack, *Literary Historicity: Literature and Historical Experience in Eighteenth-Century Britain* (Stanford: Stanford University Press, 2009), 3.

12 Chandler, *England in 1819*, 107. Cf. Mack's engagement with Chandler's argument on behalf of an earlier, eighteenth-century historicism in her *Literary Historicity*, 85–6.

13 Gottlieb, *Feeling British*, 181.

14 Scott, *Waverley*, 340.

15 Johannes Fabian, "Of Dogs Alive, Birds Dead, and Time to Tell a Story," in *Chronotypes: The Construction of Time*, eds John Bender and David E. Wellbery (Stanford: Stanford University Press, 1991), 186. Cf. James Buzard's chapter on *Waverley* in *Disorienting Fiction: The Autoethnographic Work of Nineteenth-Century British Novels* (Princeton: Princeton University Press, 2005), 63–104.

16 Keith Tribe, Introduction to Reinhart Koselleck, *Futures Past: On the Semantics of Historical Time*, trans. Tribe (New York: Columbia University Press, 2004), xi. This edition is a revision of Tribe's earlier 1985 translation, published by MIT Press.

17 Gérard Genette, *Paratexts: Thresholds of Interpretation*, trans. Jane E. Lewin (New York: Columbia University Press, 1997), 1.

18 Scott, *Ivanhoe*, 16. Cf. Chandler, *England in 1819*, 133–47.

19 Scott, *Ivanhoe*, 16.

20 Ibid., 16.

21 Ellen Meiksins Wood, *Liberty and Property: A Social History of Western Political Thought from Renaissance to Enlightenment* (London and New York: Verso, 2012), 2. The other generally agreed-upon elements of Western modernity that Wood identifies are commercial society (capitalism) and rationalization (technological progress).

22 Scott, *Waverley*, 5.

23 Scott, *Ivanhoe*, 18.

24 Ibid., 17–18.

25 Ibid., 22.

26 Koselleck, *Futures Past*, 11.

27 Ibid., 13.

28 The question of the "rise" of secularism in the West is divisive, and Koselleck's view is by no means the only one available. For a recent and in some respects divergent perspective, see Charles Taylor, *A Secular Age* (Cambridge, MA: The Belknap Press, 2007).

29 Koselleck, *Futures Past*, 14.

30 Ibid., 15–16.

31 Ibid., 18.

32 Ibid., 21.

33 Ibid., 22.

34 Foucault, *Discipline and Punish: The Birth of the Prison*, trans. Alan Sheridan (New York: Vintage, 1977), 31.

35 Scott, *The Antiquary*, ed. David Hewitt (New York: Penguin, 1998a), 3.

36 Ibid., 21–2.

37 Ibid., 24.

38 Yoon Sun Lee, *Nationalism and Irony: Burke, Scott, Carlyle* (New York: Oxford University Press, 2004), 90–104. See also Rowlinson, *Real Money and Romanticism*, 65–86.

39 Scott, *The Antiquary*, 38.

40 Ibid., 29.

41 Ibid., 31.

42 See Hewitt's explanatory notes to *The Antiquary*, 376 n. 31.6, 31.11–12.

43 Scott, *The Antiquary*, 265.

44 Koselleck, "Social History and Conceptual History," in *The Practice of Conceptual History: Timing History, Spacing Concepts*, trans. Todd Samuel Presner et al. (Stanford: Stanford University Press, 2002), 27.

45 Scott, *The Antiquary*, 107.

46 Ibid., 356.

47 Koselleck, "Social History and Conceptual History," 28.

48 Ibid.

49 Hewitt, notes to *The Antiquary*, 402 n. 137.33.

50 Scott, *The Antiquary*, 137.

51 Ibid., 92.

52 Ibid., 92–3.

53 Koselleck, "The Eighteenth Century as the Beginning of Modernity," in *Practice of Conceptual History*, 167–8.

54 Scott, *The Antiquary*, 54.

55 See Rowlinson, *Real Money and Romanticism*, 76–7.

56 Koselleck, "Social History and Conceptual History," 23–4.

57 Scott wrote a mostly admiring review of Radcliffe's oeuvre for the Ballantyne's Novelists series introduction; see the abridgement in *Sir Walter Scott on Novelists and Fiction*, ed. Ioan Williams (New York: Barnes and Noble, 1968), 102–20. For more on Scott and the Gothic, see especially Robertson, *Scott and the Gothic*; on Scott and realism, see Harry E. Shaw, *Narrating Reality: Austen, Scott, Eliot* (Ithaca, NY: Cornell University Press, 1999), esp. 168–217.

58 David Punter, "Scottish and Irish Gothic," in *The Cambridge Companion to Gothic Fiction*, ed. Jerrold E. Hogle (New York: Cambridge University Press, 2002), 109. I discuss this episode in more detail in "Sir Walter and Plain Jane: Teaching Scott and Austen Together," in *Approaches to Teaching Scott's Waverley Novels*, eds Gottlieb and Ian Duncan, 101–4.

59 On the historical functions of the concept of "crisis," see Koselleck, "Some Questions Regarding the Conceptual History of 'Crisis,'" in *Practice of Conceptual History*, 236–47.

60 For more on *St. Ronan's Well*, see especially Burgess, *British Fiction and the Production of Social Order*, 186–234.

61 See "Historical Note," in Scott, *Redgauntlet*, ed. G. A. M. Wood with David Hewitt (London: Penguin, 2000c), 381–4.

62 Koselleck, *Futures Past*, 255

63 See Foucault's well-known assertion near the end of *The Order of Things* that "As the archaeology of our thought easily shows, man is an invention of recent date. And one perhaps nearing its end" (387).

64 Cf. Rowlinson, *Romanticism and Real Money*, 86.

65 Scott, *Redgauntlet*, 373.

66 Manuel DeLanda, *A Thousand Years of Nonlinear History* (New York: Zone Books, 1997). Page references are taken from the Swerve Editions reprint (2000).

67 DeLanda, *Intensive Science and Virtual Philosophy* (London and New York: Continuum, 2002), 4.

68 This is what Meillassoux calls "correlationism" – the idea that everything humans know about reality must be correlated through our own consciousness. See his *After Finitude: An Essay on the Necessity of Contingency*, trans. Ray Brassier (New York and London: Continuum, 2008).

69 In an interview, DeLanda explains in greater detail his belief that it is possible to attempt such descriptions, without become a naïve empiricist. See "Deleuzian Interrogations: A Conversation with Manuel DeLanda, John Protevi, and Torkild Thanem," *Tamara: Journal for Critical Organizational Inquiry* 3.4 (2004): 1–36.

70 DeLanda, *Intensive Science*, 9

71 Ibid., 10. But for a critique of what he calls the "undermining" of objects by approaches like Deleuze's and DeLanda's, see Graham Harman, *The Quadruple Object* (Winchester, UK and Washington: Zero Books, 2011), 8–10.

72 DeLanda, "Deleuzian Interrogations," 2. The inclusion of "energy" and "physical information" alongside "matter" explains why DeLanda has come to prefer the term "realist" (instead of "materialist") to describe his Deleuzean ontology.

73 DeLanda, *A Thousand Years*, 258.

74 Ibid., 258.

75 Ibid., 108.

76 DeLanda, *Deleuze: History and Science* (New York and Dresden: Atropos Press, 2010), 8.

77 Ibid., 3.

78 See DeLanda, "Emergence, Causality, and Realism," in *The Speculative Turn: Continental Materialism and Realism*, eds Levi Bryant, Nick Srnicek, and Graham Harman (Melbourne: re.press, 2011), 381; DeLanda, *Deleuze: History and Science*, 4.

79 See, for example, DeLanda, *Philosophy and Simulation: The Emergence of Synthetic Reason* (London and New York: Continuum, 2011).

80 Scott, *Redgauntlet*, 89.

81 DeLanda, *A Thousand Years*, 111.

82 Ibid., 112.

83 Scott, *Redgauntlet*, 174.

84 Ibid., 181.

85 Scott, *Redgauntlet*, 188–9.

86 Ibid., 191.

87 Ibid., 293.

88 Ibid., 320.

89 Ibid., 379.

90 This is a telling example of how Scott's representation of the transmission of genetic material is highly influenced by cultural norms (a young female character with an ugly, wrinkled forehead being highly unsatisfactory for Scott and his readers). For a more traditional reading of *Redgauntlet* as a remasculinization of Scott's writing after the relative failure of *St. Ronan's Well*, see Emily Allen, "Re-Marking Territory: *Redgauntlet* and the Restoration of Sir Walter Scott," *Studies in Romanticism* 37 (Summer 1998): 163–82.

91 DeLanda, *A Thousand Years*, 273.

92 Ibid., 274.

Chapter 3

1 See Jacques Derrida, *Of Grammatology*, trans. Gayatri Chakravorty Spivak, corrected edition (Baltimore and London: The Johns Hopkins University Press, 1997b), 158. The phrase "il n'y a pas de hors-texte" appears in the context of Derrida's discussion of Rousseau's *Confessions*, in which he explains that there is no point referring the text back to the "truth" of Rousseau's life, because "there has never been anything but writing; there have never been anything but supplements, substitutive significations which could only come forth in a chain of differential references, the 'real' supervening, and being added only while taking on meaning from an invocation of the trace and from the supplement, etc." (159). The final "etc." here, I think, indicates the lack of any finality to the open, endless chains of signification that, for Derrida, characterize human meaning-making.

2 Judith Butler, *Excitable Speech: A Politics of the Performative* (New York and London: Routledge, 1997). The context here is a gloss on Toni Morrison's 1993 Nobel Lecture in Literature.

3 Foucault, *Discipline and Punish*, 24.

4 Ibid., 194.

5 Foucault, *The History of Sexuality, Volume 1: An Introduction*, trans. Robert Hurley (New York: Random House, 1979), 45.

6 Calling Foucault's analyses of the relations between power and discourse pioneering does not mean that he is without predecessors or mentors; in addition to the work of Friedrich Nietzsche (e.g. *On the Genealogy of Morals*, trans. Walter Kaufmann [New York: Vintage, 1989]) see, among others, that of Georges Canguilhem (e.g. *The Normal and the Pathological*, trans. Carolyn R. Fawcett with Robert S. Cohen [New York: Zone Books, 1991]).

7 Foucault, "The Gay Science," interview with Jean Le Bitoux, trans. Nicole Morar and Daniel W. Smith, *Critical Inquiry* 37.3 (Spring 2011): 385–403; see esp. 389–90.

8 See, for example, Foucault, *History of Sexuality*, Vol. 1, 95–6.

9 Jeffrey T. Nealon, *Foucault Beyond Foucault: Power and its Intensifications since 1984* (Stanford: Stanford University Press, 2008), 105.

10 Butler in particular has had her disagreements with psychoanalysis; see, for example, her critiques of Freud's and Lacan's systems in *Gender Trouble: Feminism and the Subversion of Identity* (New York and London: Routledge, 1990), esp. 35–78; her criticisms of the early work of Žižek in "Arguing

with the Real," in *Bodies That Matter: On the discursive limits of "sex"*,
Routledge Classics edition (New York and London: Routledge, 2011), 139–68;
and her series of exchanges with Žižek in Judith Butler, Ernesto Laclau,
and Slavoj Žižek, *Contingency, Hegemony, Universality: Contemporary
Dialogues on the Left* (London and New York: Verso, 2000).

11 François Laruelle goes further, calling difference "The most enveloping and
comprehensive [problematic] of contemporary thought" in his *Philosophies
of Difference: A Critical Introduction to Non-philosophy*, trans. Rocco
Gangle (London and New York: Continuum, 2010), xiii.

12 Walter Scott, *Rob Roy*, ed. Ian Duncan (New York: Oxford University Press,
1998c), 5.

13 Ibid., 69.

14 Shaw, *Narrating Reality*, 36; see also his *Forms of Historical Fiction*,
128–49.

15 Although he would write parts of *Redgauntlet* in epistolary and diaristic
formats, as we have seen, *Rob Roy* is his only novel to be written entirely in
the protagonist's own voice.

16 Scott, *Rob Roy*, 95.

17 Ibid., 97.

18 Ibid., 96–8.

19 Ibid., 141–2.

20 Although he does not discuss *Rob Roy* specifically, Rowlinson's discussions
of eighteenth-century Britain's monetary system in general, and Scott's
relationship with it in particular, are valuable; see *Real Money and
Romanticism*, 33–99. For a contrasting view of economic texts (including
bills) as widely diverging from more literary forms of writing over the
same period, however, see Mary Poovey, *Genres of the Credit Economy:
Mediating Value in Eighteenth- and Nineteenth-Century Britain* (Chicago and
London: University of Chicago Press, 2008).

21 Scott, *Rob Roy*, 246.

22 Ibid., 255.

23 Ibid., 273.

24 Ibid., 273; compare to "his frame was rather beneath than above the
middle size" (254).

25 Ibid., 273.

26 See Duncan, Introduction to *Rob Roy*, xxii–xxiv; and *Scott's Shadow*, 112.

27 The *locus classicus* of the "internal colonialism" model of Anglo-Scottish
relations is Michael Hechter, *Internal Colonialism: The Celtic Fringe in British
National Development*, rev. ed. (New Brunswick, NJ: Transaction, 1999); for
strong but nuanced literary applications of this approach, see, for example,
Katie Trumpener, *Bardic Nationalism*; Janet Sorensen, *The Grammar of
Empire in Eighteenth-Century Britain* (Cambridge: Cambridge University
Press, 1999). For studies that highlight the Scots' cultural agency following
the Union, see, for example, Leith Davis, *Acts of Union: Scotland and the
Literary Negotiation of the British Nation, 1707–1830* (Stanford: Stanford

University Press, 1998); Gottlieb, *Feeling British*; McNeil, *Scotland, Britain, Empire*; Juliet Shields, *Sentimental Literature and Anglo-Scottish Identity, 1745–1820* (Cambridge: Cambridge University Press, 2010).

28 Bill Ashcroft, Gareth Griffiths, and Helen Tiffin, *Post-Colonial Studies: The Key Concepts*, 2nd edn (New York and London: Routledge, 2000), 108. Their use of the term "contact zone," in turn, is borrowed from Mary Louise Pratt, *Imperial Eyes: Travel Writing and Transculturation* (London and New York: Routledge, 1992).

29 Homi Bhabha, *The Location of Culture*, Routledge Classics ed. (London and New York: Routledge, 2004), 122. This reprint, which includes a substantial new preface by Bhabha, consists (like the 1994 original volume) of essays mostly written from 1985 to 1992.

30 Ibid., 123.

31 Scott, *Rob Roy*, 277.

32 Ibid., 274.

33 Ibid., 296, 325.

34 Ibid., 297.

35 Cf. McNeil's observation that in *Rob Roy* "it is the operations of the exchange *between* the primitive and the modern *within* the nation that establish grounds for a reassessment, a rearticulation, of national collectivity" (*Scotland, Britain, Empire*, 53).

36 Bhabha, *Location of Culture*, 277. C.f. the denunciation of Bhabha's so-called "inflationary rhetoric" in Aijaz Ahmad, *In Theory: Classes, Nations, Literatures* (London and New York: Verso, 1992), 68–9.

37 Scott, *Rob Roy*, 364.

38 Raymond Williams, *Marxism and Literature* (New York and Oxford: Oxford University Press, 1977), 123.

39 Scott, *Rob Roy*, 346.

40 Margaret Bruzelius, *Romancing the Novel: Adventure from Scott to Sebald* (Lewisburg, PA: Bucknell University Press, 2007), 119.

41 Perhaps not coincidentally, Bhabha's essays in *Location of Culture* contain very few examples drawn from female authors. It has been left to other postcolonial critics, including Ania Loomba, Chandra Talpade Mohanty, and Gayatri Chakravorty Spivak, to extend or interrogate the relevance of postcolonial theory to women's experiences. See, for example, Ania Loomba, *Colonialism/Postcolonialism*, 2nd edn (London and New York: Routledge, 2005), esp. 115–43; Chandra Talpade Mohanty, *Feminism Without Borders: Decolonizing Theory, Practicing Solidarity* (Durham, NC and London: Duke University Press, 2003); Gayatri Chakravorty Spivak, "Can the Subaltern Speak?," in *Colonial Discourse and Post-Colonial Theory: A Reader*, eds Patrick Williams and Laura Chrisman (New York: Columbia University Press, 1994), 66–111.

42 Scott, *Rob Roy*, 411.

43 Ibid., 413.

44   Cf. Welsh, *Hero of the Waverley Novels*, 48–55. For a good example of how this kind of approach can be usefully updated, especially when teaching Scott in the classroom, see Diane Long Hoeveler, "Teaching the Female Body as Contested Territory," in *Approaches to Teaching Scott's Waverley Novels*, eds Gottlieb and Duncan, 105–14.

45   Bruzelius, *Romancing the Novel*, 111.

46   Scott, *Rob Roy*, 101.

47   Fiona Robertson's *Legitimate Histories, Scott, Gothic, and the Authorities of Fiction* is still the most complete study of relations between the Waverley Novels and the gothic genre.

48   Scott, *Rob Roy*, 452.

49   Butler, *Gender Trouble*, viii.

50   Ibid., 6.

51   I put "opposite" in quotation marks here to register the socially constructed nature of the so-called opposition between "masculine" and "feminine" gender identities. On this and other basic tenets of modern feminist theory, see, for example, Toril Moi's *Sexual/Textual Politics* (New York: Routledge, 1985).

52   Butler, *Bodies That Matter*, 60.

53   An even more recent phase of Butler's career, comprising a turn toward ethics and international politics in such texts as *Precarious Life: The Powers of Mourning and Violence* (London and New York: Verso, 2004) and *Frames of War: When is Life Grievable?* (London and New York: Verso, 2009), will factor briefly into this chapter's concluding observations.

54   See the essays by Derrida (and a synopsis of Searle's rejoinder) in *Limited Inc*, ed. Gerald Graff (Evanston, IL: Northwestern University Press, 1988).

55   See Louis Althusser, "Ideology and Ideological State Apparatuses," in *Lenin and Philosophy*, trans. Ben Brewster (London and New York: Monthly Review Press, 1971), 170–86.

56   Butler, *Excitable Speech*, 24.

57   Ibid., 24–5.

58   See the excellent notes to the Edinburgh Edition of Scott's *The Talisman*, ed. J. B. Ellis with J. H. Alexander, P. D. Garside, and David Hewitt (Edinburgh: University of Edinburgh Press, 2009), 362–430.

59   See Eve Kosofsky Sedgwick, *Between Men: English Literature and Male Homosocial Desire* (New York: Columbia University Press, 1985).

60   Scott, *Talisman*, 319.

61   Ibid., 153.

62   Butler, *Bodies that Matter*, xxi.

63   Scott, *Talisman*, 55.

64   For two recent examples, see Tara Ghoshal Wallace, "Thinking Globally: *The Talisman* and *The Surgeon's Daughter*," in *Approaches to Teaching Scott's Waverley Novels*, eds Gottlieb and Duncan, esp. 170–3; James Watt, "Scott, the Scottish Enlightenment, and Romantic Orientalism," in *Scotland and the Borders of Romanticism*, eds Davis, Duncan, and Sorensen, esp. 105–8.

65 Bruzelius, *Romancing the Novel*, 98.

66 Ibid., 99. Saladin, thus, forms a contrast not only with the novel's Christian knights and women, but also with the dwarf Nectanabus, whose grotesque antics repeatedly make him the object of scorn and thereby trapped within the convention of physical deformity as a sign of psychological abnormality. A more thorough study of Scott's novels through the critical lens of "disability" seems highly promising. See, for example, *The Disability Studies Reader*, ed. Lennard J. Davis (London and New York: Routledge, 2010).

67 Scott, *Talisman*, 27.

68 Butler, *Excitable Speech*, 38.

69 Scott, *Talisman*, 163.

70 Ibid., 187–8.

71 Ibid., 195–6.

72 Ibid., 202.

73 Ibid., 203.

74 Ibid., 205.

75 Ibid., 233. For more on the theory of abjection as developed by Julia Kristeva, see her *Powers of Horror: An Essay on Abjection*, trans. Leon S. Roudiez (New York: Columbia University Press, 1982).

76 Butler, *Giving an Account of Oneself* (New York: Fordham University Press, 2005), 83.

77 Scott, *Talisman*, 277.

78 Butler, *Precarious Life*, 44.

Chapter 4

1 See, for example, David Buchanan, "Popular Reception by Dramatic Adaptation: The Case of Walter Scott's *The Heart of Mid-Lothian*," *European Romantic Review* 22.6 (December 2011): 745–63. The contemporary equivalent to this phenomenon is seeing the movie before reading the book on which it is based.

2 James Hogg, *Anecdotes of Sir W. Scott*, ed. Douglas Mack (Edinburgh: Scottish Academic Press, 1983), 28. Hogg provides an expanded transliteration in the next paragraph: "We are just like the French in Sarragossa [sic] we are gaining foot by foot and room by room but we hope to get possession of the whole by and by."

3 Sutherland, *Life of Scott*, 157.

4 Fielding, *Scotland and the Fictions of Geography*, 83. But see also Kyoko Takanashi's argument that "For Scott, the national imagined community, which continues to extend its reach as roads are built and mail-coach routes are instituted, does not so much incorporate localities into a national network of communication as subordinate them"

("Circulation, Monuments, and the Politics of Transmission in Sir Walter Scott's *Tales of My Landlord*," *ELH* 79 [Summer 2012]: 290). My thanks to the author for making her article available to me in draft form.

5 Scott, *The Heart of Midlothian*, ed. Claire Lamont (New York: Oxford University Press, 1982), 15. In the text, I use Scott's manuscript spelling of his title (*Mid-Lothian*).

6 Ibid., 16.

7 For more on *Mid-Lothian*'s interest in women's bodies and the state, see Gottlieb, "'Almost the Same as Being Innocent: Celebrated Murderesses and National Narratives in Walter Scott's *The Heart of Mid-Lothian* and Margaret Atwood's *Alias Grace*," in *Scottish Literature and Postcolonial Literature: Comparative Texts and Critical Perspectives*, eds Michael Gardiner, Graeme Macdonald, and Niall O'Gallagher (Edinburgh: University of Edinburgh Press, 2011), 30–42.

8 Michel Foucault, *The Birth of Biopolitics: Lectures at the College de France, 1978–79*, ed. Michel Senellart, trans. Graham Burchell (New York: Picador, 2008), 20.

9 Foucault, *Discipline and Punish: The Birth of the Prison*, trans. Alan Sheridan (New York: Vintage, 1979), 31.

10 Foucault, *Birth of Biopolitics*, 19. For more on the political ramifications of this concept, see Brett Levinson, *Market and Thought: Meditations on the Political and the Biopolitical* (New York: Fordham University Press, 2004).

11 The secondary literature on Foucault is vast. For helpful overviews of the central ideas and questions that animate his best-known published texts, try Chapters 6 and 7 of Dews, *Logics of Disintegration* and Gary Gutting, *Foucault: A Very Short Introduction* (Oxford: Oxford University Press, 2005). For a recent genealogy of the concept of *dispositif*, see Bernard Dionysius Geoghegan, "From Information Theory to French Theory: Jakobson, Lévi-Strauss, and the Cybernetic Apparatus," *Critical Inquiry* 38.1 (Autumn 2011): 96–126.

12 Foucault, *Security, Territory, Population: Lectures at the Collège de France, 1977–78*, ed. Michael Senellart, trans. Graham Burchell (New York: Picador, 2007), 108.

13 Ibid., 108.

14 Ibid., 109.

15 Ibid., 109.

16 Ibid., 125.

17 Ibid., 165.

18 Ibid., 290–1.

19 Ibid., 290.

20 Dorothy Van Ghent, *The English Novel: Form and Function* (New York: Harper and Row, 1953), 139–53; David Hewitt, "Teaching *The Heart of Midlothian*," in *Approaches to Teaching Scott's Waverley Novels*, eds

Gottlieb and Duncan, 150–6. I have elsewhere interpreted *Mid-Lothian* as a fictional experiment in the application of sympathetic discourse to the era's political dilemmas; see Gottlieb, *Feeling British*, 188–204.

21 Charlotte Sussman, "The Emptiness at *The Heart of Midlothian*: Nation, Narration, and Population," *Eighteenth-Century Fiction* 15.1 (October 2002): 103–26.

22 Lincoln, *Walter Scott and Modernity*, 168; Lincoln then goes on to complicate productively this reading (see 169–72). On *The Tale of Old Mortality*'s portrayal of the Covenanters, see, for example, Hasler, "Framing the Covenanters (Again)" in *Approaches to Teaching Scott's Waverley Novels*, eds Gottlieb and Duncan, 140–9.

23 Scott, *Heart of Midlothian*, 153.

24 Lincoln, *Scott and Modernity*, 171. The Cameronians opposed the legitimacy of the Hanoverian dynasty for its refusal to revive the Solemn League and Covenant, on which Scottish Presbyterian hopes for a religious state had been pinned in the seventeenth century. For a complementary reading of Davie Deans that emphasizes his hypocrisy, see Julian Meldon D'Arcy, "Davie Deans and Bothwell Bridge: A Re-evaluation," *Scottish Literary Journal* 12.2 (1985): 23–34.

25 Scott, *Heart of Midlothian*, 304.

26 Ibid., 308.

27 Ibid., 310.

28 Ibid., 337.

29 Foucault, *Security, Territory, Population*, 354.

30 Scott, *Heart of Midlothian*, 412; Duncan, *Modern Romance*, 146–76.

31 Scott, *Heart of Midlothian*, 351.

32 Ibid., 410.

33 Foucault, *Security, Territory, Population*, 312–13.

34 Ibid., 315.

35 Scott, *Heart of Midlothian*, 137.

36 Ibid., 138.

37 Ibid., 160. Scott was not only trained in the law, like many Scotsmen of his generation and station, but also served as Sheriff-Depute of Selkirk for most of his adult life (although his duties were relatively light; see Sutherland, *Life of Scott*, 71–2).

38 Ibid., 175.

39 Foucault, *Security, Territory, Population*, 314.

40 Scott, *Midlothian*, 283.

41 Lumsden, *Scott and the Limits of Language*, 113.

42 See Foucault's *The Birth of Biopolitics*: "the central core of all the problems that I am presently trying to identify is what is called population. Consequently, this is the basis on which something like biopolitics could be formed" (21). An earlier version of this concept

is introduced near the end of his *History of Sexuality,* Vol. 1, where it is called "bio-power": the pressures and processes that "brought life and its mechanisms into the realm of explicit calculations and made knowledge-power an agent of transformation of human life" (143). For a brief but evocative overview of the development of the concepts of biopolitics and biopower in Foucault's thought, see the section "Appropriating the Theory Proper" in Mark Driscoll's "Looting the Theory Commons: Hardt and Negri's *Commonwealth," Postmodern Culture* 21.1 (September 2010).

43 Giorgio Agamben, *The Signature of All Things: On Method*, trans. Luca D'Isanto with Kevin Attell (New York: Zone Books, 2009a), 7. For a cogent discussion of some important differences between Foucault and Agamben, however, see Alison Ross' introduction to "The Agamben Effect," *South Atlantic Quarterly* 107.1 (Winter 2008): 1–12, esp. 5–6.

44 Agamben, *Signature of All Things*, 24.

45 Ibid., 32.

46 Ibid.

47 Agamben, "What is an Apparatus?," in *What is an Apparatus? and Other Essays*, trans. David Kishik and Stefan Pedatella (Stanford: Stanford University Press, 2009b), 3.

48 Ibid., 2–3.

49 Ibid., 22–3.

50 At the time of writing (November 2011), the outcome of this fledgling movement was still unknown, but for an encouraging analysis of its potential by Žižek, see his "Occupy First. Demands Come Later," *The Guardian*, 26 October 2011, www.guardian.co.uk/commentisfree/2011/oct/26/occupy-protesters-bill-clinton.

51 Agamben, *Signature of All Things*, 110.

52 Agamben, *Homo Sacer: Sovereign Power and Bare Life*, trans. Daniel Heller-Roazen (Stanford: Stanford University Press, 1998), 1.

53 Carl Schmitt, *Political Theology: Four Chapters on the Concept of Sovereignty*, trans. George Schwab (Chicago: University of Chicago Press, 2005), 5; quoted in a different translation in Agamben, *Homo Sacer*, 11.

54 Agamben, *Homo Sacer*, 83.

55 Ibid., 115.

56 Some theorists disagree with Agamben's condemnation of all forms of sovereignty as necessarily and essentially tending toward authoritarianism; see, for example, Wendy Brown's running critique of Agamben in *Walled States, Waning Sovereignty* (New York: Zone Books, 2010).

57 Agamben, *State of Exception*, trans. Kevin Attell (Chicago: University of Chicago Press, 2005), 2.

58 Cf. Schmitt, *Political Theology*, 12–14.

59 Agamben, *State of Exception*, 86.

60 Ibid., 86.

61   Ibid., 87. Agamben cites the USA Patriot Act, first signed into law in October 2001 (and more or less continually renewed since then despite vocal opposition from civil liberties groups), as a present-day example of the state of exception's deployment.

62   Scott, *Quentin Durward*, eds J. H. Alexander and G. A. M. Wood (Edinburgh: Edinburgh University Press, 2001), 1. All references are to this edition unless otherwise noted. Alexander and Wood provide a more poetic translation of the novel's epigraph: "War is my native land, my armour my house, and continuous fighting is my life" (508 n.), and note that Scott may be thinking here of analogous sentiments quoted in Cervantes' *Don Quixote*.

63   Scott, *Quentin Durward*, ed. Susan Manning (New York and Oxford: Oxford University Press, 1992), 4. The comparison already appears in the first chapter of the original edition, where Scott describes Louis' "Machiavellian stratagems" (26).

64   Scott, *Quentin Durward*, 27.

65   A more full discussion of *Quentin Durward*'s gypsies as embodiments of Agamben's *homines sacri* appears in the fifth chapter of my work-in-progress, *Romantic Globalism: British Literature and Modern World Order, 1750–1830*.

66   Scott, *Quentin Durward*, 43.

67   Agamben, *Homo Sacer*, 83. Cf. Eric Santner's recent *The Royal Remains: The People's Two Bodies and the Endgames of Sovereignty* (Chicago: University of Chicago Press, 2011). In addition to engaging with Agamben and Foucault, Santner draws on earlier theorists and scholars of sovereignty like Walter Benjamin, Ernst Kantorowicz, and Claude Lefort.

68   Scott, *Quentin Durward*, 75.

69   Ibid., 81.

70   Agamben, *State of Exception*, 38.

71   Ibid., 39.

72   See, for example, Agamben's reference to "the powerful theological machine of Christian *oiconomia* [sic]" near the beginning of his *The Coming Community*, trans. Michael Hardt (Minneapolis: University of Minnesota Press, 1993), 6.

73   Agamben, *The Kingdom and the Glory: For a Theological Genealogy of Economy and Government*, trans. Lorenzo Chiesa with Matteo Mandarini (Stanford: Stanford University Press, 2011a). The Aristotelian definition of *oikonomia* appears on page 17.

74   Agamben, *Kingdom and the Glory*, 1.

75   Ibid., 24.

76   Ibid., 21, 25.

77   Ibid., 35, 39.

78   Ibid., 140, 142.

79   Ibid., 143.

80   Ibid., 273–4, 283–4.

81 Scott, *Quentin Durward*, 37.

82 Ibid., 37, 143.

83 Agamben, *The Kingdom and the Glory*, 285.

84 Scott, *Quentin Durward*, 85.

85 Ibid., 301.

86 Ibid., 47, 50.

87 Agamben, *The Sacrament of Language: An Archaeology of the Oath*, trans. Adam Kotsko (Stanford: Stanford University Press, 2011b), 68–70.

88 See Agamben, *Sacrament of Language*, 68–70.

89 Ibid., 72.

90 Scott, *Quentin Durward*, 254, 371–4.

91 Ibid., 399.

Chapter 5

1 On the genre of the "national" or "regional tale," especially as distinct from the historical novel, see, for example, recent work by Miranda Burgess, "The National Tale and Allied Genres, 1770s–1840s," in *The Cambridge Companion to the Irish Novel*, ed. John Wilson Foster (Cambridge: Cambridge University Press, 2006); Ina Ferris, *The Romantic National Tale and the Question of Ireland* (Cambridge: Cambridge University Press, 2002); Anthony Jarrells, "Provincializing Enlightenment: Edinburgh Historicism and the Blackwoodian Regional Tale," *Studies in Romanticism* 48.2 (Summer 2009): 257–77; Shields, *Sentimental Literature and Anglo-Scottish Identity*, 110–38.

2 Roberto Esposito, *Communitas: The Origin and Destiny of Community*, trans. Timothy Campbell (Stanford: Stanford University Press, 2010), 1.

3 Cf. Alain Badiou's description of the twentieth century as "the totalitarian century. . . . It begins in 1917 with Lenin . . . reaches its apex in 1937 with Stalin and 1942–45 with Hitler, and to all intents and purposes comes to an end with Mao Tsetung's death in 1976" (*The Century*, trans, Alberto Toscano [Malden, MA and Cambridge: Polity, 2007], 2).

4 See, in particular, Kant's essay "Toward Perpetual Peace" (1795), in *Practical Philosophy: The Cambridge Edition of the Works of Immanuel Kant*, trans. and ed. Mary J. Gregor (Cambridge and New York: Cambridge University Press, 1996), 311–51.

5 Max Horkheimer and Theodor Adorno, "The Concept of Enlightenment," in *Dialectic of Enlightenment: Philosophical Fragments*, ed. Gunzelin Schmid Noerr, trans. Edmund Jephcott (Stanford: Stanford University Press, 2002), 21.

6 Foucault, *History of Sexuality Vol. 1: An Introduction*, 101, 157. In his final series of lectures, Foucault elaborates an idea of *parrēsia*, or "true discourse in the political realm," that arguably goes well beyond these earlier concepts; nevertheless, and perhaps tellingly for Foucault, while *parrēsia* inevitably involves more than one subject (since the truth-speaker must knowingly put herself at risk in the speech), it is still essentially an individual rather than communal endeavor. See Foucault, *The Government of Self and Others: Lectures at the Collège de France, 1982–83*, trans. Graham Burchell (New York: Palgrave Macmillan, 2010), 6, 51–7.

7 Among Baudrillard's large corpus, see in particular: *The Mirror of Production*, trans. Mark Poster (St. Louis: Telos Press, 1975); *Simulations*, trans. Paul Foss, Paul Patton, and Philip Beitchman (New York: Semiotext[e], 1983); *Forget Foucault*, no trans. (New York: Semiotext[e], 1987); *Fatal Strategies*, trans. Philippe Beitchman and W. G. J. Niesluchowski (Los Angeles: Semiotext[e], 1990).

8 See Jürgen Habermas, *The Structural Transformation of the Public Sphere: An Inquiry into a Category of Bourgeois Society*, trans Thomas Burger with Frederick Lawrence (Cambridge, MA: MIT Press, 1989).

9 Habermas, *The Philosophical Discourse of Modernity: Twelve Lectures*, trans. Frederick G. Lawrence (Cambridge, MA: MIT Press, 1985), 304.

10 See Habermas, *The Theory of Communicative Action*, 2 Vols., trans. Thomas McCarthy (Boston: Beacon Press, 1984, 1987).

11 Habermas, "Fundamentalism and Terror: A Dialogue with Jürgen Habermas," in Giovanna Borradori, *Philosophy in a Time of Terror: Dialogues with Jürgen Habermas and Jacques Derrida* (Chicago: University of Chicago Press, 2003a), 37.

12 Habermas, "Fundamentalism and Terror," 42.

13 Walter Scott, *The Bride of Lammermoor*, ed. J. H. Alexander (New York: Penguin, 1995), 19.

14 Habermas, "A Genealogical Analysis of the Cognitive Content of Morality," trans. Ciarin Cronin, in *The Inclusion of the Other: Studies in Political Theory*, ed. Ciaran Cronin and Pablo De Grieff (Cambridge, MA: The MIT Press, 1998), 29.

15 Scott, *Bride of Lammermoor*, 59.

16 Ibid., 60.

17 Lincoln, *Walter Scott and Modernity*, 190.

18 Cf. John Dwyer, *Virtuous Discourse: Sensibility and Community in Late Eighteenth-Century Scotland* (Edinburgh: John Donald, 1987); Gottlieb, *Feeling British*; Shields, *Sentimental Literature and Anglo-Scottish Identity*.

19 For a recent overview of the scholarship surrounding *The Bride*'s pre- and post-Union settings, as well as the potential meanings of Scott's shift, see D'Arcy, *Subversive Scott*, 165–8.

20 The now-classic critical text explicating the prevalence of such arrangements is Sedgwick's *Between Men*. See also Gayle Rubin's foundational critical essay, "The Traffic in Women: Notes on the 'Political Economy' of Sex," in *Toward an Anthropology of Women*, ed. Reyna Reiter (New York: Monthly Review Press, 1975).

21 See the essays collected in *The Turn to Ethics*, eds Marjorie Garber, Beatrice Hanssen, and Rebecca L. Walkowitz (New York: Routledge, 2000).

22 Jacques Derrida, "Ja, ou la faux-bond," *Digraphe* 11 (1977), 11; quoted in Dews, *Logics of Disintegration*, 35.

23 The secondary literature on Derrida is too vast to be summarized; again, Dews' chapter on Derrida in *Logics of Disintegration* is a good starting point, as are early books by Christopher Norris (*Deconstruction: Theory and Practice* [London: Methuen, 1982] and *Derrida* [Cambridge, MA: Harvard University Press, 1988]) and Jonathan Culler (*On Deconstruction: Theory and Criticism after Structuralism* [Ithaca, NY: Cornell University Press, 1982]). On the question of "phases" in Derrida's career, see Ian Balfour, "Introduction," *Late Derrida*, special issue of *South Atlantic Quarterly* 106.2 (Spring 2007): 205–17.

24 Jacques Derrida, *Of Hospitality: Anne Dufourmantelle invites Jacques Derrida to respond*, trans. Rachel Bowlby (Stanford: Stanford University Press, 2000), 83. John Caputo argues that, insofar as deconstruction has always been about "keep[ing] a constant watch for all those forces that would contain what is coming, that would forestall or prevent the invention of the other," Derrida's entire critical project is really "a form of hospitality" (*Deconstruction in a Nutshell: A Conversation with Jacques Derrida*, ed. Caputo [New York: Fordham University Press, 1997a], 109).

25 Derrida, "A Word of Welcome," in *Adieu to Emmanuel Levinas*, trans. Pascale-Anne Brault and Michael Naas (Stanford: Stanford University Press, 1999), 51. Derrida's relationship with Levinas goes back decades; see, for example, his 1964 meditation "Violence and Metaphysics: An Essay on the Thought of Emmanuel Levinas," in *Writing and Difference*, trans. Alan Bass (Chicago: University of Chicago Press, 1978), 79–153.

26 See Scott, *Bride of Lammermoor*, 81.

27 Ibid., 84; my italics.

28 For a reading of Lucy's role in *The Bride* that uses Sedgwick to speculate on repressed homosexual desire between Ravenswood and Bucklaw, see Oliver Buckton, "'This Monstrous Passion': Teaching *The Bride of Lammermoor* and Queer Theory," in *Approaches to Teaching Scott's Waverley Novels*, eds Gottlieb and Duncan, 157–63.

29 Scott, *Bride of Lammermoor*, 101.

30 Ibid., 102–3. For an analysis of the clash of various languages and discourses in *The Bride*, see Janet Sorensen, "Writing Historically, Speaking Nostalgically: The Competing Languages of Nation in Scott's *The Bride of Lammermoor*," in *Narratives of Nostalgia, Gender, and Nationalism*, eds Jean Pickering and Suzanne Kehde (Washington Square: New York University Press, 1997), 30–51.

31 Karl Marx, *The Communist Manifesto*, ed. Frederic L. Bender (New York and London: W. W. Norton, 1988), 57; Scott, *Bride of Lammermoor*, 115.

32 Scott, *Bride of Lammermoor*, 182.

33 Ibid., 17.

34 Duncan, *Modern Romance*, 142. Cf. Bruzelius' description of Lady Ashton as the "incarnat[ion] [of] uncontrollable and unregulated maternal desire, the nightmare of patriarchy" (*Romancing the Novel*, 123).

35 Ibid., 120.

36 Scott, *Bride of Lammermoor*, 247.

37 Derrida, *Of Hospitality*, 77.

38 On the host of superstitious omens in *The Bride*, see, for example, Duncan, *Modern Romance*, 142–4; and the section on *The Bride* in my own "Unvarnished Tales and Fatal Influences: Teaching the National Tale and Historical Novel," *Romantic Pedagogy Commons* (August 2008), http://www.rc.umd.edu/pedagogies/commons/novel/gottlieb.html.

39 Scott, *Bride of Lammermoor*, 136, 246.

40 Ibid., 139.

41 Ibid., 268–9.

42 Jean-Luc Nancy, *The Inoperative Community*, ed. Peter Connor, trans. Peter Connor, Lisa Garbus, Michael Holland, and Simona Sawhney (Minneapolis and Oxford: University of Minnesota Press, 1991), 1.

43 See Alfred Tönnies, *Community and Civil Society*, ed. Jose Harris, trans. Margaret Hollis (New York and London: Cambridge University Press, 2001). Cf. Raymond Williams' helpful entry on "Community" in his still-indispensable *Keywords: A vocabulary of culture and society* (London: Fontana, 1983), 75–6.

44 Habermas, *Inclusion of the Other*, xxxv.

45 Nancy, *Inoperative Community*, 11.

46 Derrida's frequent invocation in his later writings of "the democracy to come" may be understood similarly; see, for example, his *On Cosmopolitanism and Forgiveness*, trans, Mark Dooley and Michael Hughes (London and New York: Routledge, 2001). As Vincent Leitch observes, however, there is simultaneously a strong suspicion of community in Derrida's late works, such that "The intensity of broken belonging and the strength accorded the sovereign self cast a long rightward-leaning libertarian shadow over Derrida's left-wing democratic politics" (*Living With Theory* [Malden, MA and Oxford: Blackwell, 2008], 78).

47 Nancy, *Inoperative Community*, 17.

48 Scott himself played no small role in popularizing Scotland as a tourist destination for picturesque travel; see, for example, Peter Womack, *Improvement and Romance: Constructing the Myth of the Highlands* (London: Macmillan, 1989); *Literary Tourism, the Trossachs, and Walter Scott*, ed. Ian Brown (Glasgow: Scottish Literature International, 2012).

49 Walter Scott, *Chronicles of the Canongate*, ed. Claire Lamont (New York: Penguin, 2003), 72.

50 Ibid., 75.

51 Ibid., 78.

52 See Wickman, *The Ruins of Experience*.

53 Scott, *Chronicles*, 78.

54 Ibid., 85.

55 Ibid., 79.

56 Ibid., 122.

57 Ibid., 114.

58 See, for example, Linda Colley, *Britons: Forging the Nation, 1707–1837* (New Haven: Yale University Press, 1992).

59 Habermas, "What is a People? The Frankfurt 'Germanists' Assembly' of 1846 and the Self-Understanding of the Humanities in the *Vormärz*," in *The Postnational Condition: Political Essays*, trans. Max Pensky (Cambridge, MA: The MIT Press, 2001), 18.

60 For a complementary reading of the tales within *Chronicles* from the perspective of Scott's shifting economic views and experiences late in his career, see Alex J. Dick, "Walter Scott and the Financial Crash of 1825: Fiction, Speculation, and the Standard of Value," in "Romanticism, Forgery, and the Credit Crunch," ed. Ian Haywood, special issue of *Romantic Circles Praxis Series* (February 2012), http://www.rc.umd.edu/praxis/forgery/HTML/praxis.2011.dick.html.

61 Habermas, "What is a People?," 19. For a succinct account of the development of "the political good of legally secured freedoms" for citizens of what Habermas calls the modern "constitutional state," see his "Does the Constitutionalization of International Law Still Have a Chance?," in *The Divided West*, ed. and trans. Ciarin Cronin (Cambridge and Malden, MA: Polity, 2006), 129–32.

62 Scott, *Chronicles*, 130.

63 See, for example, Seamus Cooney, "Scott and Cultural Relativism: 'The Two Drovers'," *Studies in Short Fiction* 15 (1978); Zahra A. Hussein Ali, "Adjusting the Borders of the Self: Sir Walter Scott's 'The Two Drovers'," *Papers on Language and Literature* 37 (Winter 2001): 65–84; Kenneth McNeil, "The Limits of Diversity: Using Scott's 'The Two Drovers' to Teach Multiculturalism in a Survey or Nonmajors Course," in *Approaches to Teaching Scott's Waverley Novels*, eds Gottlieb and Duncan, 123–9.

64 Cf. Jacques Derrida, *The Politics of Friendship*, trans. George Collins (London and New York: Verso, 1997c).

65 Michael Hardt and Antonio Negri, *Multitude: War and Democracy in the Age of Empire* (New York: Penguin, 2004), 261.

66 This is a version of the classic Marxist conception of society as composed of an economic base and a cultural/political superstructure, in which the former determines the latter. Neither Hardt, Negri, nor most other Marxist intellectuals today subscribe to such a clear-cut view of the matter; nevertheless, some form of this materialist distinction continues to inform much of their work, especially in Italy. See, for example, Franco Berardi, *The Soul at Work: From Alienation to Autonomy*, trans. Francesca Cadel and Giuseppina Mecchia (Los Angeles: Semiotext[e], 2009); Antonio Negri, *Art & Multitude*, ed. Ed Emery (Cambridge and Malden, MA: Polity, 2011); Paolo Virno, *A Grammar of the Multitude: For an Analysis of Contemporary*

Forms of Life, trans. Isabella Bertoletti, James Cascaito, and Andrea Casson (Los Angeles: Semiotext[e], 2004).

67 Scott, *Chronicles*, 142.

68 Ibid., 145–6.

69 In this, the English attitude toward Scotland indeed agreed with justifications (both earlier and later) for European imperialism around the world. See Immanuel Wallerstein, *European Universalism: The Rhetoric of Power* (New York and London: The New Press, 2006).

70 See M. M. Bakhtin, *The Dialogic Imagination: Four Essays*, ed. Michael Holquist, trans. Caryl Emerson and Michael Holquist (Austin: University of Texas Press, 1982). Cf. McNeil, "The Limits of Diversity," in *Approaches to Teaching Scott's Waverley Novels*, eds Gottlieb and Duncan.

71 James Watt, "Scott, the Scottish Enlightenment, and Romantic Orientalism," in *Scotland and the Borders of Romanticism*, eds Davis, Duncan, and Sorensen, 94. See also Tara Ghoshal Wallace, *Imperial Characters: Home and Periphery in Eighteenth-Century Literature* (Lewisburg, PA: Bucknell University Press, 2010), 146–66.

72 Along these lines, for example, one could consider Richard Middlemas— the bastard child of an English Catholic father and Spanish Jewish mother, raised by a prudent Scottish country doctor—as another of Scott's hybrid characters.

73 Claire Lamont, "Historical Note to 'The Surgeon's Daughter'," in *Chronicles of the Canongate*, ed. Lamont, 355.

74 Scott, *Chronicles*, 198.

75 Ibid., 243.

76 Ibid., 259.

77 Ibid., 199, 242.

78 Hardt and Negri, *Multitude*, 99–101.

79 Hardt and Negri, *Multitude*, 100. See also their *Empire* and *Commonwealth* (Cambridge, MA: Belknap Press of Harvard University Press, 2009). Notable critiques of their project include *Debating Empire*, ed. Gopal Balakrishnan (London and New York: Verso, 2003) and *Empire's New Clothes: Reading Hardt and Negri*, eds Paul Passavant and Jodi Dean (London and New York: Routledge, 2003).

80 Hardt and Negri, *Multitude*, 99. As their use of "singularities" suggests, Hardt and Negri take their inspiration not just from the Marxian tradition, but also from Spinoza's philosophical materialism; see, for example, the essays by Michael Goddard and George Caffentzis in Part III of *Reading Negri: Marxism in the Age of Empire*, eds Pierre Lamarche, Max Rosenkrantz, David Sherman (Chicago and LaSalle, IL: Open Court, 2011).

81 Scott, *Chronicles*, 219.

82 Ibid., 13. Graham Tulloch notes these similarities, and a few more, between Scott and Croftangry in his Preface to Scott's *The Two Drovers and Other Stories* (London: Oxford University Press, 1987), esp. xxiv–xxv.

83 Scott, *Chronicles*, 21.

84 See Bakhtin, "Forms of Time and of the Chronotope in the Novel: Notes Toward a Historical Poetics," in *The Dialogic Imagination*, 84–258.

85 Scott, *Chronicles*, 68, 155.

86 Ibid., 287.

87 Ibid., 287–8.

88 Scott, *The Fair Maid of Perth*, eds A.D. Hook and Donald Mackenzie (Edinburgh: Edinburgh University Press, 1999a), 4.

89 Jacques Rancière, "The Politics of Literature," in *The Politics of Literature*, trans. Julie Rose (Malden, MA and Cambridge: Polity, 2011c), 21. An earlier version of this essay, also worth consulting, first appeared in *SubStance* 33.1 (2004b): 10–24.

90 For a wide-ranging, synoptic account of Scott's influence on the nineteenth-century novel in Europe and beyond, see Simon Edwards, "Home and Away with Walter Scott," in *Approaches to Teaching Scott's Waverley Novels*, eds Gottlieb and Duncan, 77–87.

91 See Rancière, *Mute Speech: Literature, Critical Theory, and Politics*, trans. James Swenson (New York: Columbia University Press, 2011b).

92 Rancière, *The Politics of Aesthetics*, 13.

93 Notably, both of the main characters in the frame introduction to *The Bride of Lammermoor*—the artist Dick Tinto and the narrator Peter Pattieson— are deceased as well; see Sorensen, "Writing Historically, Thinking Nostalgically."

94 Rancière, *Hatred of Democracy*, trans. Steve Corcoran (London and New York: Verso, 2006), 51. For the origins of Rancière's political thought— especially his break from the structural Marxism of his intellectual mentor, Louis Althusser—see the recent translation of his first major text, *Althusser's Lesson*, trans. Emiliano Battista (London and New York: Continuum, 2011a), which contains a very helpful new "Foreword to the English Edition" by Rancière. On the salient distinctions between Hardt and Negri's "multitude" and Rancière's "people," see Ernesto Laclau, "Can Immanence Explain Social Struggles?," in *Empire's New Clothes*, eds Passavant and Dean, 21–30.

Conclusion

1 Stuart Kelly, *Scott-Land: The Man Who Invented a Nation* (Edinburgh: Polygon, 2010), 3–4.

2 The question of how humanistic study in particular can better articulate its mission(s) to those outside its disciplinary boundaries—a group that includes most university administrators as well as the public at large—has become ever more pressing in our current cycle of public defunding of higher education and what Geoffrey Galt Harpham identifies as the concomitant turn toward framing university missions "solely in terms of job training, or even as information transmission"; see his *The Humanities and the Dream of America* (Chicago: University of Chicago Press, 2011), 17, with the proviso that I see a much greater role for theory in the humanities than Harpham generally does.

3 There are other ways of thinking through the differences between the poststructuralist paradigm and what is beginning to supersede it; for a compelling recent account that thinks in terms of "affirmation/ immanence" versus "negation/ transcendence," see Benjamin Noys, *The Persistence of the Negative: A Critique of Contemporary Continental Theory* (Edinburgh: University of Edinburgh Press, 2010).

4 Friedrich Nietzsche, "On Truth and Lies in a Nonmoral Sense," in *Philosophy and Truth: Selections from Nietzsche's Notebooks of the Early 1820's*, ed. and trans. Daniel Breazeale (New Jersey: Humanities Press, 1979), 84.

5 In this attitude, one senses the long shadow cast by Ludwig Wittgenstein's famous concluding aphorism that, with regard to the supposed nonsense of metaphysical propositions, "What we cannot speak about we must pass over in silence": Wittgenstein, *Tractatus Logico-Philosophicus*, trans D. F. Pears and B. F. McGuinness (London and New York: Routledge, 2001), 89.

6 Cary Wolfe, *What is Posthumanism?* (Minneapolis and London: University of Minnesota Press, 2010), xvi.

7 Foucault, *The Order of Things*, xxiii; see also Wolfe, *What is Posthumanism?*, xii.

8 In this regard, the work of Marshall McLuhan is equally pertinent; see, for example, *Understanding Media: The Extensions of Man*, rev. ed. (Cambridge, MA and London: MIT Press, 1994).

9 See, for example, Derrida, *The Animal That Therefore I Am*, ed. Marie-Louis Mallet, trans. David Wills (New York: Fordham University Press, 2008); Derrida, *The Beast and The Sovereign*, Vols. 1 and 2 of *The Seminars of Jacques Derrida*, ed. Michel Lisse, Marie-Louise Mallet, and Ginette Michaud, trans. Geoffrey Bennington (Chicago and London: University of Chicago Press, 2009, 2011); Agamben, *The Open: Man and Animal*, trans. Kevin Attell (Stanford: Stanford University Press, 2004); Baudrillard, *Impossible Exchange*, trans. Chris Turner (London and New York: Verso, 2001); Habermas, *The Future of Human Nature*, trans. William Rehg, Max Pensky, and Hella Beister (Polity: Cambridge and Malden, MA, 2003b). For recent studies that seek to unpack the varieties of posthumanism in many of these theorists' oeuvres, see Gerald L. Bruns, *On Ceasing to Be Human* (Stanford: Stanford University Press, 2011); Timothy C. Campbell, *Improper Life: Technology and Biopolitics from Heidegger to Agamben* (Minneapolis and London: University of Minnesota Press, 2011).

10 DeLanda, *Intensive Science and Virtual Philosophy*, 5.

11 Jane Bennett, *Vibrant Matter: A Political Ecology of Things* (Durham, NC and London: Duke University Press, 2010), x. Cf. Gilles Deleuze and Félix Guattari, "Treatise on Nomadology – The War Machine," in *A Thousand Plateaus: Capitalism and Schizophrenia* Vol. 2, trans. Brian Massumi (Minneapolis and London: University of Minnesota Press, 1987), 351–423.

12 On the relevance of the various ramifications of matter as "multiplicity"—the concept plays an important role in Deleuze's thought as early as his primary doctoral thesis, published in English as *Difference and Repetition*, trans. Paul Patton (New York: Columbia University Press, 1994)—see DeLanda, *Intensive Science and Virtual Philosophy*, 9–55. Deleuze's secondary doctoral thesis, also first published in French in 1968, focused on Spinoza. The phrase "Radical Enlightenment" is from Jonathan L. Israel's magisterial (albeit controversial) three-volume historical exploration; see especially, his *Enlightenment Contested: Philosophy, Modernity, and the Emancipation of Man, 167–1752* (Oxford and New York: Oxford University Press, 2006).

13 William Wordsworth, "Lines written a few miles above Tintern Abbey, on revisiting the banks of the Wye during a tour, 13 July 1798," ll. 103–5, in Duncan Wu (ed.), *Romanticism: An Anthology*, 4th edn (Oxford and Malden, MA: Wiley-Blackwell, 2012), 418.

14 Timothy Morton, *Ecology Without Nature: Rethinking Environmental Ethics* (Cambridge, MA and London: Harvard University Press, 2007). Žižek has recently been making a similar point, albeit without Morton's references to the Romantics; see, for example, his interview in *The Examined Life: Excursions with Contemporary Thinkers*, ed. Astra Taylor (New York and London: The New Press, 2009), 155–83.

15 Michel Serres, *The Parasite*, new edition, trans. Lawrence R. Schehr (Minneapolis and London: University of Minnesota Press, 2007), 225. Cary Wolfe's introduction to this edition is especially useful.

16 Serres, *The Five Senses: A Philosophy of Mingled Bodies*, trans. Margaret Sankey and Peter Cowley (London and New York: Continuum, 2008), 61.

17 The closest Scott might be said to approach a similar sense of interconnectedness between humanity and the natural world is probably in the famous passages at the start of Canto VI of *The Lay of the Last Minstrel* (1805): "Oh Caledonia . . . What mortal hand/ Can e'er untie the filial band/ That knits me to thy rugged strand?" (VI.ii.1, 5–7). But, this representation of the intimate relationship between man and landscape is heavily mediated by the discourse of nationalism (*Romanticism: An Anthology*, ed. Wu, 600).

18 King Richard explains that "the Almighty, who gave the dog to be companion of our pleasure and our toils, hath invested him with a nature noble and incapable of deceit. . . . He hath a share of man's intelligence, but no share of man's falsehood" (Scott, *The Talisman*, 225).

19 Lockhart, *Life of Scott*, 282.

20 Donna Haraway, *When Species Meet* (Minneapolis and London: University of Minnesota Press, 2008), 42.

21 Deleuze and Guattari, *Anti-Oedipus: Capitalism and Schizophrenia* [Vol 1.], trans. Robert Hurley, Mark Seem, and Helen R. Lane (Minneapolis: University of Minnesota Press, 1983), 5–6.

22 Ibid., 8.

23 See Haraway, "A Cyborg Manifesto: Science, Technology, and Socialist-Feminism in the Late Twentieth Century," in *Simians, Cyborgs and Women:*

The Reinvention of Nature (London and New York: Routledge, 1991). See also, for example, N. Kathleen Hailes, *How We Became Posthuman: Virtual Bodies in Cybernetics, Literature, and Informatics* (Chicago and London: University of Chicago Press, 1999).

24 See, for example, Allison Muri, *The Enlightenment Cyborg: A History of Communications and Control in the Human Machine, 1660–1830* (Toronto, Buffalo, and London: University of Toronto Press, 2007); Julie Park, *The Self and It: Novel Objects in Eighteenth-Century England* (Stanford: Stanford University Press, 2010). On the Romantic culture of science, broadly conceived, see Richard Holmes, *The Age of Wonder: How the Romantic Generation Discovered the Beauty and Terror of Science* (New York: Vintage, 2010).

25 Cf. Shawn Malley, "Walter Scott's Romantic Archeology: New/Old Abbotsford and *The Antiquary*," *Studies in Romanticism* 40.3 (Summer 2001): 233–51.

26 Scott, *The Fortunes of Nigel*, ed. Frank Jordan (Edinburgh: Edinburgh University Press, 2004), 25.

27 Friedrich Kittler, *Optical Media: Berlin Lectures 1999*, trans. Anthony Enns (Cambridge and Malden, MA: Polity, 2010), 72. See also Barbara Maria Stafford, *Body Criticism: Imaging the Unseen in Enlightenment Art and Medicine* (Cambridge, MA and London: MIT Press, 1991).

28 Ian Duncan, "The Trouble with Man: Scott, Romance, and World History in the Age of Lamarck," in *Romantic Frictions*, special issue of *Romantic Circles Praxis Series*, ed. Theresa M. Kelley (September 2011), www.rc.umd.edu/praxis/frictions/HTML/praxis.2011.duncan.html.

29 Scott, *Count Robert of Paris*, ed. J. H. Alexander (Edinburgh: University of Edinburgh Press, 2006), 170–1.

30 Agamben, *The Open*, 37, 22.

31 Deleuze and Guattari, *Anti-Oedipus*, 6.

32 Deleuze and Guattari, *What is Philosophy?*, trans. Hugh Tomlinson and Grant Burchell (New York: Columbia University Press, 1994), 5.

33 Deleuze and Guattari, *A Thousand Plateaus*, 7.

34 Ibid., 371.

35 Gerald Raunig, *A Thousand Machines: A Concise Philosophy of the Machine as Social Movement*, trans. Aileen Derieg (Los Angeles: Semiotext[e], 2010), 32.

36 See Bruno Latour, *Reassembling the Social: An Introduction to Actor-Network-Theory* (New York: Oxford University Press, 2005), 54–5; Latour, *We Have Never Been Modern*, trans. Catherine Porter (Cambridge, MA: Harvard University Press, 1993), 5

37 Latour, *We Have Never Been Modern*, 6.

38 See Levi Bryant, *The Democracy of Objects* (Ann Arbor, MI: Open Humanities Press, 2011); Graham Harman, *The Quadruple Object*; Meillassoux, *After Finitude*; Isabelle Stengers, *Cosmopolitics I*, trans. Robert Bononno (Minneapolis and London: University of Minnesota Press, 2010). Ian Bogost's *Alien Phenomenology, or What It's Like to* *be a Thing* (Minneapolis and London: University of Minnesota Press, 2012) surveys many of the current ideas in this field, as well as makes its own contributions, for example, this helpful gloss on Bryant's "flat ontology": "all things equally exist, but not all things exist equally" (11). The increasingly innovative work of Peter Sloterdijk, whose three-volume trilogy on the relations between humans and their built environments has just begun to appear in English, is also relevant here; see *Spheres* Vol. 1: *Bubbles*, trans. Wieland Hoban (Los Angeles: Semiotext[e], 2011).

39 See, for example, James P. Carson, *Populism, Gender, and Sympathy in the Romantic Novel* (New York: Palgrave Macmillan, 2010), 45–74; Anthony Hasler, "Framing the Covenanters (Again)," in *Approaches to Teaching Scott's* Waverley Novels, eds Gottlieb and Duncan, 140–9; Stephen Arata, "Scott's Pageants: The Example of *Kenilworth*," *Studies in Romanticism* 40.1 (Spring 2001): 99–108; Lumsden, *Walter Scott and the Limits of Language*, 208–13.

40 See, for example, Niklas Luhmann, *Social Systems*, trans. John Bednarz Jr. with Dirk Baecker (Stanford: Stanford University Press, 1995); Manuel DeLanda, *A New Philosophy of Society: Assemblage Theory and Social Complexity* (New York and London: Continuum, 2006); Immanuel Wallerstein, *World-Systems Analysis: An Introduction* (Durham, NC and London: Duke University Press, 2004). For a characteristically polemical argument for the greater utility and relevance of these approaches as compared to more traditional forms of theoretical critique, see Latour, "Why Has Critique Run out of Steam? From Matters of Fact to Matters of Concern," *Critical Inquiry* 30 (Winter 2004): 225–48.

41 Alain Badiou, *Logics of Worlds: Being and Event II*, trans. Alberto Toscano (London and New York: Continuum, 2009), 4. For an ingenious alignment of Badiou's "truths," which constitute something human that is nevertheless in excess of "bodies" and "languages," with Lacan's *objet a*, see Zupančič, *Odd One In*, 52.

42 See Badiou, *Being and Event*, trans. Oliver Feltham (New York and London: Continuum, 2006a). For each of these treatises, Badiou has written a condensed version that presents its ideas in a more accessible, less technical format: see his *Manifesto for Philosophy*, trans. Norman Madarasz (Albany, NY: State University of New York Press, 1999) and *Second Manifesto for Philosophy*, trans. Louise Burchill (Cambridge and Malden, MA: Polity, 2011). In my opinion, however, the best introductory volume written by Badiou remains his *Ethics: An Essay on the Understanding of Evil*, trans. Peter Hallward (London and New York: Verso, 2001).

43 See Badiou, "Truth: Forcing and the Unnameable," in *Conditions*, trans. Steve Corcoran (London and New York: Continuum, 2008), esp. 130–3.

44 Cf. Badiou's assertion that "An evental fidelity is a real break (both thought and practiced) in the specific order within which the event took place (be it political, loving, artistic, or scientific . . .)" (*Ethics* 42). Badiou's notion of the "truth event" can be compared with that of Žižek's Act; see Todd McGowan, "Subject of the event, subject of the act: The difference between Badiou's and Žižek's systems of philosophy," *Subjectivity* 3.1 (April 2010): 7–30.

45 Badiou, "Politics as a Truth Procedure," in *Theoretical Writings*, ed. and trans. Ray Brassier and Alberto Toscano (London and New York: Continuum, 2006b), 155–7. This third feature is what distinguishes politics as a truth procedure from the other three (love, art, science): "only in politics is the deliberation about the possible (and hence about the infinity of the situation) constitutive of the process itself" ("Politics," 156–7).

46 Scott, *Waverley*, 339.

47 Badiou, *Ethics*, 70.

48 For calls to reinstate "pleasure" as a legitimate criterion of literary and cultural analysis, see, for example, Harpham, "The Next Big Thing in Literary Studies: Pleasure," in *Humanities and the Dream of America*, esp. 113–22; Catherine Belsey, *A Future for Criticism* (Oxford and Malden, MA: Wiley-Blackwell, 2011), 1–17.

49 Scott, *Waverley*, 5.

Bibliography

Agamben, Giorgio (1993). *The Coming Community*, trans. Michael Hardt. Minneapolis and London: University of Minnesota Press.

—(1998). *Homo Sacer: Sovereign Power and Bare Life*, trans. Daniel Heller-Roazen. Stanford, CA: Stanford University Press.

—(2002). *Remnants of Auschwitz: The Witness and the Archive*, trans. Daniel Heller-Roazen. New York: Zone Books.

—(2004). *The Open: Man and Animal*, trans. Kevin Attell. Stanford, CA: Stanford University Press.

—(2005). *State of Exception*, trans. Kevin Attell. Chicago and London: University of Chicago Press.

—(2009a). *The Signature of All Things: On Method*, trans. Luca D'Isanto with Kevin Attell. New York: Zone Books.

—(2009b). *What is an Apparatus? and Other Essays*, trans. David Kishik and Stefan Pedatella. Stanford, CA: Stanford University Press.

—(2011a). *The Kingdom and the Glory: For a Theological Genealogy of Economy and Government*, trans. Lorenzo Chiesa with Matteo Mandarini. Stanford, CA: Stanford University Press.

—(2011b). *The Sacrament of Language: An Archaeology of the Oath*, trans. Adam Kotsko. Stanford, CA: Stanford University Press.

Ahmad, Aijaz (1992). *In Theory: Classes, Nations, Literatures*. London and New York: Verso.

Ali, Z. A. H. (2001). "Adjusting the Borders of the Self: Sir Walter Scott's 'The Two Drovers'." *Papers on Language and Literature* 37 (Winter): 65–84.

Allen, Emily (1998). "Re-Marking Territory: *Redgauntlet* and the Restoration of Sir Walter Scott." *Studies in Romanticism* 37 (Summer): 163–82.

Althusser, Louis (1971). *Lenin and Philosophy*, trans. Ben Brewster. London and New York: Monthly Review Press.

Arata, Stephen (2001). "Scott's Pageants: The Example of *Kenilworth*." *Studies in Romanticism* 40.1 (Spring): 99–108.

Ashcroft, Bill, Gareth Griffiths, and Helen Tiffin (2000). *Post-Colonial Studies: The Key Concepts*, 2nd edn. London and New York: Routledge.

Badiou, Alain (1999). *Manifesto for Philosophy*, trans. Norman Madarasz. Albany, New York: State University of New York Press.

—(2001). *Ethics: An Essay on the Understanding of Evil*, trans. Peter Hallward. London and New York: Verso.

—(2006a). *Being and Event*, trans. Oliver Feltham. London and New York: Continuum.

—(2006b). *Theoretical Writings*, eds and trans. Ray Brassier and Alberto Toscano. London and New York: Continuum.

—(2007). *The Century*, trans. Alberto Toscano. Malden, MA and Cambridge: Polity.

—(2008). *Conditions*, trans. Steve Corcoran. London and New York: Continuum.

—(2009). *Logics of Worlds: Being and Event II*, trans. Alberto Toscano. London and New York: Continuum.

—(2011). *Second Manifesto for Philosophy*, trans. Louise Burchill. Cambridge and Malden, MA: Polity.

Bakhtin, Mikhail M. (1982). *The Dialogic Imagination: Four Essays*, ed. Michael Holquist, trans. Caryl Emerson and Michael Holquist. Austin, TX: University of Texas Press.

Balakrishnan, Gopal, ed. (2003). *Debating Empire*. New York and London: Verso.

Balfour, Ian (2007). "Introduction." *South Atlantic Quarterly* 106.2 (Spring): 205–17.

Baudrillard, Jean (1975). *The Mirror of Production*, trans. Mark Poster. St. Louis, MO: Telos Press.

—(1983). *Simulations*, trans. Phil Beitchman, Paul Foss, and Paul Patton. New York: Semiotext(e).

—(1987). *Forget Foucault*, no trans. New York: Semiotext(e).

—(1990). *Fatal Strategies*, trans. Phillipe Beitchman and W. J. G. Niesluchowski. Los Angeles: Semiotext(e).

—(2001). *Impossible Exchange*, trans. Chris Turner. London and New York: Verso.

Beiderwell, Bruce, ed. (2002). "Romantic Enlightenment: Sir Walter Scott and the Politics of History." Special issue of *European Romantic Review* 13.3: 223–324.

Belich, John (2009). *Replenishing the Earth: The Settler Revolution and the Rise of the Anglo-World, 1783–1939*. Oxford and New York: Oxford University Press.

Belsey, Catherine (2011). *A Future for Criticism*. Oxford and Malden, MA: Wiley-Blackwell.

Bender, John and David E. Wellbery, eds (1991). *Chronotypes: The Construction of Time*. Stanford, CA: Stanford University Press.

Bennet, Jane (2010). *Vibrant Matter: A Political Ecology of Things*. Durham, NC and London: Duke University Press.

Berardi, Franco (2009). *The Soul at Work: From Alienation to Autonomy*, trans. Francesca Cadel and Giuseppina Mecchia. Los Angeles: Semiotext(e).

Bhabha, Homi (2004). *The Location of Culture*. Routledge Classics ed. London and New York: Routledge.

Bogost, Ian (2012). *Alien Phenomenology, or What It's Like to Be a Thing*. Minneapolis and London: University of Minnesota Press.

Borradori, Giovanna (2003). *Philosophy in a Time of Terror: Dialogues with Jürgen Habermas and Jacques Derrida*. Chicago and London: University of Chicago Press.

Bourg, Julian (2007). *From Revolution to Ethics: May 1968 and Contemporary French Thought*. Montreal and Kingston, ON: McGill-Queens University Press.

Brown, Ian, ed. (2012). *Literary Tourism, the Trossachs, and Walter Scott*. Glasgow: Scottish Literature International.

Brown, Marshall, ed. (2009). "Romancing Scotland." Special issue of *Modern Language Quarterly* 70.4 (December): 403–525.

Brown, Wendy (2010). *Walled States, Waning Sovereignty*. New York: Zone Books.

Bruns, Gerald L. (2011). *On Ceasing to Be Human*. Stanford, CA: Stanford University Press.

Bruzelius, Margaret (2007). *Romancing the Novel: Adventure from Scott to Sebald*. Lewisburg, PA: Bucknell University Press.

Bryant, Levi (2011). *The Democracy of Objects*. Ann Arbor, MI: Open Humanities Press.

Buchanan, David (2011). "Popular Reception by Dramatic Adaptation: The Case of Walter Scott's *The Heart of Mid-Lothian*." *European Romantic Review* 22.6 (December): 745–63.

Buckton, Oliver (2009). "'This Monstrous Passion': Teaching *The Bride of Lammermoor* and Queer Theory." In *Approaches to Teaching Scott's Waverley Novels*, eds Evan Gottlieb and Ian Duncan. New York: Modern Language Association of America, 157–63.

Burgess, Miranda (2000). *British Fiction and the Production of Social Order*. Cambridge: Cambridge University Press.

—(2006). "The National Tale and Allied Genres, 1770s–1840s." In *The Cambridge Companion to the Irish Novel*, ed. John Wilson Foster. Cambridge: Cambridge University Press, 39–59.

Butler, Judith (1990). *Gender Trouble: Feminism and the Subversion of Identity*. London and New York: Routledge.

—(1997). *Excitable Speech: A Politics of the Performative*. London and New York: Routledge.

—(2004). *Precarious Life: The Powers of Mourning and Violence*. London and New York: Verso.

—(2005). *Giving an Account of Oneself*. New York: Fordham University Press.

—(2009). *Frames of War: When is Life Grievable?* London and New York: Verso.

—(2011). *Bodies That Matter: On the Discursive Limits of "Sex."* Routledge Classics Edition. London and New York: Routledge.

Butler, Judith, Ernesto Laclau, and Slavoj Žižek (2000). *Contingency, Hegemony, Universality: Contemporary Dialogues on the Left*. London and New York: Verso.

Butler, Marilyn (1981). *Romantics, Rebels, and Reactionaries: English Literature and its Background, 1760–1830*. Oxford and London: Oxford University Press.

Buzard, James (2005). *Disorienting Fiction: The Autoethnographic Work of Nineteenth-Century British Novels*. Princeton: Princeton University Press.

Campbell, Timothy (2011). *Improper Life: Technology and Biopolitics from Heidegger to Agamben*. Minneapolis and London: University of Minnesota Press.

Canguilhem, Georges (1991). *The Normal and the Pathological*, trans. Carolyn R. Fawcett with Robert S. Cohen. New York: Zone Books.

Carson, James P. (2010). *Populism, Gender, and Sympathy in the Romantic Novel*. Basingstoke and New York: Palgrave Macmillan.

Chandler, James (1998). *England in 1819: The Politics of Literary Culture and the Case of Romantic Historicism*. Chicago: University of Chicago Press.

Cockshut, A. O. J. (1969). *The Achievement of Sir Walter Scott*. New York: New York University Press.

Colley, Linda (1992). *Britons: Forging the Nation*. New Haven and London: Yale University Press.

Cooney, Seamus (1978). "Scott and Cultural Relativism: 'The Two Drovers'." *Studies in Short Fiction* 15: 1–9.

Copjec, Joan (1994a). *Read my Desire: Lacan against the Historicists*. Cambridge, MA and London: MIT Press.

—ed. (1994b). *Supposing the Subject*. London and New York: Verso.

Crawford, Robert (1992). *Devolving English Literature*. Oxford: Oxford University Press.

Culler, Jonathan (1982). *On Deconstruction: Theory and Criticism after Structuralism*. Ithaca, NY: Cornell University Press.

—(2000). *Literary Theory: A Very Short Introduction*. Oxford: Oxford University Press.

Cusset, François (2008). *French Theory: How Foucault, Derrida, Deleuze, & Co. Transformed the Intellectual Life of the United States*, trans. Jeff Fort. Minneapolis and London: University of Minnesota Press.

Daiches, David (1951). "Scott's Achievement as a Novelist." *Nineteenth Century Fiction* 6.2–3: 81–95, 153–73.

D'Arcy, Julian Meldon (1985). "Davie Deans and Bothwell Bridge: A Re-evaluation." *Scottish Literary Journal* 12.2: 23–34.

—(2005). *Subversive Scott: The Waverley Novels and Scottish Nationalism*. Reykjavik: Vigdís Finnbogadóttir Institute and University of Iceland Press.

David, Lennard J., ed. (2010). *The Disability Studies Reader*. London and New York: Routledge.

Davis, Colin (2010). *Critical Excess: Overreading in Derrida, Deleuze, Levinas, Žižek, and Cavell*. Stanford, CA: Stanford University Press.

Davis, Leith (1998). *Acts of Union: Scotland and the Literary Negotiation of the Anglo-Scottish Union, 1707–1830*. Stanford, CA: Stanford University Press.

Davis, Leith, Ian Duncan, and Janet Sorensen, eds (2004). *Scotland and the Borders of Romanticism*. Cambridge: Cambridge University Press.

de Certeau, Michel (1988). *The Writing of History*, trans. Tom Conley. New York: Columbia University Press.

DeLanda, Manuel (1997). *A Thousand Years of Non-Linear History*. New York: Zone Books.

—(2002). *Intensive Science and Virtual Philosophy*. London and New York: Continuum.

—(2006). *A New Philosophy of Society: Assemblage Theory and Social Complexity*. London and New York: Continuum.

—(2010). *Deleuze: History and Science*. New York and Dresden: Atropos Press.

—(2011a). "Emergence, Causality, and Realism." In *The Speculative Turn: Continental Materialism and Realism*, eds Levi Bryant, Nick Srnicek, and Graham Harman. Melbourne: re.press, 381–92.

—(2011b). *Philosophy and Simulation: The Emergence of Synthetic Reason*. London and New York: Continuum.

DeLanda, Manuel, John Protevi, and Torkild Thanem (2004). "Deleuzian Interrogations: A Conversation with Manuel DeLanda, John Protevi, and Torkild Thanem." *Tamara: Journal for Critical Organizational Inquiry* 3.4: 1–36.

Deleuze, Gilles (1994). *Difference and Repetition*, trans. Paul Patton. New York: Columbia University Press.

Deleuze, Gilles and Félix Guattari (1983). *Anti-Oedipus: Capitalism and Schizophrenia*, trans. Robert Hurley, Mark Seem, and Helen R. Lane. Minneapolis: University of Minnesota Press.

—(1987). *A Thousand Plateaus: Capitalism and Schizophrenia* Vol. 2, trans. Brian Massumi. Minneapolis and London: University of Minnesota Press.

—(1994). *What is Philosophy?*, trans. Hugh Tomlinson and Grant Burchell. New York: Columbia University Press.

Derrida, Jacques (1978). *Writing and Difference*, trans. Alan Bass. Chicago: University of Chicago Press.

—(1988). *Limited Inc*, trans. Samuel Weber et al. Evanston, IL: Northwestern University Press.

—(1991). *On Cosmopolitanism and Forgiveness*, trans. Mark Dooley and Michael Hughes. London and New York: Routledge.

—(1997a). *Deconstruction in a Nutshell: A Conversation with Jacques Derrida*, ed. John Caputo. New York: Fordham University Press.

—(1997b). *Of Grammatology*, trans. Gayatri Chakravorty Spivak. Corrected ed. Baltimore and London: The Johns Hopkins University Press.

—(1997c). *The Politics of Friendship*, trans. George Collins. London and New York: Verso.

—(1999). *Adieu to Emmanuel Levinas*, trans. Pascale-Anne Brault and Michael Naas. Stanford, CA: Stanford University Press.

—(2000). *Of Hospitality: Anne Dufourmantelle Invites Jacques Derrida to Respond*, trans. Rachel Bowlby. Stanford, CA: Stanford University Press.

—(2003). "Autoimmunity: Real and Symbolic Suicides – A Dialogue with Jacques Derrida." In *Philosophy in a Time of Terror*, ed. Giovanna Borradori. Chicago, IL: University of Chicago Press, 85–136.

—(2006). *Specters of Marx: The State of the Debt, the Work of Mourning, and the New International*, trans. Peggy Kamuf. Routledge Classics ed. London and New York: Routledge.

—(2008). *The Animal That Therefore I Am*, ed. Marie-Louise Mallet, trans. David Wills. New York: Fordham University Press.

—(2009, 2011). *The Beast and the Sovereign*, Vols. 1 and 2: *The Seminars of Jacques Derrida*, eds Michel Lisse, Marie-Louise Mallet, and Ginette Michaud, trans. Geoffrey Bennington. Chicago and London: University of Chicago Press.

Dews, Peter (1987). *Logics of Disintegration: Post-Structuralist Thought and the Claims of Critical Theory*. London and New York: Verso.

Dick, Alex J. (2012). "Walter Scott and the Financial Crash of 1825: Fiction, Speculation, and the Standard of Value." In "Romanticism, Forgery, and the Credit Crunch," ed. Ian Haywood. Special issue of *Romantic Circles Praxis Series* (February), http://www.rc.umd.edu/praxis/forgery/HTML/praxis.2011. dick.html.

Driscoll, Mark (2010). "Looting the Theory Commons: Hardt and Negri's *Commonwealth*." *Postmodern Culture* 21.1 (September), http://muse.jhu. edu/login?auth=0&type=summary&url=/journals/postmodern_culture/ v021/21.1.driscoll.html.

Duncan, Ian (1992). *Modern Romance and Transformations of the Novel: The Gothic, Scott, Dickens*. Cambridge: Cambridge University Press.

—(2007). *Scott's Shadow: The Novel in Romantic Edinburgh*. Princeton and Oxford: Princeton University Press.

—(2011). "The Trouble with Man: Scott, Romance, and World History in the Age of Lamarck." In "Romantic Frictions," ed. Theresa M. Kelley. Special issue of *Romantic Circles Praxis Series* (September), www.rc.umd.edu/praxis/frictions/ HTML/praxis.2011.duncan.html.

Duncan, Ian, Ann W. Rowland, and Charles Snodgrass, eds (2001). "Scott, Scotland, and Romantic Nationalism." Special issue of *Studies in Romanticism* 40.1: 3–168.

Dwyer, John (1987). *Virtuous Discourse: Sensibility and Community in Late Eighteenth-Century Scotland.* Edinburgh: John Donald.

Edwards, Simon (2009). "Home and Away with Walter Scott." In *Approaches to Teaching Scott's Waverley Novels*, eds Evan Gottlieb and Ian Duncan. New York: Modern Language Association of America, 77–87.

Esposito, Roberto (2010). *Communitas: The Origin and Destiny of Community*, trans. Timothy Campbell. Stanford, CA: Stanford University Press.

Ferris, Ina (1991). *The Achievement of Literary Authority: Gender, History, and the Waverley Novels.* Ithaca and London: Cornell University Press.

—(2002). *The Romantic National Tale and the Question of Ireland.* Cambridge: Cambridge University Press.

Fielding, Penny (2008). *Scotland and the Fictions of Geography: North Britain, 1760–1830.* Cambridge: Cambridge University Press.

Forster, Edward M. (1985). *Aspects of the Novel.* New York: Houghton Mifflin Harcourt.

Foucault, Michel (1970). *The Order of Things: An Archaeology of the Human Sciences.* New York: Vintage.

—(1978). *The History of Sexuality,* Vol. 1: *An Introduction*, trans. Robert Hurley. New York: Vintage.

—(1979). *Discipline and Punish: The Birth of the Prison*, trans. Alan Sheridan. New York: Vintage.

—(2007). *Security, Territory, Population: Lectures at the Collège de France, 1977–1978*, ed. Michel Senellart, trans. Graham Burchell. New York: Picador.

—(2008). *The Birth of Biopolitics: Lectures at the Collège de France, 1978–1979*, ed. Michel Senellart, trans. Graham Burchell. New York: Picador.

—(2010). *The Government of Self and Others: Lectures at the Collège de France, 1982–1983*, ed. Michael Senellart, trans. Graham Burchell. New York: Palgrave Macmillan.

—(2011). "The Gay Science," trans. Nicole Morar and Daniel W. Smith. *Critical Inquiry* 37.3 (Spring): 385–403.

Frye, Northrop (1976). *The Secular Scripture: A Study of the Structure of Romance.* Boston: Harvard University Press.

Garber, Marjorie, Beatrice Hanssen, and Rebecca L. Walkowitz, eds (2000). *The Turn to Ethics.* New York: Routledge.

Garside, Peter (1975). "Scott and the 'Philosophical Historians'." *Journal of the History of Ideas* 36: 497–512.

—(1991). "Hidden Origins of Scott's *Waverley*." *Nineteenth Century Literature* 46.1 (June): 30–53.

Genette, Gérard (1997). *Paratexts: Thresholds of Interpretation*, trans. Jane E. Lewin. New York: Columbia University Press.

Geoghegan, Dionysius (2011). "From Information Theory to French Theory: Jakobson, Lévi-Strauss, and the Cybernetic Apparatus." *Critical Inquiry* 38.1 (Autumn): 96–126.

Goode, Mike (2003). "Dryasdust Antiquarianism and Soppy Masculinity: The Waverley Novels and the Gender of History." *Representations* 82: 52–86.

Gottlieb, Evan (2007). *Feeling British: Sympathy and National Identity in Scottish and English Writing, 1707–1832.* Lewisburg, PA: Bucknell University Press.

—(2008). "Unvarnished Tales and Fatal Influences: Teaching the National Tale and Historical Novel." *Romantic Pedagogy Commons* (August). http://www.rc.umd. edu/pedagogies/commons/novel/gottlieb.html.

—(2009). "Sir Walter and Plain Jane: Teaching Scott and Austen Together." In *Approaches to Teaching Scott's Waverley Novels*, eds Evan Gottlieb and Ian Duncan. New York: Modern Language Association of America, 101–4.

—(2011). "'Almost the Same as Being Innocent: Celebrated Murderesses and National Narratives in Walter Scott's *The Heart of Mid-Lothian* and Margaret Atwood's *Alias Grace*." in *Scottish Literature and Postcolonial Literature*, eds Michael Gardiner, Graeme Macdonald and Niall O'Gallagher. Edinburgh: Edinburgh University Press, 30–42.

Gottlieb, Evan and Ian Duncan, eds (2009). *Approaches to Teaching Scott's Waverley Novels*. New York: Modern Language Association of America.

Gutting, Gary (2005). *Foucault: A Very Short Introduction*. Oxford: Oxford University Press.

Habermas, Jürgen (1984 and 1987). *The Theory of Communicative Action*, trans. Thomas McCarthy. 2 Vols. Boston: Beacon Press.

—(1987). *The Philosophical Discourse of Modernity: Twelve Lectures*, trans. Frederick G. Lawrence. Cambridge, MA: MIT Press.

—(1989). *The Structural Transformation of the Public Sphere: An Inquiry into a Category of Bourgeois Society*, trans. Thomas Burger with Frederick Lawrence. Cambridge, MA: MIT Press.

—(1998). *The Inclusion of the Other: Studies in Political Theory*, eds Ciaran Cronin and Pablo De Grieff, trans. Ciaran Cronin. Cambridge, MA: MIT Press.

—(2001). *The Postnational Condition: Political Essays*, ed. and trans. Max Pensky. Cambridge, MA: MIT Press.

—(2003a). "Fundamentalism and Terror – A Dialogue with Jürgen Habermas." In *Philosophy in a Time of Terror*, ed. Giovanna Borradori. Chicago: University of Chicago Press, 25–43.

—(2003b). *The Future of Human Nature*, trans. Max Pensky et al. Malden, MA and Cambridge: Polity.

—(2006). *The Divided West*, ed. and trans. Ciarin Cronin. Malden, MA and Cambridge.

Hailes, Kathleen N. (1999). *How We Became Posthuman: Virtual Bodies in Cybernetics, Literature, and Informatics*. Chicago and London: University of Chicago Press.

Hamilton, Paul (2003). *Metaromanticism: Aesthetics, Literature, Theory*. Chicago and London: University of Chicago Press.

Haraway, Donna (1991). *Simians, Cyborgs and Women: The Reinvention of Nature*. New York and London: Routledge.

—(2008). *When Species Meet*. Minneapolis and London: University of Minnesota Press.

Hardt, Michael and Antonio Negri (2000). *Empire*. Cambridge, MA and London: Harvard University Press.

—(2004). *Multitude: War and Democracy in the Age of Empire*. New York: Penguin.

—(2009). *Commonwealth*. Cambridge, MA and London: Belknap Press.

Harman, Graham (2011). *The Quadruple Object*. Winchester, UK and Washington: Zero Books.

Harpham, Galt G. (2011). *The Humanities and the Dream of America*. Chicago: University of Chicago Press.

Hart, Francis R. (1966). *Scott's Novels: The Plotting of Historical Survival.* Charlottesville, VA: University of Virginia Press.

Hasler, Anthony J. (2009). "Framing the Convenanters (Again): Teaching *Old Mortality* in Context." In *Approaches to Teaching Scott's Waverley Novels*, eds Evan Gottlieb and Ian Duncan. New York: Modern Language Association of America, 140–9.

Hayden, John O. (1995). *Sir Walter Scott: The Critical Heritage.* London: Routledge.

Hechter, Michael (1999). *Internal Colonialism: The Celtic Fringe in British National Development*, rev. ed. New Brunswick, NJ: Transaction.

Hewitt, David (2009). "Teaching *The Heart of Midlothian*." In *Approaches to Teaching Scott's Waverley Novels*, eds Evan Gottlieb and Ian Duncan. New York: Modern Language Association of America, 150–6.

Heydt-Stevenson, Jill and Charlotte Sussman, eds (2008). *Recognizing the Romantic Novel: New Histories of British Fiction, 1780–1830.* Liverpool: University of Liverpool Press.

Hill, Richard J. (2010). *Picturing Scotland through the Waverley Novels: Walter Scott and the Origins of the Victorian Illustrated Novel.* Burlington, VT and Farnham, UK: Ashgate.

Hoeveler, Diane L. (2009). "Teaching the Female Body as Contested Territory." In *Approaches to Teaching Scott's Waverley Novels*, eds Evan Gottlieb and Ian Duncan. New York: Modern Language Association of America, 105–14.

Hogg, James (1983). *Anecdotes of Sir W. Scott*, ed. Douglas Mack. Edinburgh: Scottish Academic Press.

Hogle, Jerrold, ed. (2002). *The Cambridge Companion to Gothic Fiction.* Cambridge and New York: Cambridge University Press.

Holmes, Richard (2010). *The Age of Wonder: How the Romantic Generation Discovered the Beauty and Terror of Science.* New York: Vintage.

Horkheimer, Max and Theodor Adorno (2002). *Dialectic of Enlightenment: Philosophical Fragments*, ed. Gunzelin S. Noerr, trans. Edmund Jephcott. Stanford, CA: Stanford University Press.

Israel, Jonathan L. (2006). *Enlightenment Contested: Philosophy, Modernity, and the Emancipation of Man, 1670–1752.* London and New York: Oxford.

Jarrells, Anthony (2009). "Provincializing Enlightenment: Edinburgh Historicism and the Blackwoodian Regional Tale." *Studies in Romanticism* 48.2 (Summer): 257–77.

Jones, Catherine (2003). *Literary Memory: Scott's Waverley Novels and the Psychology of Narrative.* Lewisburg, PA: Bucknell University Press.

Jones, Colin and Dror Wahrman, eds (2002). *The Age of Cultural Revolutions: Britain and France, 1750–1820.* Berkeley: University of California Press.

Kant, Immanuel (1996). *Practical Philosophy: The Cambridge Edition of the Works of Immanuel Kant*, ed. and trans. Mary J. Gregor. Cambridge and New York: Cambridge University Press.

Kelly, Gary (1989). *English Fiction of the Romantic Period, 1789–1830.* London and New York: Longman.

Kelly, Stuart (2011). *Scott-Land: The Man Who Invented a Nation.* Edinburgh: Polygon.

Kerr, James (1989). *Fiction against History: Scott as Storyteller.* Cambridge: Cambridge University Press.

Kittler, Friedrich (2010). *Optical Media: Berlin Lectures 1999*, trans. Anthony Enns. Cambridge and Malden, MA: Polity.

Koselleck, Reinhart (2002). *The Practice of Conceptual History: Timing History, Spacing Concepts*, trans. Todd S. Presner et al. Stanford, CA: Stanford University Press.

—(2004). *Futures Past: On the Semantics of Historical Time*, trans. Keith Tribe. New York: Columbia University Press.

Kristeva, Julia (1982). *Power of Horror: An Essay on Abjection*. trans. Leon S. Roudiez. New York: Columbia University Press.

Laclau, Ernesto (2004). "Can Immanence Explain Social Struggles?" In *Empire's New Clothes*, eds Paul A. Passavant and Jodi Dean. New York: Routledge, 21–30.

Lamarche, Pierre, Max Rosenkrantz, and David Sherman, eds (2011). *Reading Negri: Marxism in the Age of Empire*. Chicago: Open Court Press.

Langan, Celeste (2009). "'The Poetry of Pure Memory': Teaching Scott's Novels in the Context of Romanticism." In *Approaches to Teaching Scott's Waverley Novels*, eds Evan Gottlieb and Ian Duncan. New York: Modern Language Association of America, 67–76.

Laruelle, François (2010). *Philosophies of Difference: A Critical Introduction to Non-Philosophy*, trans. Rocco Gangle. London and New York: Continuum.

Latour, Bruno (1993). *We Have Never Been Modern*, trans. Catherine Porter. Cambridge, MA: Harvard University Press.

—(2004). "Why Has Critique Run out of Steam? From Matters of Fact to Matters of Concern." *Critical Inquiry* 30 (Winter): 225–48.

—(2005). *Reassembling the Social: An Introduction to Actor-Network-Theory*. Oxford and New York: Oxford University Press.

Lee, Yoon Sun (2004). *Nationalism and Irony: Burke, Scott, Carlyle*. New York and Oxford: Oxford University Press.

Leitch, Vincent (2008). *Living with Theory*. Oxford and Malden, MA: Blackwell.

Levinson, Brett (2004). *Market and Thought: Meditations on the Political and the Biopolitical*. New York: Fordham University Press.

Lincoln, Andrew (2007). *Walter Scott and Modernity*. Edinburgh: Edinburgh University Press.

Lockhart, Gibson J. (1906). *The Life of Sir Walter Scott*. London: J. M. Dent & Sons.

Loomba, Ania (2005). *Colonialism/Postcolonialism*, 2nd edn. London and New York: Routledge.

Luhmann, Niklas (1995). *Social Systems*, trans. John Bednarz Jr. with Dirk Baecker. Stanford, CA: Stanford University Press.

Lukács, Georg (1962). *The Historical Novel*, trans. Hannah Mitchell and Stanley Mitchell. London: Merlin Press.

Lumsden, Alison (2010). *Walter Scott and the Limits of Language*. Edinburgh: Edinburgh University Press.

Lynch, Shauna D. (1998). *The Economy of Character: Novels, Market Culture, and the Business of Inner Meaning*. Chicago and London: University of Chicago Press.

Mack, Douglas and Suzanne Gilbert (2009). "Scottish history in the Waverley Novels." In *Approaches to Teaching Scott's Waverley Novels*, eds Evan Gottlieb and Ian Duncan. New York: Modern Language Association of America, 26–37.

Mack, Ruth (2009). *Literary Historicity: Literature and Historical Experience in Eighteenth-Century Britain.* Stanford: Stanford University Press.

Malley, Shawn (2001). "Walter Scott's Romantic Archeology: New/Old Abbotsford and *The Antiquary.*" *Studies in Romanticism* 40.3 (Summer): 233–51.

Marx, Karl (1988). *The Communist Manifesto*, ed. Frederic L. Bender. New York and London: W. W. Norton.

Maxwell, Richard (2001). "Inundations of Time: A Definition of Scott's Originality." *ELH* 68.2: 419–68.

—(2008). "The Historical Novel." In *Cambridge Companion to Fiction in the Romantic Period*, eds Richard Maxwell and Katie Trumpener. Cambridge: Cambridge University Press, 52–86.

Maxwell, Richard and Katie Trumpener, eds (2008). *The Cambridge Companion to Fiction in the Romantic Period.* Cambridge and New York: Cambridge University Press.

McCracken-Flesher, Caroline (2005). *Walter Scott and the Story of Tomorrow.* Oxford: Oxford University Press.

McGann, Jerome (2004). "Walter Scott's Romantic Postmodernity." In *Scotland and the Borders of Romanticism*, eds Leith Davis, Ian Duncan, and Janet Sorensen. Cambridge: Cambridge University Press, 113–29.

McGowan, Todd (2010). "Subject of the Event, Subject of the Act: The Difference between Badious's and Žižek's Systems of Philosophy." *Subjectivity* 3.1 (April): 7–30.

McLuhan, Marshall (1994). *Understanding Media: The Extensions of Man*, rev. ed. Cambridge, MA and London: MIT Press.

McMaster, Graham (1981). *Scott and Society.* Cambridge: Cambridge University Press.

McNeil, Kenneth (2007). *Scotland, Britain, Empire: Writing the Highlands, 1760–1860.* Columbus: Ohio State University Press.

—(2009). "The Limits of Diversity: Using Scott's 'The Two Drovers' to Teach Multiculturalism in a Survey or Nonmajors Course." In *Approaches to Teaching Scott's Waverley Novels*, eds Evan Gottlieb and Ian Duncan. New York: Modern Language Association of America, 123–9.

Meek, Ronald L. (1967). "The Scottish Contribution to Marxist Sociology." In *"Economics and Ideology" and Other Essays.* London: Chapman and Hall, 34–66.

Meillassoux, Quentin (2008). *After Finitude: An Essay on the Necessity of Contingency*, trans. Ray Brassier. New York and London: Continuum.

Miles, Robert (2008). *Romantic Misfits.* Basingstoke: Palgrave Macmillan.

Millgate, Jane (1984). *Walter Scott: The Making of the Novelist.* Toronto: University of Toronto Press.

Mohanty, Talpade C. (2003). *Feminism Without Borders: Decolonizing Theory, Practicing Solidarity.* Durham, NC and London: Duke University Press.

Moi, Toril (1985). *Sexual/Textual Politics.* New York: Routledge.

Moretti, Franco (1998). *Atlas of the European Novel, 1800–1900.* London and New York: Verso.

—(2000). *The Way of the World: The Bildungsroman in European Culture*, new edn. London and New York: Verso.

Morton, Timothy (2007). *Ecology Without Nature: Rethinking Environmental Ethics.* Cambridge, MA and London: Harvard University Press.

Muri, Allison (2007). *The Enlightenment Cyborg: A History of Communications and Control in the Human Machine, 1660–1830.* Toronto and Buffalo: University of Toronto Press.

Nancy, Jean-Luc (1991). *The Inoperative Community*, ed. Peter Connor, trans. Peter Connor, Lisa Garbus, Michael Holland, and Simona Sawhney. Minneapolis and Oxford: University of Minnesota Press.

Nealon, Jeffrey T. (2008). *Foucault Beyond Foucault: Power and its Intensifications since 1984.* Stanford, CA: Stanford University Press.

Negri, Antonio (2011). *Art & Multitude*, ed. Ed Emery. Malden, MA and Cambridge: Polity.

Nietzsche, Friedrich (1979). "On Truth and Lies in a Nonmoral Sense." In *Philosophy and Truth: Selections from Nietzsche's Notebooks of the Early 1820's*, ed. and trans. Daniel Breazeale. New Jersey: Humanities Press, 79–91.

—(1989). *On the Genealogy of Morals*, ed. Walter Kaufmann. New York: Vintage.

Norris, Christopher (1982). *Deconstruction: Theory and Practice.* London: Methuen.

—(1988). *Derrida.* Cambridge, MA: Harvard University Press.

Noys, Benjamin (2010). *The Persistence of the Negative: A Critique of Contemporary Theory.* Edinburgh: Edinburgh University Press.

Osborne, Peter (2011). "Philosophy after Theory: Transdisciplinarity and the New." In *Theory After 'Theory,'* eds Jane Elliott and Derek Attridge, London and New York: Routledge, 19–33.

Park, Julie (2010). *The Self and It: Novel Objects in Eighteenth-Century England.* Stanford, CA: Stanford University Press.

Piper, Andrew (2009). *Dreaming in Books: The Making of the Bibliographic Imagination in the Romantic Age.* Chicago and London: University of Chicago Press.

Poovey, Mary (2008). *Genres of the Credit Economy: Mediating Value in Eighteenth- and Nineteenth-Century Britain.* Chicago and London: University of Chicago Press.

Pratt, Mary Louise (1992). *Imperial Eyes: Travel Writing and Transculturation.* London and New York: Routledge.

Rancière, Jacques (2004a). *The Politics of Aesthetics*, trans. Gabriel Rockhill. London and New York: Continuum.

—(2004b). "The Politics of Literature." *SubStance* 33.1: 10–24.

—(2006). *Hatred of Democracy*, trans. Steve Corcoran. London and New York: Verso.

—(2011a). *Althusser's Lesson*, trans. Emiliano Battista. London and New York: Continuum.

—(2011b). *Mute Speech: Literature, Critical Theory, and Politics*, trans. James Swenson. New York: Columbia University Press.

—(2011c). *The Politics of Literature*, trans. Julie Rose. Malden, MA and Cambridge: Polity.

Raunig, Gerald (2010). *A Thousand Machines: A Concise Philosophy of the Machine as Social Movement*, trans. Aileen Derieg. Los Angeles: Semiotext(e).

Rigney, Ann (2001). *Imperfect Histories: The Elusive Past and the Legacy of Romantic Historicism.* Ithaca, NY: Cornell University Press.

—(2012). *The Afterlives of Walter Scott: Memory on the Move.* Oxford and New York: Oxford University Press.

Robertson, Fiona (1994). *Legitimate Histories: Scott, Gothic, and the Authorities of Fiction.* Oxford: Clarendon.

—ed. (2012). *The Edinburgh Companion to Sir Walter Scott.* Edinburgh: Edinburgh University Press.

Ross, Allison (2008). Introduction to "The Agamben Effect." Special issue of *The South Atlantic Quarterly* 107.1 (Winter): 1–14.

Ross, Kristin (2002). *May '68 and its Afterlives.* Chicago: University of Chicago Press.

Rowlinson, Matthew (2010). *Real Money and Romanticism.* Cambridge: Cambridge University Press.

Rubin, Gayle (1975). "The Traffic in Women: Notes on the 'Political Economy' of Sex." In *Toward an Anthropology of Women*, ed. Reyna Reiter. New York: Monthly Review Press, 157–210.

Santner, Eric (2011). *The Royal Remains: The People's Two Bodies and the Endgames of Sovereignty.* Chicago: University of Chicago Press.

Sarup, Madan (1993). *An Introduction to Post-Structuralism and Postmodernism*, 2nd edn. Athens, GA: University of Georgia Press.

Schmitt, Carl (2005). *Political Theology: Four Chapters on the Concept of Sovereignty*, trans. George Schwab. Chicago and London: University of Chicago Press.

Scott, Walter (1982). *The Heart of Midlothian*, ed. Claire Lamont. Oxford and New York: Oxford University Press.

—(1986). *Waverley*, ed. Claire Lamont. Oxford and New York: Oxford University Press.

—(1987). *The Two Drovers and Other Stories*, ed. Graham Tulloch. London: Oxford University Press.

—(1995). *The Bride of Lammermoor*, ed. John H. Alexander. London and New York: Penguin.

—(1996). *Ivanhoe*, ed. Ian Duncan. Oxford and New York: Oxford University Press.

—(1998a). *The Antiquary*, ed. David Hewitt. London and New York: Penguin.

—(1998b). *The Journal of Sir Walter Scott*, ed. W. E. K. Anderson. Edinburgh: Canongate Books.

—(1998c). *Rob Roy*, ed. Ian Duncan. Oxford and New York: Oxford University Press.

—(1999a). *The Fair Maid of Perth*, eds Andrew. D. Hook and Donald Mackenzie. Edinburgh: Edinburgh University Press.

—(1999b). *Kenilworth*, ed. John H. Alexander. London and New York: Penguin.

—(2000a). *Ivanhoe*, ed. Graham Tulloch. London and New York: Penguin.

—(2000b). *Quentin Durward*, ed. Susan Manning. Oxford and New York: Oxford University Press.

—(2000c). *Redgauntlet*, ed. G. A. M. Wood with David Hewitt. London and New York: Penguin.

—(2001). *Quentin Durward*, eds John H. Alexander and G. A. M. Wood. Edinburgh: Edinburgh University Press.

—(2003). *Chronicles of the Canongate*, ed. Claire Lamont. London and New York: Penguin.

—(2004). *The Fortunes of Nigel*, ed. Frank Jordan. Edinburgh: Edinburgh University Press.

— (2006). *Count Robert of Paris.* ed. J. H. Alexander. Edinburgh: Edinburgh UP.

—(2009a). *The Talisman*, eds J. B. Ellis with John H. Alexander, P. D. Garside, and David Hewitt. Edinburgh: University of Edinburgh Press.

— (2009b). *The Betrothed.* eds J. B. Ellis with John H. Alexander and David Hewitt. Edinburgh: Edinburgh University Press.

Sedgwick, Eve K. (1985). *Between Men: English Literature and Male Homosocial Desire.* New York: Columbia University Press.

Serres, Michel (2007). *The Parasite*, new edn, trans. Lawrence R. Schehr. Minneapolis and London: University of Minnesota Press.

—(2008). *The Five Senses: A Philosophy of Mingled Bodies*, trans. Margaret Sankey and Peter Cowley. London and New York: Continuum.

Shaw, Harry (1983). *The Forms of Historical Fiction: Sir Walter Scott and His Successors.* Ithaca: Cornell University Press.

—(1999). *Narrating Reality: Austen, Scott, Eliot.* Ithaca, NY: Cornell University Press.

Shields, Juliet (2010). *Sentimental Literature and Anglo-Scottish Identity, 1745–1820.* Cambridge: Cambridge University Press.

Simpson, David (2008). "'Which is the merchant here? and which the Jew?': Friends and Enemies in Walter Scott's Crusader Novels." *Studies in Romanticism* 47 (Winter): 437–52.

Sloterdijk, Peter (1987). *Critique of Cynical Reason*, trans. Michael Eldred. Minneapolis: University of Minnesota Press.

—(2011). *Spheres, Vol. 1: Bubbles*, trans. Wieland Hoban. Los Angeles: Semiotext(e).

Sorensen, Janet (1997). "Writing Historically, Speaking Nostalgically: The Competing Languages of Nation in Scott's *The Bride of Lammermoor.*" In *Narratives of Nostalgia, Gender, and Nationalism*, eds Jean Pickering and Suzanne Kehde. New York: New York University Press, 30–51.

—(1999). *The Grammar of Empire in Eighteenth-Century Britain.* Cambridge: Cambridge University Press.

Spivak, Chakravorty G. (1994). "Can the Subaltern Speak?" In *Colonial Discourse and Post-Colonial Theory: A Reader*, eds Patrick Williams and Laura Chrisman. New York: Columbia University Press, 66–111.

St Clair, William (2004). *The Reading Nation in the Romantic Period.* Cambridge: Cambridge University Press.

Stafford, Maria B. (1991). *Body Criticism: Imaging the Unseen in Enlightenment Art and Medicine.* Cambridge, MA and London: MIT Press.

Stengers, Isabelle (2010). *Cosmopolitics I*, trans. Robert Bononno. Minneapolis and London: University of Minnesota Press.

Stephen, Leslie (1892). *Hours in a Library*, Vol. 1. London: Smith, Elder, and Co.

Sussman, Charlotte (2002). "The Emptiness at *The Heart of Midlothian*: Nation, Narration, and Population." *Eighteenth-Century Fiction* 15.1 (October): 103–26.

Sutherland, John (1995). *The Life of Sir Walter Scott: A Critical Biography.* Malden, MA and Oxford: Blackwell.

Sutherland, Kathryn (1987). "Fictional Economies: Adam Smith, Walter Scott and the Nineteenth-century Novel." *ELH* 54: 97–127.

Takanashi, Kyoko (2012). "Circulation, Monuments, and the Politics of Transmission in Sir Walter Scott's *Tales of My Landlord*." *ELH* 79 (Summer): 289–314.

Taylor, Charles (2007). *A Secular Age*. Cambridge, MA: Belknap Press.

Tönnies, Alfred (2001). *Community and Civil Society*, ed. Jose Harris, trans. Margaret Hollis (New York and London: Cambridge University Press.

Trumpener, Katie (1997). *Bardic Nationalism: The Romantic Novel and the British Empire*. Princeton: Princeton University Press.

Van Ghent, Dorothy (1953). *The English Novel: Form and Function*. New York: Harper & Row.

Virno, Paulo (2004). *A Grammar of the Multitude: For an Analysis of Contemporary Forms of Life*, trans. Isabella Bertoletti, James Cascaito, and Andrea Casson. Los Angeles: Semiotext(e).

Wagner, Peter (2012). *Modernity: Understanding the Present*. Oxford and Malden, MA: Polity.

Wallace, Tara Ghoshal (2009). "Thinking Globally: *The Talisman* and *The Surgeon's Daughter*." In *Approaches to Teaching Scott's Waverley Novels*, eds Evan Gottlieb and Ian Duncan. New York: Modern Language Association of America, 170–6.

—(2010). *Imperial Characters: Home and Periphery in Eighteenth-Century Literature*. Lewisburg, PA: Bucknell University Press.

Wallerstein, Immanuel (2004). *World-Systems Analysis: An Introduction*. Durham, NC and London: Duke University Press.

—(2006). *European Universalism: The Rhetoric of Power*. New York and London: The New Press.

Warhman, Dror (2004). *The Making of the Modern Self: Identity and Culture in Eighteenth-Century England*. New Haven and London: Yale University Press.

Warner, William B. (1998). *Licensing Entertainment: The Elevation of Novel Reading in Britain, 1684–1750*. Berkeley and Los Angeles: University of California Press.

Watt, James (2004). "Scott, the Scottish Enlightenment, and Romantic Orientalism." In *Scotland and the Borders of Romanticism*, eds Leith Davis, Ian Duncan, and Janet Sorensen. Cambridge: Cambridge University Press, 94–112.

Welsh, Alexander (1992). *The Hero of the Waverley Novels: With New Essays on Scott*. Princeton, NJ: Princeton University Press.

West, David (2010). *Continental Philosophy: An Introduction*, 2nd edn. Cambridge and Malden, MA: Polity.

White, Hayden (1973). *Metahistory: The Historical Imagination in Nineteenth-Century Europe*. Baltimore and London: Johns Hopkins University Press.

Wickman, Matthew (2006). *The Ruins of Experience: Scotland's "Romantick" Highlands and the Birth of the Modern Witness*. Philadelphia: University of Pennsylvania Press.

Williams, Ioan, ed. (1968). *Sir Walter Scott on Novelists and Fiction*. New York: Barnes and Noble.

Williams, Raymond (1977). *Marxism and Literature*. Oxford and New York: Oxford University Press.

—(1983). *Keywords: A Vocabulary of Culture and Society*. London: Fontana.

Wilt, Judith (1985). *Secret Leaves: The Novels of Sir Walter Scott*. Chicago: University of Chicago Press.

Wittgenstein, Ludwig (2001). *Tractatus Logico-Philosophicus*, trans. David F. Pears and Brian F. McGuinness. London and New York: Routledge.

Wolfe, Cary (2010). *What is Posthumanism?* Minneapolis and London: University of Minnesota Press.

Womack, Peter (1989). *Improvement and Romance: Constructing the Myth of the Highlands*. London: Macmillan.

Wood, Ellen Meiksins (2012). *Liberty and Property: A Social History of Western Political Thought from Renaissance to Enlightenment*. London and New York: Verso.

Wu, Duncan, ed. (2012). *Romanticism: An Anthology*, 4th edn. Malden, MA and Oxford: Wiley-Blackwell.

Žižek, Slavoj (1989). *The Sublime Object of Ideology*. London and New York: Verso.

—(1991). *Looking Awry: An Introduction to Jacques Lacan through Popular Culture*. Cambridge, MA and London: MIT Press.

—(1992a). *Enjoy Your Symptom! Jacques Lacan in Hollywood and Out*. London and New York: Routledge.

—ed. (1992b). *Everything You Always Wanted to Know about Lacan . . . But were Afraid to Ask Hitchcock*. London: Verso.

—(1993). *Tarrying with the Negative: Kant, Hegel, and the Critique of Ideology*. Durham, NC and London: Duke University Press.

—(1999). *The Ticklish Subject: The Absent Centre of Political Ontology*. New York and London: Verso.

—(2000). *The Fragile Absolute: or, Why is the Christian Legacy worth Fighting for?* London and New York: Verso.

—(2002a). *For They Know Not What They Do: Enjoyment as a Political Factor*, 2nd edn. London and New York: Verso.

—(2002b). *Welcome to the Desert of the Real: Five Essays on September 11 and Related Dates*. London and New York: Verso.

—(2005). *Interrogating the Real*, eds Rex Butler and Scott Stephens. London and New York: Continuum.

—(2006a). *The Parallax View*. Cambridge, MA and London: MIT Press.

—(2006b). *The Universal Exception: Selected Writings*, Vol. 2, eds Rex Butler and Scott Stephens. New York and London: Continuum.

—(2008). *In Defense of Lost Causes*. London and New York: Verso.

—(2009). "Ecology." In *The Examined Life: Excursions with Contemporary Thinkers*, ed. Astra Taylor. New York and London: The New Press, 155–83.

—(2011). "Occupy First. Demands Come Later." *The Guardian*, 26 October 2011, www.guardian.co.uk/commentisfree/2011/oct/26/occupy-protesters-bill-clinton.

Zupančič, Alenka (1993). *The Shortest Shadow: Nietzsche's Philosophy of the Two*. Cambridge, MA: MIT Press.

—(2000). *Ethics of the Real: Kant and Lacan*. London and New York: Verso.

—(2008). *The Odd One In: On Comedy*. Cambridge, MA and London: MIT Press.

Index